Where to Next?

To	The explorer in you.
From	The first readers of this inspiring and uplifting story about a life beyond borders.

Where to Next? is a soul-searching page-turner, a must-have and must-read for anyone wanting to explore the world and its amazing horizons.

Alice Miller Dupas
France, United States, Germany

What an amazing adventure! This book widened my horizons, causing me to laugh and cry as I turned the pages.

Alison Small
United Kingdom

See the world and the meaning of life through Solène's eyes. Witnessing her emotional rollercoaster of a journey makes you think about what you want to do and who you'd like to be. This book is a must-read for anyone looking for new adventures.

Amélie Pha
France, Austria, Libya, Germany

A tribute at the altar of wanderlust, this story takes the reader on an emotional rollercoaster of not belonging where you are and constantly searching for your mythical place in the world. A testament that life shouldn't be lived trying to 'keep up with the Joneses', but rather, listening to your instinctual gut feeling and following your own individual path. An emotionally honest and raw memoir told in short, witty snippets – the memories, milestones, challenges, and anecdotes – that make up a life, and the lessons learnt along the way.

Andrea Agrotis
Australia, Cyprus, United Kingdom, France, Greece

We don't always get what we want in life, but if you try your hardest, you become wiser, stronger and more compassionate. This book traces Solène's life journey and her courageous outlook for adventure. I can't wait to find out what's next!

Bonnie Chao
United States, China

This is the most inspiring book I have read in a long time! Be ready to travel the world and embark on a new adventure every time you turn a page.

Céline Maimaran
France, Morocco, United Kingdom, United States, Norway, Australia

With *Where to Next?* the author shares her burning desire to travel the world as well as her determination to make her dreams come true. From childhood to adulthood, country after country, follow her footsteps, witness her joy, pain and life-changing moments. Reading this book will give you a boost and leave you positive, driven and energised.

Joanne Profeta
France, Norway

Living through the writer's adventures was pure entertainment! Not only did this book inspire me to travel more, it also encouraged me to improve in everyday life.

Lindsay Fave
United States, Australia

Where to Next? will take you on the author's journey from childhood to adulthood through many countries, cultures and people. Reading it will remind you of how much you love both your family and your partner. You will discover funny anecdotes, beautiful landscapes, worldwide friendships, emotional love stories... And above all, it will bring you out of your comfort zone and leave you wondering how you contribute to making the world more unified.

Nina Coutéat
France, French Polynesia, New Zealand, Ireland, Morocco

Written in a beautiful and raw manner, *Where to Next?* invites us to reflect on and connect to our own life experiences and dreams as well as to define what 'home' truly means to us.

Olivia Ryan
Ireland, Spain, Australia, India

A gripping and lively contemporary autobiography about the international journey of a young woman in her quest to find what 'home' means to her. Follow her from France to Australia as she grows up to become a self-made storyteller. Whether you are a frequent flyer or an aspiring traveller, I am convinced that you will relate to and enjoy her story as much as I did.

Oriane Freund
France, Germany, China

One word: Inspiring! I really enjoyed how this book challenged me and how much I could relate to it at the same time. Through her experience, the author reminded me that stepping out of your comfort zone is always the right thing to do.

Ouissem Belgacem
France, Tunisia, United States, United Kingdom, Spain

This book is an essential read for anyone who feels alone, lost, frustrated and misunderstood. Read this story and understand that taking a chance, persevering and not accepting the status quo will take you on a journey to become a better you.

Simon Taylor
United Kingdom, Australia, United States, Greece, China

Where to Next?

A Memoir Beyond Borders

SOLÈNE ANGLARET

Published in Australia by
BeBeyondBorders
Elsternwick, VIC 3185
Tel: 0478692529
Email: bebeyondborders@yahoo.com
Website: www.bebeyondborders.com

First published in Australia 2018
Copyright © Solène Anglaret 2018

All rights reserved. No part of this publication may be reproduced, stored in a retrieval system, or transmitted, in any form or by any means without the prior written permission of the publisher, nor be otherwise circulated in any form of binding or cover other than that in which it is published and without a similar condition being imposed on the subsequent purchaser.

 A catalogue record for this book is available from the National Library of Australia

Anglaret, Solène
WHERE TO NEXT?

ISBN: 978-0-6482432-0-5 (paperback)
ISBN: 978-0-6482432-1-2 (epub)

Cover layout and design by HRM Graphics (India, Guj, Rajkot)
Book typesetting by Nelly Murariu of pixbeedesign.com
Printed by Ingram Spark

Disclaimer
All care has been taken in the preparation of the information herein, but no responsibility can be accepted by the publisher or author for any damages resulting from the misinterpretation of this work. All contact details given in this book were current at the time of publication, but are subject to change.

The advice given in this book is based on the experience of the individuals. Professionals should be consulted for individual problems. The author and publisher shall not be responsible for any person with regard to any loss or damage caused directly or indirectly by the information in this book.

"All changes, even the most longed for, have their melancholy; for what we leave behind us is a part of ourselves; we must die to one life before we can enter another."

Anatole France

Contents

Chapter 1
Home is Louviers   13

Chapter 2
Home is Here   47

Chapter 3
Is Home Home?   77

Chapter 4
Home isn't Here   89

Chapter 5
Home isn't Home   109

Chapter 6
Home is Them   123

Chapter 7
Home is Me   195

Chapter 8
Home is the World   283

Acknowledgments   299

About the Author   301

CHAPTER 1

Home is Louviers

Entrance
Paris. August 1988. Twenty-first day of the month. It's warm and comfortable, but like most good things – or so I would understand much later on – it must come to an end. I'm not willing to make a smooth entrance into the world. Instead, it's bum first that the doctor finds me. A caesarean is the only option. Hours later, I scream my lungs out. Where am I? Tiny, shivering and with hips twisted inwards, I'm not a pretty sight. "Looks like we have a little rebel on our hands," Mum and Dad say to each other shortly after my grand entrance. Little do they know how right they'll turn out to be.

Right
I live near Paris for the first two years of my existence, but I have no recollection of it. Then, my parents decide to move to Normandy. They buy a house at the edge of a small town called Louviers. It has a large and steep garden that ends in a forest. Right now, this house is home to me. It's a familiar, organised mess in which comfort reigns. My favourite room of all is the corridor.

Corridor
Every so often, I transform it into a fashion runway. I wear my prettiest dresses, one after the other. Each time, I walk up and down in a straight line posing at either end of the room. It's so much fun! Regardless of the fact my little sister can barely walk, I'm determined to make her do the same. I think she hates it. We're only two years apart but couldn't be more different. Sometimes, I wish I could go back to being an only child but then I feel bad because that's mean. Everything changed after she was born. My whole universe seems to have been turned

upside down. I'm no longer the centre of attention. She is. Slim, with huge, beautiful dark eyes and long straight hair, she looks perfect. Plus, she is so well-behaved. She sleeps, eats, and stays quiet. I'm the opposite. Chubby, with messy curly hair, and loud. I stand out for all the wrong reasons. My favourite hobbies are dancing, eating desserts, and flying.

Flying
I love flying. I hate flying. I love it because it takes me to places I've never been before. I hate it because my ears hurt when we take off and when we land. I'm four years old, and together with Mum, Dad, and my sister, we're going to the Canary Islands for a family holiday. Waiting in line to enter this giant bird of steel, I'm nervous. On board, I sit in one of the enormous chairs between Mum and Dad. A beautiful lady in a blue suit asks if I'm ok. I am. Soon after, I hear a loud roar and feel the airplane take off. We're flying! I'm flying! Through the window, I can see white and fluffy clouds against the bright blue sky. They look like cotton candy. I can't stop staring. The view is so beautiful! I never want it to end. Why stay on earth when you can be in the sky? A burning desire to fly all over the world rises within me.

Burning
I hear the wood crackling. I watch the flames lengthening. I feel my body warming. It's a typically cold, winter day. Dad is looking after the fire while Mum is cooking dinner for the four of us. It smells so good. Caramelised onions, eggplants, courgettes, peppers, tomatoes, thyme, rosemary... a ratatouille is in the making. One of my favourite dishes ever. If it's followed by baguette with cheese and a chocolate fondant, I'll be in food

heaven! She's never said, but I think cooking might be Mum's way of showing us her love.

Mum
"Mum, one day I'll travel the world, meet a lot of people and tell their stories." I'm a six-year-old little girl who has big plans and a big mouth.

"Sure," she says.

Feeling the distance in her voice, I think either she doesn't believe me or she isn't really listening. It happens sometimes when she comes back from work. Apparently, it's stress and fatigue. Unless she's had enough of me and my endless declarations. I don't blame her.

After school, I often try to tell her about my day but she shrugs and says, "It's just little girl stories."

So I tell Martine instead. Martine is the kind lady who picks my sister and I up from school, cleans the house, and looks after us until Mum and Dad come back in the evening. They work hard and sometimes very late, Dad especially.

Dad
Every year at school the teacher asks us what our parents do, what their job is. Now that I'm seven years old, I think I should be able to understand, so I decide to question Dad. I try so hard to focus. I really want to make sense of his words. But all I gather is that I should say he's an engineer. I have no idea what it means. All I know is: Dad wears suits, uses complicated words and travels all the time. I wish I could ask him again but I'm afraid it will seem as though I didn't pay attention, or I didn't understand the first time around. Neither are good things. I can't wait to grow up! First, because I'm sure everything will be obvious then.

Second, because I, too, want to wear fancy clothes, use incomprehensible language, and visit other countries. It must be so exciting!

Exciting

Today, we're going on a family holiday to the United States. That's where Granddad and Step-Grandma live. I saw on the blue, round globe at school that it's really far away. None of my friends have been there. It will be the longest plane ride I've ever been on. Mum wrote a packing list. I followed it and made sure I gathered all the essentials: my favourite jumper covered in bears, my pretty blue and white dress and, most importantly, Boutchou, my teddy bear. It was given to me by Mum's grandma when I was one. I can't make up my mind whether it's a boy or a girl. So yesterday it wore trousers and today it's wearing a pretty pink dress with a little scarf Grandma sewed. It doesn't matter which gender it is – at least not to me – as long as it's fluffy. I carry Boutchou everywhere. Well, everywhere apart from school. That would be embarrassing. As we board the plane, I'm hyper-active and over-excited. I hug Boutchou tightly in my arms because it's scared of flying. Once again, the engine roars and the airplane takes off. I can't wait to see Granddad and Step-Grandma!

Step-Grandma

She is Granddad's second wife. She is American. Although she is friendly to me, I'm not sure whether I'm allowed to like her or not. I've heard the story so many times. Grandma's story. When Mum was in her twenties, Grandma received an anonymous letter through the mail saying that her husband was cheating on her. As it turned out he'd been seeing another woman on the other side of the Atlantic for the past ten years. Exposed, he decided to leave Grandma and move to the United States where he married his mistress. That's how she became Mum's Step-Mum and my Step-Grandma. To be honest, it's fine by me. I'm not even sure if this story is true or if this is my interpretation of what I was told. The only problem is that it makes me sad to see Grandma sad. Every time I visit Grandma, she tells me that one day he will come back. I don't think it's true, but I don't want to be the one to tell her. Maybe I should do so when I'm older, as this is definitely grown-up talk. In the meantime, I've decided that I will be nice to Step-Grandma because she is nice to me too. I've also made a mental note of never liking a boy as much as Grandma liked Granddad because break-ups look painful and pointless. Anyway, I don't talk to boys.

Talk
Step-Grandma's French isn't great. She just asked us to help clean the ceiling instead of the floor. *Plafond* versus *plancher*. Close enough. We're all laughing out loud. But behind my smile, there is determination. One day, I too want to be able to master this language of hers that right now sounds like a mysterious code to me. Last night, I overheard Dad and Granddad saying it's the most spoken language in the world. The world, that's what I want to see. Becoming fluent in English is something I must add to my 'grown-up' list.

List
Mum makes lists for trips to the supermarket, things to mend in the house, and what to pack for holidays. Dad makes lists of the bottles of wine in his cellar, the comic books he buys, and the number of kilometres he cycles per year. It seems as though

making lists is the only way to get things done, so I decide that eight years old is a good age to start. In my head, I begin a list of all the things I'd like to do when I grow up. Thus far it reads:
- Travel the world
- Become fluent in English
- Never lose Boutchou
- …

That's all I can come up with for now. It's not much. Do other kids also have 'grown-up' lists? Will I ever be able to complete what's on it? What if I don't? All these questions come to my mind as I lie in bed hoping for a night without nightmares.

Nightmares

Every time we come back from holidays, I have the same nightmare. We're driving back home from the airport at night while my sister and I are sleeping soundly at the back of the car. Johnny Halliday's 'Allumer le Feu'[1] is playing in the background but it doesn't bother us. As we approach our house, I hear Mum gasp. The sound she makes isn't loud but rather unusual. I open my eyes to see what it's about and ask her what's wrong. That's when I realise we've almost arrived. I start to distinguish our house from afar. Something is odd. It looks like the wood in our fireplace on typical winter days. I see orange, red, yellow and suddenly realise that our house is covered in flames. Yet, I can't hear anything. Silence. Dad parks the car in front of the door and all four of us jump out. We can't go far though. Standing on the sidewalk, I'm freezing cold despite the heat of the fire. I

---

[1] The title of this famous French song 'Allumer le feu' interpreted by the late Johnny Halliday and released in 1998 has two meanings. A literal meaning: to light a fire and a figurative meaning: to get the party started.

should do something! I have to move. But I'm stuck, stunned, frozen. We're too late. We have to watch it burn. Staring right at it, I think about everything I own and care about turning to ashes. It's unbearable. Suddenly, I wake up. Same nightmare again. Sitting on the bed, I think to myself… perhaps it's better not to have a home so you never worry about it burning down.

Worry
Sleeping in itself is ok, though it feels like an utter waste of time. Imagine all you could do if you didn't sleep: draw, dance, learn, laugh, talk, travel, and so much more. But that's not the point. The point is that I hate going to bed because that's when the thoughts creep in and the inner voice gets louder. It tells you that you are not smart enough, not pretty enough, not talented enough, simply not good enough. I can't remember exactly when the inner voice started. I think it was sometime around my ninth birthday, a few months ago. Before that, I believed I could achieve anything I put my mind to and become anyone I wanted to be.

Anyone
There are two things I like about going to school: learning new things and getting good grades. Both make me feel really happy! However, there is one thing I don't like about school: being bullied. It wasn't too bad at first, just kids being themselves and making jokes about each other. That was until a few of my classmates agreed on a nickname for me. I think it's mean. They think it's funny. 'The whale' is what they call me now. They point at me and laugh right in my face. They say it, sing it, rap it. It's not just one or two of them, the entire class uses it, even the one who just yesterday told me I was her best friend.

Even her. She is one of them now, pointing and laughing. I wish I could liquefy and disappear.

Disappear

If only I could jump on a plane to a place where no one knows me or at least not as the largest marine mammal on earth. I can't bear the thought of not having friends. I feel left out and alone. I need to find a way to make them like me again. Every swimming day, I cry before going to bed and then again in the morning. Mum asks why but I don't want to tell her. It's so embarrassing. What if she thinks they're right? After all, maybe I'm as fat as they say.

Fat

I guess it's a fact, I'm fat. Food is everything to me. It's my best and only friend now. If I'm happy, I eat chocolate to celebrate. If I'm sad, I eat cookies to make it better. If I feel empty, I eat to fill the void. If I'm full, I eat more because I'm greedy. I know it's wrong, so I eat in secret after school. Please don't tell Mum and Dad... The more I eat, the bigger I become. The bigger I become, the more bullied I am. The more bullied I am, the more I eat. Never-ending vicious cycle. I don't know how to break it. Every day, I wish I could escape this harsh reality. Or perhaps I could slim down as I get older? Not a bad idea. So one night, after yet another horrible day at school, I decide to add it to my mental 'grown-up' list which now reads:

- Travel the world
- Become fluent in English
- Never lose Boutchou
- Be skinny and beautiful
- ...

Repeating these in my head one by one as I fall asleep, I feel as though the list is missing something: a dream job. What do I actually want to do when I grow up?

Dream
We're watching television as a family one night. I'm ten and I absolutely love TV! Watching it is a weekend treat. During the week, the rules are strict: no TV and no sleep overs, just homework and reading. That's the theory anyway. I've convinced Martine to let us watch the fun kids' programmes once we've finished our homework and before Mum and Dad come home. Plus, I know she won't be around for that long. I'm getting old enough to look after my sister. I can't wait to do my homework in front of my favourite shows. I'll have to make the little one swear she won't tell, but I think that will be easy. I'll just threaten to hit her. I've followed this through before and I can tell she is scared. Well, that's only when Dad's not around, because if he is, she screams and I'm the one who ends up receiving the blow. Smart brat. Anyway, tonight is not like that. It's a lovely evening and for some reason, there and then, I'm sure of it. So I turn to my parents and say: "One day this will be me." The lady I'm pointing at is the famous French newsreader Claire Chazal. That's it: my dream job is to be a journalist on TV. Imagine, I could travel the world, learn so much and meet thousands of amazing people! Plus, everyone would watch me on their small screen. They would be forced to take back all their mean words then. There's no doubt about it. One more for the list:
- Travel the world
- Become fluent in English
- Never lose Boutchou
- Be skinny and beautiful

- Be a journalist on TV
- …

Now I need to find out how to turn my dreams into reality. It seems to happen in all the Disney© movies so there must be a way.

Reality

In my family, everyone is some form of scientist. Not that they have Einstein's haircut or anything like that, but they are either engineers or doctors and are factual and rational. Granddad, who lives in the United States, is a famous researcher and a professor in chemistry. I've always wondered if it's his job that makes him so cold and arrogant or if he was born this way. Both my parents are successful engineers. Even my cousin, who's three years older than me, has already decided that's what she'll be when she grows up. In this environment, I stick out like a sore thumb with my dreams of reporting, presenting, writing and travelling. Sometimes I can't help but think that I was adopted or swapped at birth. I don't belong to this family, to this house and to this life. That's one of the things I tell Dad when we argue. It makes him even angrier, but I can't help it.

Angrier

I'm angry. I'm angry because I feel trapped. Trapped within this small town. Trapped within the fattening body that is mine. Trapped within my conflicted mind. So I scream, I insult, I hit. My sister, my parents, the walls, anything that's within reach becomes a target. What makes me so angry? Why can't I be a normal 11 year old? How can I escape?

Escape
Today I'm in Venice with Granddad, Step-Grandma and my older cousin. I love being abroad. I love exploring a new city. I love eating all the Italian food I want. Venice is one of the most beautiful places I've ever seen! Behind every corner there is something new to discover: winding waterways full of gondolas, St Mark's Square covered by thousands of pigeons, Rialto Bridge and its countless little shops... Just after midday, the four of us hop in a taxi to a local restaurant. There, we sit outside waiting for our lunch to be served. It's a gorgeous, sunny day. I close my eyes and feel the warmth of the sun on my face and the murmur of the wind in my ears. I grab a bunch of hair and stick it in my mouth. I don't know when or why I started doing that. There's something reassuring, relaxing and soothing about it. My mind starts to wander, when suddenly and surprisingly Step-Grandma decides to tell me off for eating my hair. She says other people have died from it because some hair ended up blocking their airways or stomach or something. I no longer recall the exact details of her argument and, to be honest, I couldn't care less. I'm not listening anymore. I can feel the heat of anger rising in my belly, like a volcano just before an eruption. Who does she think she is? She is not my Mum. She is not even my Grandma. She has no right. But I know these words are dreadful. There would be no coming back from saying them out loud. So before the anger strikes, I stand and I run away.

Run
At first, I run as fast as I can. When I can't see them anymore, I slow down a little. Walking swiftly along the streets of Venice, which are completely foreign to me, I feel free and in control of my destiny. I look for sign posts and I recognise shops and

junctions. "I'm twelve. I'm an adult. I can do this," is what I say to myself quietly and it works. I have no idea how, but I find my way back to our hotel. Luckily, I kept a room key in my pocket. I sit on the bed and at first, I'm so happy and proud. I made it! I didn't get angry and I showed her not to mess with me. But as the minutes tick by I start to realise what I've done, and guilt consumes me. This is not the first time I've run away. I've done it before back home. In a pointless desire to avoid the anger, I flee. I just disappear for a few minutes, hours, up to an afternoon. Naively I think my family might love me more when I come back. It seems to work in the movies so why wouldn't it work in real life? Well, where I'm from, it simply doesn't. My parents become so irritated instead. I think they don't understand that in those moments it would just be worse if I stayed. I would say and do things I'd later regret. And regret is one thing I don't want to have. Ever.

Regret

By the time Granddad, Step-Grandma and my cousin return to the hotel, I feel so bad about what I've just done. Understandably, Step-Grandma is annoyed but what's worse is Granddad's silence. Not a word. Ashamed, I apologise quietly. Disappointing someone feels so awful. That night, hiding under the hotel's fresh sheets, I promise myself that in the future, I will always warn those I love before I leave.

Warn

"As soon as I turn eighteen, I will leave home," I tell my parents after I return from the trip. Six years' notice is plenty, isn't it? It might sound harsh but is it cruel if it's the truth?

Truth
The truth is, I have no idea what it means to leave home or where home is in the first place. As I lie on my bed tonight under the beams of my bedroom ceiling, listening to the rain pouring on the skylights, I wonder how this could be home when it doesn't feel like I belong. My eyes are wide open. I can't sleep. But as I finally drift away, dreams of adventures and discoveries come to life. A few hours later, my alarm rings and brings me back to reality. I sit up on the bed and look at myself. I'm not fit. I'm far from beautiful. I'm not that smart. I'm nobody. Why would my dreams come true? I most certainly don't deserve it so, why would I be so lucky?

Lucky
Mum is Protestant. Dad is atheist. Sometimes I pray to God. Sometimes I wish for luck. To be honest, I think I'm actually pretty lucky! My family is healthy and caring. I live in a lovely house in a small town in Normandy. I'm bright at school, never top of the class but never far from it either. I do various extra-curricular activities: dancing, tennis, music. I go away on holidays; sometimes somewhere in France, other times further away. Perfect.

Perfect
That's the perspective I get when I force myself to look at the bigger picture. Doing so feels like pulling my mind and my body apart, as if I were able to look at myself from above and smile. I wonder if other people do that too. Do you? Or perhaps it's just me. But recently it hasn't been easy. I've just been feeling really unlucky and self-pity has kicked in. Last year, I broke my left wrist in a poor attempt at roller-skating, and just last

week I twisted my right knee in an even poorer attempt at snowboarding. The knee is worse because doctors can't seem to be able to figure out exactly what's wrong. I've been to orthopaedists, sports specialists and physiotherapists. I've had x-rays, MRIs and even an arthroscopy. I spent a few weeks on crutches at school. It was fun, at first, walking with your arms and being asked by everyone if you're ok. But after a couple of days, I was already bored of it. I know my knee could be a lot worse and I'll be ok soon, but last night I had another nightmare. I was 30 years old and in a wheel chair. I woke up sweating, shaking, and decided that if I can walk, I must walk; if I can run, I must run; if I can move, I must move. This morning, that went straight onto my 'grown-up' list:

- Travel the world
- Become fluent in English
- Never lose Boutchou
- Be skinny and beautiful
- Be a journalist on TV
- Keep moving
- ...

This latest addition might need to be further defined. How will I keep moving? And in which direction? With or against the flow of life?

Flow

I absolutely love dancing! Put on some music and you'll have me jump, shake and, most importantly, smile. Dance class used to be one of my favourite moments of the week but since the knee injury and now that I'm getting bigger, I just look like a bull in a china shop, ready to destroy everything one hip movement at a time. I don't fit in and I can't follow.

Can't
Is life a permanent struggle, or is it just me?
Why do I feel as if something within me is missing?
Am I putting too much pressure on myself or not enough?
Will I ever stop feeling like I'm underachieving?
Will I ever believe that I'm enough?
Will I ever succeed?
What is success anyway?
Am I over thinking?
Am I overanalysing?
Am I…? I can't. Stop.
Inner Voice.
Please. Just. Stop.

Stop
My inner voice gets quieter when I'm going somewhere, focusing on something or talking to someone. That's why I don't like to be alone at home. I'd rather be surrounded by people, family, friends, strangers, basically anyone. I've just turned 13 and when I look around me, I can see quite a few friends… or should I say 'friends'. They're the kind of people you laugh with but don't become too close to. They're the ones you wouldn't share secrets with but are good to have around to break the silence and enjoy the moment. They're easy to make and just as easy to forget. Or so I thought.

Thought
Friendships take time to form and flourish. That's what I've learnt over the past year. A few of the 'friends' I'd made have become actual friends now. We've grown closer. Hanging out with them is so much fun! In our little group, a few stand out. Three girls – popular girl, smart girl and clumsy girl – are

amongst them. Popular girl has become my best friend. We call each other almost every day after school. Oblivious of the time, we speak for hours and hours. Our parents complain as they can't use their own house phone when they need or want to. Too bad! She is amazing, beautiful, smart and has so many stories to tell. I admire her immensely and can't believe someone like her would even consider hanging out with me. From what I gather, I make her laugh. Is this who I am: funny girl?

Funny

Popular girl receives a lot of attention from the boys in our class. The boy I really liked last year told me he wasn't interested as he would rather go out with her. I didn't even get angry this time. Fair enough, I thought. If only some of her aura and charisma could rub off on me. Perhaps it has... I've been spending more and more time with one of the boys in our group lately. I like him a lot. At first, I thought it was just friendship, but it's been evolving into something else. He makes me laugh till I cry. He looks at me like I'm some sort of treasure and when he's gone I miss him so much it hurts. That's what I told him yesterday. I'm so nervous about seeing him this morning. I have no idea what will happen... I've never kissed a boy before. I've been trying to practice on my pillow – which is what they suggested on the radio show I listen to past midnight – but I found it disgusting so I stopped. What if I didn't do it properly? What if I hurt him with my braces? What if he changed his mind?

Changed

He is here! I look down as he walks towards me slowly. Our bodies are inches apart. I can feel electricity between us. Shaking and shy, he takes me into his arms and we hug for ages. Out of the blue, he breaks his embrace and kisses me. Seconds later, his tongue finds mine. Butterflies fill my stomach. If that's what love feels like, he is all I need for the rest of my life. I have no idea what this boy sees in me but his confidence in my greatness and his endless compliments make me feel worthy. For the first time in a long time, I'm genuinely happy and can't wait to find out what the future holds. It's him and me against the world, and together we're invincible. The best part is he agrees. "*Je t'aime*,"[2] he whispers in my ear. "*Je t'aime encore plus*,"[3] I reply. At 14, I can confidently say that I've never cared about anyone in this way before. Things are complicated in his family, and he often feels overwhelmed by worry and self-doubt. Being someone he can lean on and talk to means the world to me, and seeing him happy is all I could wish for. With him, my own anxiety seems long gone.

Gone
Mum, Dad, my sister and I are getting ready for a family holiday to the small island of Malta. Usually I'd be jumping for joy at the idea of flying off somewhere new, but this time is different. The thought of being separated from him is unbearable. What's even worse is not being able to communicate with him for seven days. It seems like an eternity.

Eternity
Lying down by the pool of our hotel, all I can think about is him. Closing my eyes, I can feel his arms around me, his kisses on my lips and his body against mine. If only I could go back to the last time I saw him or, even better, back to the first time

---

[2] '*Je t'aime*' in French means 'I love you' in English.
[3] '*Je t'aime encore plus*' in French means 'I love you even more' in English.

we kissed. I knew love could hurt but I never thought the mark he'd leave on my heart would be so intense and everlasting. Without him, I can barely breathe. Everything I eat tastes bland. Everything I touch feels rough. Everything I see looks desolate.

Desolate
Six months of romantic texts, long phone calls and secret meet-ups later, our parents tell us we won't be going to the same high school. He says long distance will be tough, so we should consider breaking up. We only live a 30-minute walk away! There must be someone else in his life, I think to myself. Even if there isn't, my ego takes over. I'd rather end things myself if he has doubts. Why wait for him to make up his mind and worry every step of the way? Looking straight into his eyes, I say, "It's over…" secretly hoping he won't let me go through with it.

Through
The moment I put an end to our relationship, I regret it. My heart is broken, and I only have myself to blame. Proud and childish, that's typical of me, sadly. If only I could go back in time and tell him once more how much I love him. Perhaps we'll meet again somewhere someday… I hope we do. In the meantime, I know I'll never forget him.

Forget
"You always forget something!" my sister says. She is right. No matter how far in advance I pack, no matter if I follow Mum's list or not, I always seem to forget an essential item. Toothbrush, plug adapter, underwear – there's always something I've missed. But not this time. This time, I'm ready. Mum and I have been through the list at least three times though it feels like many more.

I'm beyond excited! I'm going to Ireland for three weeks to learn English. I'll be staying with an Irish family. In their house! Today is the first time I will travel on my own.

Travel

At the airport, a lady in uniform puts a blue and orange square document holder around my neck and escorts me to the aircraft. I think I'm too old for this nonsense and could walk around by myself but apparently "procedures are procedures." If she'd asked, I would have answered that some rules are there to be broken. But she didn't. Too bad. As I wave goodbye to my family, I can feel a pinch in my heart, but I don't cry. I have to be strong. I don't know how but I'm sure this is the first of many airport goodbyes. After being escorted along endless corridors, I finally sit on the plane and buckle up. Waiting for the aircraft to take off, a wave of anxiety spreads over me. Why am I doing this? What if it all goes horribly wrong?

Wrong

I hadn't defined 'wrong' on the plane but as I sit in my bedroom at the host-family's house, I know that this is it: loneliness. No one speaks French and my English isn't that good. I struggle to understand, and even more to be understood. I don't have a mobile phone yet and overseas calls are expensive, so I'm only allowed to ring my parents once a week. I've already read all the books I brought with me. I've thought about everything I could possibly imagine. Perhaps this was a bad idea after all. Staying at home in Louviers is so much easier and more comfortable.

Comfortable
Every morning, I have a two-hour English class with the mum of the host family. Though pretty strict with grammar and spelling, she is always so kind and patient with me. Thanks to her guidance, I improve every day, little by little. Each afternoon is free time. I stay in my bedroom the first few days but having had enough of the loneliness, I decide it's time for a change. At first, with her permission, I follow her around everywhere she goes. Then, one day, she's visiting her friend so I go out to explore on my own. As soon as I leave the house, that feeling reappears. It's the same as in Venice: a sense of freedom and adventure. Kinsale is such a pretty little town with its yacht-filled harbour, narrow colourful streets and historical forts. And the people are so lovely. I walk past a butcher's, a pharmacy, a hairdresser's and a local pub. The next shop catches my attention. They sell souvenirs. I decide to buy a few for my family and some postcards too. When I realise I will need stamps for these, I gather the courage to ask the shop assistant. I can't quite believe it myself, but he understands me and I understand him! A few of these small victories under my belt, I start to feel more confident. I love Ireland! Endless green fields with thousands of sheep. Gaelic songs playing in bars and restaurants. Friendly local faces walking around town. When I get back from my walk that afternoon, I relax on the sofa and reflect on my little success. I've left home's comfort, lost then regained confidence and finally re-discovered comfort in a different place and surrounded by different people. I'm both amazed and delighted. I wish I could stay longer. I'd love to live here for a while! That way I could learn even more about this country, its people and its culture. As I bid Ireland and my host family goodbye, I hope that one day I'll be back.

Back
I'm home! It's so good to see everyone again and hear French around me. I can't wait to eat Mum's food! She and I are driving from the airport back to Normandy when suddenly an appalling driver pulls in front of us and I scream "Jesus Christ!" It comes out instinctively, so naturally even I'm surprised. Mum isn't impressed to say the least! Her daughter, cursing in English in her car, is more than she bargained for. I'm smiling nonetheless, I can't help it because I know where this shout comes from. It's what the mum of the Irish host family used to yell at drivers when she thought they weren't behaving appropriately. It looks like I picked it up from her. Strangely, I feel as if a little piece of me has become Irish and I wonder… is it possible for more than one place to be home?

Home
When I look around, I feel as though everything is the same. Everything but me. This experience has changed me somehow. It's reinforced my wish to explore the world and ignited my quest to find out where home actually is. But before I know it, my deep thoughts are interrupted by the daily routine slowly settling back in.

Routine
Wake-up, go to school, walk home, do homework, have dinner, go to bed. Repeat. Days merge into weeks. Weeks merge into months. Months merge into years. Dressed in black most days, my sadness is obvious. It's been more than a year now, but I can't seem to get over him. My first love. As it turns out, sadness attracts sadness. Most of the friends I'd made have gone their own way. Popular girl now hangs out with prettier and funnier

people. Once again, I'm alone. After school, I sit in my room and write poems. At 16, poetry has become my way of escaping reality until I can actually leave this small town for good and start afresh. Two years to go.

Two

To my greatest surprise, not everyone is put off by my moody attitude. One of the boys in class often sits next to me and tries to make me laugh. Looking at him now, he is actually rather attractive. Tall and skinny, his longish, curly brown hair partially hides his mischievous eyes and cheeky smile. His jokes often result in him getting in trouble with our teachers. It doesn't seem to affect him in the slightest though. Even if it did, he's way too cool to let it show. I admire his carefree attitude. The two of us are polar opposites. We complement each other. Around him, I feel re-energised and more daring than ever.

Daring

He introduces me to something called MSN Messager© and we start chatting online for hours and hours every day after school. What begins as innocent banter turns into a game of seduction. Suddenly, I feel alive again. His presence calms me down and brightens up my life. There is little I wouldn't be prepared to do to make him smile. Though he is my second love, with him come all the firsts. Day by day, I fall for him stronger and deeper. He is the musician of whom I'd like to be the muse. Chatting one evening, we realise that we share the same passion for travel and both dream of living abroad. He says he'll explore the world by boat someday. I secretly hope he'll take me with him. Together, we talk endlessly about our exciting adventures ahead. We can't wait for high school to end!

End
I've received my *Baccalauréat*[4] results today. They're not too bad, pretty good in fact. I think my parents are happy, but I can't know for sure. Words used around the house are more factual and functional than emotional. That night, I'm sitting on the living room sofa when I overhear Mum speaking to Granddad over the phone. He is asking why I won't be pursuing scientific studies despite such a good grade in physics and chemistry. "What a waste," he says. I feel as though I've been stabbed in the heart. I've disappointed him again. However, this time, his judgment feels harsh and unfair. You can be successful even if you're not a mathematician, an engineer or a doctor, is what I tell myself. I'm determined to prove him wrong and ready to jump into the unknown with my eyes and heart wide open.

Heart
He is 'The One'. I've heard that you know when you know, and I do know. Simple as that. We've been together for two years already and this summer is the most important of my life to date. I'm stressed. I snap easily. Everyone around me is a potential target, especially those I love the most: my family and him – my boyfriend. We've argued a lot recently. I've even ended up hitting a table with my thigh the other day. Extreme anger rose within me, and I was like a demon possessed. The table, one of those old wooden ones, was so heavy it didn't even move. My leg, on the other hand, still hurts. The bruise is enormous. It's gone from blue to purple and I guess it will turn yellow soon. I can't even remember why we were arguing and I'm over it

---

[4] *Baccalauréat* is the academic qualification French students take at the end of high school. It is required to pursue university studies.

already. I'm not the kind to hold a grudge. I usually get everything out in the open and then blank it out. There are so many things I have to learn and remember these days, why should I store bad memories and use up all this potentially useful space in my brain? Plus, he knows I love him regardless of the fights we have. What's done is done.

Done

Today I took my driving test. It went well, I think, though I'll have to wait a few days for the official results to come through. *Baccalauréat* – done. Driving test – done. Only one to go: the exams to enter into Sciences Po, one of France's prestigious *Grandes Ecoles*[5]. The best of its kind. The one where most successful journalists in the country have studied. The ideal path to my dream job. It's in three days. I'm quite nervous and extremely committed.

Committed

However, back home from the driving test, I can't focus on my books. I haven't heard from my boyfriend since last night. Not a single text. He has neither wished me good luck nor has he asked how it went. He knew it was today. I messaged him a few hours ago asking, 'What's going on?' in vain. Complete radio silence. I'm torn between anger and worry. Finally, as the sun goes down, I receive a message from him: 'We have to talk'. Immediately I know something is wrong.

---

[5] French *Grandes Ecoles* (literally Grand Schools) are selective and prestigious higher-education establishments outside of the main university system. They can be entered post *Baccalauréat* or after one to three years of dedicated preparatory classes.

Something
I fear the worst but, at the same time, it's unthinkable to me. He and I, we're soul mates. So many times, I've told him, "*Je t'aime pour toujours.*"[6] I meant it then and I mean it now. So whatever it is, I'm convinced it will pass. I don't say anything to Dad as I ask him to drive me over to my boyfriend's parents' place. Silent, I look out the window hoping I'll manage to hold in the tears until I get there. It's nothing. It has to be. I couldn't bear it.

Bear
When I arrive at his parents' house, my heart is beating out of my chest, my brain can't decide between panic and rage, and my legs are on auto-mode climbing the stairs to his room. He is standing there waiting for me. He doesn't come over to kiss me as usual. Next, a whole bunch of words spill out of his mouth. The only part I remember is when he says it's been months since he stopped loving me. Two weeks ago, he treated me to a candlelight birthday dinner at a Parisian restaurant and showered me in gifts he couldn't afford. I'm still wearing his promise ring around my finger. Last night, he even texted me '*Je t'aime*'. Was he lying then?

Lying
I slap him as hard as I can. He doesn't budge. There is no way I will show him how I truly feel. He doesn't deserve it. So I call Dad and ask him to pick me up. I've only been here 10 or 15 minutes, but he must have sensed something was wrong as he doesn't ask any questions and says he'll come over right away. I wait outside

---

[6] '*Je t'aime pour toujours*' in French means 'I love you forever' in English.

for him. Keep it together girl. Keep it together. My now ex asks for one last kiss. A false, loud laugh breaks from me. Are you kidding? No way! "I never want to see you again," is all I manage to mutter instead. A few minutes later, I jump into Dad's car and as we turn right at the end of the street, I can't hold it anymore and burst into tears. 'Les Histoires d'A'[7]. by Les Rita Mitsouko is playing in my head. I've heard this song so many times. I should have been prepared. I wasn't at all. Now, I'm lost.

Lost
Who am I? For the past two years I've listened to the music he liked, I've watched the movies he enjoyed, and I've eaten the food he fancied. Now, as we part ways, I feel as though I don't know myself in the slightest. The only thing I'm certain of is that I'm hurting more than ever. Every morning when I wake and every night when I go to bed, I think of him. The memory of his presence is everywhere. I obviously wasn't good enough for him to stay. Sadly, I'd fallen in love with him just like Grandma fell in love with Granddad years before. Finally, I understand her. Love does what love wants.

Love
I've been crying myself to sleep every night for the last three days. I'm miserable. I'm pathetic. But today and tomorrow are exam days. I'm on my way to the centre of Arcueil, a dodgy suburb just outside Paris. The weather reflects how I feel: cloudy and wet. My inner voice is divided. It's as if I was in one of these silly cartoons.

---

[7] 'Les Histoires d'A.' is a song by Les Rita Mitsouko. It was released in 1986 and is famous for its lyrics 'Love stories end badly'.

On one side, the little angel in my head says, "You can do this, just stay focused and keep going."

On the other side, the devil replies, "What are you on about? Why bother? You'll never make it."

Devil

A couple of weeks later, I'm at home with my parents waiting for the results. The car is full and ready to go. I passed the entry exams for Sciences Po Bordeaux but I'm yet to find out whether I was accepted at Sciences Po Paris. What's the difference? Well, first of all, they are located in two different cities. As you might have guessed, one is in Bordeaux and the other in Paris. However, that's not all. Sciences Po Paris is undeniably the most prestigious of the two. Being accepted would not only be amazing, it would also be a great way of getting back at all those who doubted me, myself included. My fingers and my toes are crossed as I refresh the results page time and time again. Sadly, the devil wins this battle. Bordeaux it will be. No time to ponder. Off we go.

Go

Dad and I jump in the car and make our way south. The trip goes so fast that I don't really have time to think or feel. Right now, that's all I could ask for. I'm 18 years old, heartbroken, lost, and a little too self-centred. I can't wait to get as far away as I can from everything and everyone I used to know. Driving on the highway to the south-west of France with music blasting and windows open to the wind gives me an incredible feeling of freedom. So much so that I don't really want to arrive. I'd rather keep enjoying the journey! Dad and I speak the whole way. Looking straight at the sun unapologetically shining, I can't help but feel grateful for the simplicity of its warmth.

Grateful

My parents rarely show their emotions. Rational and composed, their demeanour drives me insane most days. But as I'm about to move away on my own, I finally realise what they've done for me and how much they actually care. We're in my studio flat now building IKEA© furniture. Dad hates it. I know he does. Looking at him struggle with the instructions and cursing his way through the whole process, I suddenly feel so appreciative and a bit guilty too. They did their best and more.

Best

That's it, I've left home! I'm living somewhere new, I'm studying for a degree that could lead to my dream job, and I have the opportunity to reinvent myself and be whomever I want to be! My heart aches though and my brain is full of memories. It's like I've moved geographically but I haven't been able to flee. I'm stuck somewhere in the past. I'd like to think I'm trying my best to move forward but it's not happening yet. Hopefully this isn't the best time of my life as people say university should be. For if it is, what will be the worst?

Worst

Blending in. Being part of a group. Becoming popular. That's my plan for this first year at university. I don't know who I am, and I don't intend to find out. So I go out, party, drink, sign-up for loads of student clubs, hang out with the 'cool' crowd and pretend to be one of them. I'm putting on weight, but I'm not bothered. I'm making a fool of myself, but I'm not bothered. I'm just not that bothered. Today and tomorrow is our 'integration weekend'. A bunch of third, fourth, and fifth year students have organised it for us newbies. Sitting in a large bus, we drive a couple of hours to the beach. Once there, we split into teams and play drinking games. I've never had a drink before. Unexpected for an 18 year old I guess. But as a child, I was full of principles. One of them was to never drink. I saw it as a useless loss of control. Not anymore! After a few glasses, we're playing a game on the beach. One by one, we have to run, turn around a bucket buried in the sand 10 times and rush back. Seven turns later, I faint head first in the sand. As I regain consciousness, I see that everyone around me is finding it funny, so I laugh along with them. From then on, I become known as 'the girl who passed out head first in the sand'. For some obscure reason, I really like it. It feels like a promising token of acceptance.

Acceptance

A few months later, I'm part of several student groups. One of them is the club that organises this year's gala event. I'm sure it's going to be an epic party! I want everyone to know I'm involved so badly. I suppose I'm hoping for validation and ultimately looking for anything that can help me forget about my solitude, so I give all I have and say yes to everything. As the party comes to an end in the early hours of the morning, I'm still drunk. Utterly exhausted, I drive myself back to my apartment. I can feel my eyes getting heavier and heavier. When they close, the car starts veering off the road. At the last minute I snap them open again and steer the car back on the road. I'm risking my life. Why? For what? For whom? Since when did being popular become an item on my mental 'grown-up' list? I have no idea. The list seems to be a relic of the past, although I'm uncertain it should be. Right now, I feel like I'm at my worst and rock bottom isn't far.

Far

In our second year, we all have the opportunity to study or do an internship abroad. I'm thrilled at the idea! There is a long list of options of countries and cities available. We've been asked to rank them according to our preference. Historically, students achieve one of their top three choices. Mine are Ireland, the United States, and the United Kingdom. Since the three weeks I spent in Ireland when I was 14, I've been really keen to go back and further improve my English. More than a mysterious code, it now feels like the key that I need to unlock my dreams of travelling the world. Today I'll find out where life will take me, and I couldn't be more impatient.

Impatient

I'm at home getting ready to take the tram and head to campus when my phone rings. It's one of my friends so I answer cheerily, as I always do.

"Hey, how's it going?" I ask.

"Good and you?" he responds in a quiet voice.

Straight away, I know something is up. Hesitantly, he asks me whether I want the good or the bad news first. I opt for the bad.

"Results are in. You didn't get any of your top choices," he says. "You'll be going to Bergen."

As if the strength in my body was leaving me, I feel myself falling to the floor. Where is Bergen anyway? Was it on my list of choices? I can't remember. I can't think. I can't breathe. I even forget to ask him for the good news before hanging up and melting down.

Down
Bergen, which apparently is the second largest city in Norway, was on my list. It was number 17. Since the launch of the exchange programme, no one has ever gotten lower than their third choice. I got my 17th. Seventeen. Seventeen. Seventeen. The number is playing on repeat in my head. I feel like an absolute failure. Another girl got her 15th choice and somehow everyone, including her, seems to think that it's cool. I envy her detachment. There is no way I can be like that. I care too much, always have and probably always will. But if I care so much about the results, why didn't I care about the process? Why didn't I study enough to get the grades that would allow me to secure my first choice? Why am I not studying at all now? I don't know. It seems like I'm caught in a downward spiral.

Downward
It's easier to blame life and luck, easier than taking my destiny in my own hands and breaking the vicious cycle I seem to keep falling into. I secretly hope that doing the strict minimum will be enough to pass. It is for many people, or so it seems. Everyone around me says they never study. Apparently, they prefer to enjoy life and party instead. So I take a chance too. Today, is the day I find out the results of my first year at university. I'm not worried. Standing in front of the names lists, I can't find mine. Suddenly, I stumble upon it. I didn't pass. Everyone else around is celebrating their own success and discussing their exciting summer plans. A buffet lunch has been prepared outside for all to enjoy. Discreetly, I hide in a corner at the end of the hall and call my parents. I tell them I won't be coming home as planned. The job Mum helped me secure has to be cancelled and I'll miss this year's family holiday. I don't know if they are

disappointed in me or if I'm projecting my own disappointment onto them. Either way, this is terrible news. I'm sure they expected more of me and I know I expected so much more of myself. I'll have to stay in Bordeaux for one more month to retake six subjects. A second chance, which I hope I'll seize successfully. If not, I'll have to do the first year all over again and I won't be moving to Bergen.

Moving
To be honest, right now, moving to Bergen sounds like the best thing that could ever happen to me. Ironic, isn't?

CHAPTER 2

Home is Here

Yes

Bergen, Bergen, Bergen, here I come! I studied as diligently as I could and passed… eventually! Finally, I can put this dreadful first year at university behind me. It's time for a new chapter, a new place, a new me. All the disappointment I felt when I found out I was going to Bergen has turned into all-consuming excitement. It's like I'm standing at the edge of a chasm, ready to jump into the unknown and somehow convinced that something good will come of it. The only thing I know about the place is what I remember from the Wikipedia© page[1]: 'It rained every day from the 29th of October 2006 to the 21st of January 2007, 85 consecutive days'. Today is the 11th of August 2007. I'm 18 and I'm ready to leave!

Leave

I've packed two large suitcases. I've gathered all the essentials, including Boutchou, though that must remain a secret. Six of us from Bordeaux will be studying in Bergen for a year. Six girls. Despite having spent our first year at the same university, we don't really know each other. The only one I've met before I don't particularly get along with. She is tall, stunning, and smart. We clearly don't have anything in common. When one of the others contacted me to see if I'd fly over with a couple of them I said yes, of course! This morning, the three of us are meeting at the airport. It's a little awkward at first. We've all come with our families, so we wave at each other from afar. While I hug and kiss my parents goodbye with a smile from ear to ear, from the corner of my eye I notice the others are doing the same, but they

---

[1] To find out more about the city and its appalling weather, here is the link to the Wikipedia© page: https://en.wikipedia.org/wiki/Bergen#Climate

are in tears. Am I heartless? Once on-board the aircraft, I try to comfort the girls but my eagerness to arrive is hard to conceal.

Arrive

As the plane lands, I'm ready to jump out. Airports truly are the gateway to a country. Each of them has a different smell. Bergen is no exception, but it seems as if I'm the only one to notice. The airport is small, so after only a few minutes, the girls and I are already at baggage claim waiting for our suitcases. I can feel their anxiety rising but we don't talk about it. We just joke around and get to know each other. From what I discover, one is pretty cheeky and the other extremely caring. Next, we need to find the bus that will take us to our new temporary home. The caring one takes the lead and asks around. I don't say anything but deep down I'm extremely grateful for her initiative. We've just arrived, and I don't feel very confident about my English. A few years have passed since I visited Ireland and I'm a bit rusty. Miraculously, we hop on the right bus and get off at the correct stop. From there, a walk over a bridge and up a hill awaits us. I'm struggling so much with my suitcases.

Suitcases

Astoundingly, the weather is nice and warm. It's very different from what the Wikipedia© page led us to believe, which is fantastic! I'm sweating from the heat. After a few minutes, that feel like an eternity, I take a small break along the way. That's when I see the girls coming back down to give me a hand. Relief and appreciation fill my heart. Looking at the two of them smiling right at me, I decide that no matter what, I'll have their back. All I hope is that they'll have mine too. Together, we walk towards our new home: Fantoft.

Home

We could see them from afar but weren't sure they were it. The three gigantic towers of grey concrete stick out like sore thumbs in the surprisingly blue sky. We're here now, standing beneath them and looking up at what reminds us of Russian Communist architecture straight from our history books. Not what we pictured Norway to look like and very different from the images we found online when searching for Bergen. Never mind. We head to the admin office to obtain our keys. Each standing in a different queue, we don't know whether we'll end up neighbours or whether they'll split us up. This isn't something we've had time to discuss. I'm trying to figure out which option I'd actually prefer when the lady at the reception desk in front of me screams "NEXT!" She looks through all my paperwork and asks a couple of questions. Then, after about 15 minutes, that's it. I have the key to my new home! I really hope it comes with a new life.

New

I wait for the girls and we realise that we're all on the same floor of the same building: 7D. A smile grows across my face and then I know that's what my heart wanted. Dragging our luggage, we make our way to the elevator. It's covered in graffiti from top to bottom. What is this place we have arrived at? Once on the seventh floor, we walk past the shared kitchen. I take a quick look at it and realise it's pretty gross. We keep walking along the corridor to find our rooms. They're next to each other and all look the same. They include a single bed, a table, a chair and a desk. Everything is wooden – plain and simple. Each room also comes with a small private bathroom. It's dark in there but as my eyes adapt to the twilight, I realise it's an 'all-in-one'. I've never seen that before. Basically, there is no separation between the shower, sink and toilet. Everything is on top of each other. I guess the wonderful thing is that you could take a shower while sitting on the toilet and brushing your teeth... Efficient, I suppose. All three of us meet in the corridor and share our first impressions. We can't help but laugh hysterically at the bathroom situation. Once we've caught our breath, we decide to head to IKEA© to equip and decorate our stern rooms.

Decorate

We spend ages in there. We look at everything and make each other giggle constantly. As it turns out, they love this store just as much as I do. Interior design is awesome! Plus, the incomprehensible names on all the furniture and decoration items are hilarious. Are they Swedish or Norwegian? We have no idea. After a good three hours, we catch the bus back with our new treasures. It's time for a make-over. Our mission accomplished, we invite each other for a tour. I'm quite proud of my little set-up. I've acquired a white and purple duvet and a collection of matching candles. It smells good and feels pretty cosy. The girls agree. I love their rooms too! It's funny how we all went to the same store at the same time but ended up buying totally different items. The colourful cushions the cheeky one went for are gorgeous, I'm a fan! After dinner, we're exhausted so we wish each other good night and return to our rooms.

Night

Back in my own little world, I open the top drawer of my wardrobe to grab my pyjamas. As I do so, a cockroach comes out. Blood goes straight to my head; my heart jumps out of my chest and after freezing for a second I grab a shoe and kill it. I'm swearing and shaking. Could this suddenly hostile and generally unfamiliar environment ever feel like home? Slowly drifting to sleep a while later, I'm so glad the girls are around. It's as if I could sense their reassuring presence through the walls.

Girls
We're quite different but here our difference rhymes with irrelevance. We all have one essential thing in common: we've just landed in a completely foreign environment. Everything around us is new. The place we live in, the people we encounter, the language they speak, the food options... It's a lot to take in and get used to. Plus, there is so much to do: open a local bank account, get a Norwegian SIM card and phone number, register at the university, request a national insurance number and the list goes on. There is no doubt about it, I'm struggling to remember what to do and when to do it. Luckily, three brains are far stronger than one, so we lean on each other. From practical tips to helpful advice and intimate secrets, we share everything.

Share
When the cheeky one breaks up with her boyfriend, we bring her a giant bag of candy and do everything in our power to cheer her up. When the caring one struggles to finish her essay on time, we bring her coffee every half hour or so and do everything in our power to cheer her on. When my bank card is swallowed by an ATM at the mall, it's Dad I call first, crying my eyes out. But from where he is there isn't much he can do to help. In the end, it's the girls who make me laugh until my tears dry out and who lend me money for a while. Bearing in mind some of the sad friendship stories of my childhood, this is quite a change for me. Have I landed in one of those American sitcoms where friends

are able to overcome all obstacles together? Am I in *Sex and the City*[2] Norwegian edition? Or is this actually normal? I hope it is as I'm enjoying every single minute of our emerging friendship. Gradually, the three of us grow into a tighter unit.

Unit

We do everything together. 'Three for one' is what other people should call us if they don't already. Day and night, we hang out. We debate, we gossip, and we joke around. Being with them is such fun. I can't remember the last time I laughed so hard. The other day, we ended up speaking about our poop. Don't worry, I won't be sharing any of the details… I've read somewhere that 'with your friends you speak about sex but with your best friends you speak about poop'. I guess our conversation was a good sign then! Later that night, the cheeky one put on a karaoke video and we all started singing our lungs out. Since then, we've been singing both when we drink and when we don't. We've been singing everywhere, all the time and have become known as 'the singing girls of 7D'. A few days later, I convinced them to organise a runway show in the corridor. It brought back some old memories and ended up in a hilarious photo shoot. When none of these options entertain us enough, we host parties.

Parties

Monday to Friday is the week. Saturday and Sunday, the weekend. Not for us. It doesn't matter which day of the week it is anymore. We party when we fancy and this evening we're ready for our first big night out! A small group of us head to the closest

---

[2] *Sex and the City* is an American sitcom about the life of four best friends who live in New York City. It was broadcast between 1998 and 2004.

Vinmonopolet. In Norway, any alcohol stronger than beer isn't sold at supermarkets but in wine shops called Vinmonopolet, as they are the monopoly of the state. Quite different from France. Anyway, at this stage all we care about is buying alcohol rather than from where we buy it. Once we arrive, we look at our options and pretty quickly realise that all we can afford between the five of us is half a bottle of vodka. Shock and dread can be read across all our faces. This ERASMUS[3] year is supposed to be all about crazy parties. That's what everyone told us before we left. What are we going to do now? No one will be getting drunk tonight. But we decide to stay positive, buy our half bottle of vodka and head back. Fantoft, where we stay, is located 20 minutes away from the city centre. As it turns out, it's where all the foreigners, students and migrants live. We don't mind. Quite the opposite! It's great to be surrounded by people who are in the same boat.

Same
This evening, sitting around our kitchen table, there are more nationalities than I've ever spent time with before. German, French, Portuguese, Palestinian, Belgian, Chinese and Canadian. We don't know each other. We don't speak the same mother tongue. We weren't born or brought up in the same country. But tonight, we're ready to party together as one! This is the first time, and I'm sure it won't be the last. We play German drinking games, learn Portuguese words, sing French songs, eat Palestinian

---

[3] Desiderius Erasmus Roterodamus (1466 – 1536) was a Dutch Catholic priest, scholar and humanist. The ERASMUS programme (EuRopean Community Action Scheme for the Mobility of University Students) is a European student exchange programme which was named after him. It was founded in 1987.

cake – hands down the best desert E.V.E.R! I feel like I'm travelling all over the world while simply sitting here. It's extraordinary! A few short hours later, we all jump on the bus and head to a club in Bergen's town centre.

Bus
The girls are singing out loud while other people are dancing and jumping around. A few bystanders are watching in disbelief… I take a minute to look around. This is the happiest I've been in ages. In the middle of this animated crowd, I unexpectedly feel as though I'm exactly where I need to be. I'm somewhere wonderful, somewhere I belong, somewhere I can be myself without the fear of being judged. Most importantly, I'm part of something bigger than just me, bigger than this bus and bigger than all of us. I close my eyes for a moment and take in the warmth and contentment that flows through my veins. Doing so, my heartbeat quickens. I'm alive! I'm here! I'm me!

Here
Once in town, we make our way to the club as quickly as we can. There is a queue outside, so we wait in the freezing cold for a while. It's only the end of August but summer seems to already be gone. More than 30 minutes later, we're finally standing at the entrance door. Before we can get in, the security guards stop us and ask to see our IDs. Most people in the group say it never happens in their home countries. I guess they're more diligent here.

Diligent
Compliant, I show my passport to one of them. Staring at my date of birth, he chuckles discreetly. "No" is all he says. Annoyed,

I ask why and begin to argue. I'm 18, almost 19, and the little rebel in me wants in! I'm convinced that in France, I would be allowed in wherever I want. As it turns out, in Norway, that's not the case. Twenty is the minimum age required to enter most bars and clubs. Damn. The girls and I wave goodbye to everyone else and walk back to the night bus. Alcohol is too expensive, and we can't get into clubs. We need a plan.

Plan

Perhaps we should be putting our energy into something other than figuring out how to party. I'm sure we will, but not this year! Regarding our first problem – alcohol – we have come up with two solutions: make our own in the basement of our tower block and import some from other countries. Regarding our second problem, getting into clubs, we have one: use one of the girl's ID for everyone. She is 20. Here is how it's going to work:
1. She shows her ID at the entrance of the club while we wait hidden around the corner.
2. As she enters, she gets a stamp on her wrist.
3. She then comes out again discreetly and passes her ID to the next person.
4. She returns to the club by showing her stamp. No ID needed.
5. The next person repeats the scheme until we're all in.

Scheme

We would probably get into all sorts of trouble if we were caught. But it's as though we've been hit by a temporary brain malfunction. It doesn't even cross our minds. All we seem to be able to focus on is making this year the most unforgettable of our lives. We put the plan in motion and surprisingly enough, it works! Every time someone travels outbound, they're tasked with bringing alcohol back. And every club we go to, we all enter with the same ID, one by one. Soon enough, these devilish schemes become part of our routine.

Routine
Get up late. Go to university downtown. Come home. Train at the gym (sometimes). Have dinner. Party. Repeat. That's most days. Actually, that's not quite true… Very few days are the same here. That's one of the things I love the most about living abroad. There are always new things to do, new places to explore and new dishes to taste. Plus, the girls keep coming up with the most random ideas. We've tried a wide range of strange food items from the supermarket and even attempted to make our own iced tea a couple of days ago. The tea turned out to be disgusting but the process was great fun. Yet another aspect of this lifestyle I adore is having the ability and luxury to travel around.

Travel
The three of us and a few other friends are keen to find out what Norway has to offer. We start by exploring our local surroundings. Together, we hike up Mont Ulriken and witness a breathtaking sunset from above. A few weeks later, we drive to Stavenger. Standing at the top of Preikestolen, 604 metres above Lysefjorden and without a single barrier in sight, makes us feel like we're on top of the world! Ignoring the snowfall, we even jump into the ocean for a few seconds. The thrill of it barely takes the cold away. It's as freezing as it's fun! Another weekend trip takes us to Hardangerfjord, the second largest fjord in Norway. There, the reflection of the mountains in the water is an image I'll never forget. Determined to make the most of our year in the

region, we then expand our horizons and start exploring other Scandinavian countries. Sweden is the first I travel to, this time on my own. One of my friends from university is spending his ERASMUS year in Stockholm so I'm visiting him for a few days. Luckily, I'm able to sleep on an inflatable mattress in his room. Staying with friends or at cheap B&B is the only way we can afford our ambitious travel plans. Plus, I think receiving advice from a local or someone who lives there is brilliant.

Brilliant
My friend has turned into a tour guide and takes great pleasure in showing me around 'his Stockholm'. His enthusiasm is contagious, and the city is gorgeous. Winding waterways, colourful buildings, beautiful people… A short weekend later, Stockholm has won me over. Back in Bergen, I'm already planning other trips. The girls and I are speaking about going to Denmark and Poland together. I would also like to visit friends in Hungary, Austria and Czech Republic. So many exciting adventures ahead! Meanwhile, we make the most of our time in Bergen. We try as many awesome activities as we can come up with: rafting in 5 degrees Celsius, paintballing in the rain, and watching the final of Norway's Football league on a giant screen. There is practically no time for boredom.

Boredom
When I was in Bordeaux, I used to find most of my university classes pretty boring but over here, I think studying is actually interesting. Plus, determined not to let the tragedy of my first year repeat itself, I'm committed to putting in the effort and studying. That's why, at the start of the semester, I decide to take on a lot of extra credits. Although it means I have more classes

to attend than most of my friends, I don't mind. All the teachers bring their subject to life in a unique and relatable way. The international relations teacher is extremely charming and makes the funniest political jokes I've ever heard. The media teacher is fascinating and reinforces my dreams of a career in journalism. The Scandinavian geography teacher is totally inspiring. At 80-something, he actually climbs mountains faster than I do. Last but not least, the Norwegian teacher is pretty surprising.

Surprising

Today is my first Norwegian class. The girls chose not to join so I don't know anyone. Once all the students have arrived, the teacher welcomes us cheerfully. She tells the class that she would like to start by teaching us the most useful word of the Norwegian language and asks us to try and guess what that might be.

Someone says he thinks it will be "Hello!"

Another person reckons it is going to be "Yes."

A third wonders whether it might be "What's your name?"

At each of their guesses, the teacher shakes her head gently. That's not it. With a spark in her eye, she eventually turns to the board and writes *øl*. A few seconds of awkward silence later, she lets out a contagious laugh and exclaims "Beer!" Everyone joins in her laughter. I'm not sure whether this is a teacher's bait or an actual insight on the local culture. Regardless, I instantly like her and can't wait to learn more Norwegian.

Norwegian

When I first heard Norwegians speak to each other I thought it sounded as though they were singing. I could neither make out the beginning nor the end of each sentence. Words were just musical notes that blended together into one melody.

Like English used to be a few years ago, Norwegian right now seems like a mysterious code to me. Once again, I can't help but feel an inherent motivation to crack it. Plus, I'm convinced that learning the local language will allow me to understand the culture better, become more integrated into the local community and ultimately make the most of living here. Who knows, I might even be able to make Norwegian friends along the way. The girls and I were lying under a lamp last night pretending it was the sun we miss so dearly and chatting about how we've been living in Bergen for about four months but don't really know any Norwegians. Shocking, don't you think? I guess living in Fantoft, away from the town centre where the student life is, has a lot to do with it. Also, locals tend to already have their own circle of friends and, to be brutally honest, they sometimes come across as quite cold towards us. Perhaps it has something to do with the weather.

Weather
It's been so miserable recently. Slowly but surely, the gorgeous white snow turns into huge puddles of grey slush, the freezing wind cuts through anything we wear, and the rain pours down endlessly. All our shoes are damp and damaged. Truth is, we haven't bought rubber boots yet. After spending our first few weeks mocking the locals who wear them and insisting that French ladies must always put style over comfort, I don't know about the other two, but I'm starting to regret my words. Perhaps the time has come to embrace local customs more and put our French-minded judgments on hold.

Local
Like the three musketeers, the girls and I have a plan of attack and scenarios for everything. We most definitely have too much

time on our hands! After a silly drunken attempt at romance with an ugly German giant, I'm currently the 'most' single of the three of us. The caring one has just started dating a handsome Portuguese guy, and the cheeky one has been in a relationship on and off with a guy back in France. I'm also the only one in a separate seminar group, by choice. I wanted to have the opportunity to meet more people. The others didn't approve at first but they now see it as a great tactical advantage in our quest to expand our circle. Anyway, we've decided – though I can't remember having much of a say in this – that the responsibility of meeting more locals has fallen to me. Truth is, they're keen for me to find a Norwegian boyfriend, and I am too.

Boyfriend
My self-esteem is still pretty low, but hanging out with the girls and meeting all these people from many parts of the world has helped me feel a little better about myself. They think I'm smart and funny. Perhaps there's some truth in that. Also, finally, after over a year, my heart has started to mend. I'm not sure I'm ready to put it on the line again but I must admit, I'm not indifferent to one of the Norwegian guys in my seminar group. He keeps staring at me in class with his intense grey eyes. Very intelligent, he is always asking meaningful questions and steering the debate. Plus, he seems to have a lot of close friends too. I can't recall having met anyone who could master both being smart and sociable. He might be the exception that confirms the rule.

Exception
The girls and I have discovered something new. People 'in the know' call it a social network, we just use its name: Facebook©.

Basically, it's an online platform through which you can connect with people, whether it'd be old friends or new acquaintances. Now that we've created our profiles, we spend our time uploading new photos, sending each other private messages and sharing all about our lives in lengthy status updates. It's not like anyone sees it anyway. It's so new that very few people are on it. At least, that's what I thought until I received a message from the cute guy in my seminar group out of the blue. 'You spend waaaaaaaaaaaaaaaaay too much time on Facebook©' is what it reads. Interesting approach, I thought to myself, intrigued.

Intrigued
There is no doubt about it, my first impression was right, this guy is extremely smart. Politics and current affairs are his passion. He reads the news every day and is curious about everything and everyone around him. His quest for knowledge is unstoppable and so endearing. On our first date, we speak for hours about where we think the world is going and where we believe our place is within it. His undeniable charisma and clever sense of humour seduce me. Tonight is our second date and I've dressed up for the occasion. I've even put on my cute black heels. Walking in them isn't easy but wearing them makes me stand a little taller and feel more confident. I can't wait to see him! I have butterflies in my stomach as I walk towards the restaurant he's invited me to.

Restaurant
The place is warm and cosy. There he is, sitting behind a small table at the centre of which stands a romantic candle. Once again, we talk for hours. Staring into his intense grey eyes, I catch a glimpse of the immensity of his kindness. There is no doubt

about it, he is a stand-up guy and I'm the luckiest girl in the world! With him, I learn so much about Norwegian history and culture. Time goes by unbelievably quickly until the waitress finally informs us that the restaurant is about to close.

Close

As we stand up to leave, we realise that it's snowing outside. There is about a metre of white powder on the ground. We turn to each other in disbelief. Our dinner was so wonderful that we completely missed what was going on out there. If walking in heels was tough earlier, it's now an absolute mission. He chuckles at my gait, so I throw a snowball at his face in revenge. We're both laughing now. Somehow, his hand has found mine and slowly, we make our way to the bus stop. Once there, we kiss passionately. Jokingly, he says I made the first move but I beg to differ. Let's just say it was a joint effort for the utmost enjoyment of both parties. The arrival of the bus interrupts our banter. Thinking of him as I lie in bed that night, I feel as though this is the beginning of a promising relationship based on tenderness, trust, and mutual respect.

Respect

At university, lecturers and students are on first name terms and interact informally. It's very different from what I've experienced in France thus far. Being able to have a chat with renowned professors openly, honestly and without a certain level of fear or intimidation is so refreshing and inspiring. University isn't the only place I've witnessed such manifestations of what I like to call 'Norwegian respect'. The more I learn about the local culture, the more I find people open-minded and accepting of all backgrounds, races, religions and genders.

Genders
Talking about gender, Norwegian girls are so beautiful – tall, slender, athletic, blond with blue eyes. I'm torn between admiration and envy. Regardless of the weather and of their shape or size, their party outfits involve next to no fabric. At first, these daring attires shocked me. But pretty soon it's the reaction they receive that baffled me more. None at all. Men seem to simply respect these northern amazons. No comments, no questions, no insults. Just respect. And that's not the only example.

Example
The other day, I saw a student carrying her baby around her waist as she entered the library. Her baby sleeping quietly against her chest, she sat down and studied for a few hours. I'd never seen a pregnant student at university before, let alone one with a child. In response to my interrogations, the Norwegian teacher explained that here, women who have children during their studies are provided with sufficient financial support. That way, they don't have to choose between learning and raising children. That's one of the country's many measures to ensure gender equality. I've come across several others over the past few months. Reflecting on it, I wish these aspects of Norwegian culture could expand to the rest of the world. If it works here, why wouldn't it work elsewhere?

Work
Nothing is perfect. If there is one thing I could change about Norway, it would be how expensive living here is. Luckily, we were provided with a small grant as part of the ERASMUS programme and my parents have been helping me too. But I feel like the time has come for me to contribute to my own life.

A few other foreign students found jobs so why not give it a try? I decide to share my thoughts with a new French girlfriend of mine. She looks at me and says, "We both want a job so let's just get one!" I laugh out loud. This girl is officially mad for thinking it'll be that simple. Looking at her again, I realise she is actually being serious.

Serious
From what we've heard, a few people have secured waitressing jobs at Grieghallen – Bergen's cultural centre. They work for a company that hosts a wide range of events there throughout the year. We're at the library. It's only a 10-minute walk. Off we go! She is leading while I feel as though I'm being dragged along behind. On the way over, I warn her that I have no experience in hospitality and I'm a terrible liar. There is no way this is going to end well. She is so positive though, so I decide not to express that last point. Instead, I smile at her like parents smile at their over-imaginative children. Standing at the front door, I feel a mix of fear and adrenaline. Could this actually work out? What if?

If
The security guard opens the door and asks us what we want. Luckily, he speaks English quite well. She explains that we're looking for a job and have heard they're currently hiring. I know she is making it up, so I just focus on nodding and looking friendly. He asks us to wait a moment and picks up the phone to call someone. Let's hope it's not more security to kick both of us out. After a few minutes, a 50-something-year-old man comes down the stairs. He's smartly dressed in a black suit and white shirt. We shake hands. Politely but firmly he asks us to follow him to his office. On the way, he shows us the kitchen and asks a few

questions. "Do you have any hospitality experience?" I remain quiet as she answers that she's worked at a music festival before. I think it's true, but I can't be sure. She is really good at this!

Good

He grabs a piece of paper and hands it to her.

"Can you speak some Norwegian?" he asks.

"Well, we're both studying Norwegian at university at the moment…" she starts to explain.

He interrupts her. "Please translate what's on the menu of tonight's event."

She freezes. As I look down the list, I realise I recognise most of the words. For the first time since we've arrived, I speak up and translate what I know.

"Ok," he utters abruptly and ushers us into his office.

Suddenly appearing in a rush, he explains that he has a very important appointment coming up and fetches two employment contracts from his drawer. All we have to do is date and sign on the last page and the jobs are ours. My joy is so hard to contain. We sign, hand the contracts back to him and make our way out. Right there, on the pavement, barely hidden from the security guard, we scream and jump in each other's arms. We did it! Our first job! Symbol of adulthood. Symbol of freedom. Symbol of power over our own lives and our own destiny. I can't wait to begin.

Begin

I've only been in Norway six months as I look back and reflect. If I were to give a name to this first half of the year, I would choose the word 'beginning'. It might seem strange but, in my mind, it describes and encompasses perfectly everything that's happened to date: new country, new job, new friendships, new language and the promising ability to love again. The other thing I've learnt thus far is that hard work does pay off. Thanks to all the extra classes I took at the start, I've managed to pass my whole ERASMUS year in only one semester. My daydreaming is interrupted by the girls' knock on my door. The caring one is wearing her skinny jeans and the cheeky one her little black dress. I pop my head out and yell, "Let's get the party started!" I never want this to end...

End

The caring one found scales. She saw it in the basement of the building, where the laundry room is. We haven't weighed ourselves in ages. I know I might have put on a few kilograms but up until this moment, I hadn't given it a second thought. It's been all about having fun, being young and living life to the fullest! The caring one is keen to find out. She says she's been worrying about her weight a lot recently, though she looks absolutely stunning to me.

"Are you coming?" she asks.

The cheeky one declines. My brain freezes. I can't decide.

"Come on, let's go!" she continues.

Fine. I follow her to the laundry room. It's not a pleasant place, far from it actually. I often wonder how our clothes can come out of here clean when the smell and the appearance of the room are equally repellent. There it is. The scales. It is staring at me like it always does, and I feel as though it has already started mocking me. I swear I can hear it say, "Look at you fatty, step on me and I'll show you who the whale is!" The caring one goes first and sighs. A few kilograms, something like two or three, is what she's put on. I hope the outcome will be the same for me. Fingers crossed. I'm petrified.

Petrified
Left foot forward. Right foot forward. The arrow shifts further and further away from zero. I hate numbers. You can't argue with them. The truth is what they give you. Seventy-six. That's one number I'll never forget. I've put on 10 kilograms in less than six months. I'm pretty much as heavy as Dad. But I only measure 169 centimetres, that's a lot less than he does. What am I going to do? We walk back up in silence and I go straight to my room. Once again, Dad is who I call right away. He is the only one who can understand. He was overweight when he was younger, but he lost it all. I've always admired that. I tell him what happened and then I make a promise – to both of us – that I will lose weight and that I will never be this heavy ever again. I have no idea how to go about it, but I'm fully committed this time. This must be the end of 'the whale'. It has to be. It will be.

Whale
Whale is actually one of the many strange things they eat over here. Other delicacies include reindeer sausage, salmon from a tube, sheep head. Some of these dishes I'm keen to try but others, like the latter, no thanks! Whale though, I thought I'd give it a go for old time's sake. Well, whale… I found it very strange. It looks like red meat from the outside so that's what your brain expects it to taste like. But when you start chewing it, you realise that it tastes more like fish. Disturbing. Not something I'll order again. Having said that, we eat all sorts of random things in France too.

Random
We're pretty famous for our strange dishes actually. Frogs' legs, snails, tongue, intestines, steak tartare and the list goes on.

Though I don't think of myself as a fussy eater, I don't particularly like any of these. There are also quite a few drinks I'm not fond of, such as coffee and red wine. When I tell people about this, their first reaction is usually shock. Often, they reply something along the lines of "You're not REALLY French then." My family tree would contradict them but the thought of perhaps being more than French is growing on me.

Growing

We've just come back from our Christmas break and I feel a little different. My priorities seem to have shifted. There isn't much time left to do all the things I'd like to do and see all the places I'd like to see, so I've made a wish list:

1. Explore Bergen and Norway more
2. Improve my Norwegian
3. Deepen my relationships
4. Become slimmer and healthier
5. Work harder

As I write it down, it reminds me of my 'grown-up' list. I guess the principle is the same though the content is a little different. Perhaps as one gets older, things do change.

Change

As the days, weeks, and months go by, I spend more and more time with my boyfriend. It's so amazing to be able to call him that. Between us, it's moving fast and it's going really well. His kindness and encouragement make me want to become a better version of myself. I thus begin to change deliberately. Step-by-step, I start watching what I eat, exercising more and looking after myself a little better.

Better
The road towards a better me isn't without a few hiccups though, like tonight's party. I skipped dinner and I promised myself I wouldn't drink too much, as I thought that'd be good for my weight loss. This evening is the first time I meet all of my boyfriends' friends and he meets all of mine so I need to behave. It's going according to plan until the girls arrive, ready to party! Pretty quickly, I lose track of both what and how much I've drunk. Beer, homemade white wine, other wine, rum, more wine and now tequila. After the sixth shot of the latter, I know I'm going to be sick so I run to the bathroom, head for the toilet and it all comes out. From the nose even. I had no idea that was possible. Considering how much it hurts, I wish I still didn't know it was. Exhausted and embarrassed, I run through the living room and hide in my boyfriend's room.

Embarrassed
He opens the window to give me some fresh air. I'm going to be sick again. Sadly, there is no time for me to go to the bathroom and the alcohol has blurred my judgment, so I throw up through the window instead. A few minutes later, someone knocks on the door. At that moment, I'm way too drunk to realise what's happening. Dropping in and out of consciousness for a while, I finally fall asleep. The next day, my boyfriend fills me in. The downstairs neighbours are the ones who knocked. They were upset because someone threw up on their windowsill... He pretended to know nothing about it and told them to speak to the people who live one floor above. He chuckles while telling me the story. I, on the other hand, am mortified. At least I presume I made an unforgettable first impression.

Unforgettable
The weather is finally getting better. The city looks so beautiful in the sun. Along the harbour, the fish market is buzzing. Around the corner, the little houses of Bryggen seem so colourful. Looking up, the majestic Mount Fløyen makes me want to go for a hike. I love it all! I love life! I love him! University is going well and so is my job. Every day that passes is a day I feel like I belong here a little more. I even ended up colouring my hair blond. It's as if a part of me was slowly becoming Norwegian.

Becoming
It's decided, I'm going to stay here for longer. After university ends and the girls return to France, I'll move into my boyfriend's flat. He lives with three friends, two guys and one girl. They're all really welcoming though they don't speak to me much as my Norwegian isn't great. But I'm improving. Last night I was having dinner with them. Despite not understanding much of the conversation, I managed to make a joke in Norwegian. Not only was it a first for me, they actually found it hilarious! Something about tomatoes that doesn't translate well. Regardless, imagine how happy that made me! The little things sometimes, they're the real game changers.

Real
Today is the 17th of May or *syttende mai* as the locals call it. It's the Norwegian Constitution Day or in other words, the country's national day. Most nations have one I suppose but this is something different. Back in France, on Bastille day, I might watch the parade on TV and check out the fireworks in the evening. Alternatively, I could just stay at home and chill or even travel somewhere. It doesn't really matter. If it wasn't a

bank holiday, it'd feel like any other day. When I said that to my boyfriend and his housemates last night, they were baffled. Everyone here, including them, seems to take the 17th of May very seriously. Norway only became fully independent in 1905. That's just over one hundred years ago. Quite understandably, this relatively young nation is eager to celebrate its identity.

Celebrate
We're getting ready now and I can't wait to be part of it all! At six o'clock this morning we heard canons being fired from the mountains. Since then, the sound of the parade has gotten louder and louder. It's smartly dressed that we finally rush downstairs. Outside it's a festival of colours. Most people are wearing their traditional attire. Some are dressed in green, others in red and a few in blue. They all look absolutely beautiful. The silver jewellery women are sporting reflects the rays of the sun. Their earrings, broaches, and hair pieces are delicate and elegant. Making our way through the crowd, we walk closer and closer to the heart of the action. The music is louder than ever. I can feel the drums beating through my whole body. My eyes and ears are wide open as I try to take it all in. With an endearing smile, my boyfriend hands me a small Norwegian flag. I wave it proudly above my head in sync with everyone else. The girls are here, and so are his friends. Together, in the middle this dense crowd, we are one, we are Norwegian.

One
One year. The end is around the corner. The last few months have gone by so incredibly fast. I've followed my priority list to the letter and I've loved every minute of it. My travels have taken me all over the place, even all the way to the north of Norway,

beyond the polar circle. What an incredible experience! My favourite memory is the day I went cross-country skiing with my boyfriend and his mum.

Skiing

We parked the car in the middle of nowhere and walked for a few metres. There it was. Snow. We couldn't see the end of it. It was like staring at a desert except this one was pure white and unbelievably cold. About -25 degrees Celsius his mum said in a very monotone voice, as if there was nothing unusual about it. The colour and temperature were striking but what surprised me the most was the total absence of tracks. It seemed as though no animals or humans had dared to walk into this cotton candy looking landscape. The three of us were about to change that. Skis on our feet and sticks in our hands, we stepped into the flawless white immensity ahead of us. Right, left, right, left, right, left. Moving through the snow was a lot tougher than I'd imagined, especially as it came up to our knees. I struggled but it didn't bother me. The view was absolutely gorgeous. It took my breath away. At one point I remember asking my boyfriend to pinch me.

Pinch

Used to this incredible landscape he'd grown-up with, my astonishment seemed odd to him. Perhaps it gave him a fresh outlook on these familiar surroundings. I never asked. I wish I had. This reminds me how much I love observing kids as they explore their environment and discover new things. The amazement in their eyes helps me remember to actually look at the beauty around me. Spending time in the north of Norway, I feel like a kid. Not only do I marvel at everything, I'm also slowly starting to get a grasp of the language. I've probably gone from speaking it like a four year old to reaching the level of a ten year old. I've even just finished reading my first Norwegian book. It's helped me communicate with my boyfriend's family and friends. Although they all speak English very well, they seem to enjoy hearing my attempts at their melodic language. I couldn't be more grateful for their patience and hospitality. Here, so far away from everything I knew before, they've somehow managed to make me feel at home. This trip has also brought me even closer to him. Seeing where he grew up, meeting his loved ones and listening to all his childhood stories has been such a wonderful experience.

Wonderful
There was no need to be as anxious as I was before the trip. It felt so natural to be here. Could he be 'The One'? I don't know. I've actually stopped believing in 'The One' and have made a conscious effort not to use the word 'forever' since my last car crash of a relationship. However, I'm certain he is one of the ones. 'The One' for the present. Honestly, all I really know right now is that I couldn't be happier, and I can't wait for the summer!

Summer
Waitress at Grieghallen in Bergen. Intern at a radio station in Rouen. Human Resources Assistant at a pharmaceutical company in Normandy. That's the plan. Though it might seem boring or daunting to some, it's incredibly exciting to me. I'll have the opportunity to learn new things, meet new people and hopefully move a little bit closer to my dreams. However, before that, I have to say goodbye to a place, a country and people who have changed me.

Goodbye

The person I was when I arrived here is different from the person I am now. Sitting on a bench at the top of Mount Fløyen, looking down at the whole city and munching on my last favourite take-away calzone, I reflect on everything that's happened. The last year of my life has been unique. I will never be able to repeat such an incredible experience. Living in Bergen was like being in a bubble, one filled with friends, laughter, success, and love. Although I have no idea what the future holds, I'm convinced that if I get a chance to grow old, I'll often refer to this chapter of my life as the best. All that's left for me to say is "Thank you and goodbye Norway, I'll be back someday."

CHAPTER 3

Is Home Home?

Back

Guess who's back? Me, myself and I! Landing at an airport and knowing that people you love are waiting for you past customs and baggage claim is one of the most uplifting feelings ever. As the doors of the terminal open, my eyes catch a glimpse of Mum and Dad. Next thing I know; I'm throwing myself into their arms. "Welcome home!" they say at exactly the same time. I'm so happy to be here right now. They seem equally delighted to see me. In their arms, I feel so safe. If I didn't know better, I'd swear my heart has just become warmer, coated in a dense layer of their love. I smile and sigh. Reunions are such precious moments, I think to myself, as we head back to Louviers.

Louviers

Walking into the house, I feel like a totally different person. My room, on the other hand, hasn't changed at all. It's like I've never actually left. Inside, everything is the same as it was a year ago. The walls are still blue. The bed hasn't moved from under those beams I adore. The carpet is as fluffy as ever, and all the decorative items are exactly where they were before. Looking around me slowly, I feel as though I've stepped back in time.

Time

Dozens of memories suddenly flood back to me – the good, the bad and the ugly. The past isn't somewhere I particularly want to be. Never mind the fact that it's summer, the time has come for a spring clean! I decide to unpack as quickly as possible and then start sorting things out. I keep a few items as souvenirs. The rest, I clear out. Toys that I've far outgrown, clothes that are finally too big and, most importantly, gifts from my ex are amongst the items that don't make the cut. Putting all these things away gives me a joint sense of empowerment and liberation. With a clearer room comes a clearer mind, is what I take away from this process.

Process
Someone's trash is someone else's treasure. That's why I'll be taking everything I don't keep to a local charity. Staring at the piles around me, I reflect on the fact that all these things have treasure potential, just not for me anymore.

Potential
Tomorrow is my first day of internship at the radio station. I can't sleep at all. I'm twisting and turning in bed. This could be the start of my dream career! I must impress. I must succeed. I must sleep.

Sleep
After a restless night, I wake up early and quickly get ready. The drive from Louviers to Rouen, where the radio station is, only takes 40 minutes. I'm so anxious. "No panic attack, no panic attack, no panic attack," I mutter to myself as I get off the highway and into the city. It takes me three attempts to park. Finally, I'm standing in the front of the building. From then on, things accelerate. I meet my boss who gives me a full tour of the premises. Everything looks fascinating, especially in the studio. There are buttons everywhere. I have no idea what they do, and I can't wait to find out. Throughout his introduction, my boss complains and complains and complains. I don't understand how someone can be so negative in such a wonderful environment. This is the dream and he gets paid to live it! However, now is not the time for my rebellious side to come out, so I listen patiently and take thousands of notes.

Is Home Home?

Notes

I'll have to come to the station really early in the morning every day, most times by six o'clock, sometimes by five. My boss will be conducting interviews, attending press conferences and writing news while I follow him around. Extremely eager to learn, shadowing him in such a way sounds perfect to me.

Learn

That's exactly what happens for the first few days, but it doesn't take long before he realises that I can do more and sends me out on my own. Quickly, I begin to compartmentalise tasks. On the one hand, there are those I thoroughly enjoy like doing research, writing scripts, coming up with new ideas, interviewing people and audio editing. My absolute favourite is broadcasting. I can't believe I've had the opportunity to be on air a few times! It's not something interns are normally allowed to do but apparently, I have a nice voice… It was so awful to hear myself at first but I'm slowly becoming used to it and I've started noticing and practicing ways to improve.

Improve

On the other hand, there are the tasks I'd happily do without. Actually, there is one in particular which I dread: vox pop[1]. That's what I have to do today at the Armada. The Armada is an event that takes place every four to six years along Rouen's famous docks. Around 50 ships from all over the world and their 8,000 sailors gather on either side of the river. Every type of vessel can be seen – from traditional sail ships to modern warships.

---

[1] Vox pop are unprompted and spontaneous interviews of people. They often take place on the street or at events and involve stopping random people and asking them a few questions on record.

On the last day, the parade gathers millions of spectators. It's an event the radio station must cover. My boss thought vox pop would be a good option to show the scale of what's happening and how excited people are about it. This makes sense, but I loathe vox pop. Interrupting people while they're having a good time and asking them to answer my questions feels intrusive and extremely uncomfortable. When he's around, his stare is enough to make me push through the awkwardness and get on with it but doing it alone today will be so tough.

Tough
I approach a few people and get rejection after rejection. They don't want to answer. They don't like the station I work for. They don't have time. I don't blame them, but it doesn't help my confidence. After just a few failed attempts, I decide to give up. I'm struggling. I'm so close to quitting the internship all together. When I return to the studio, my boss asks to listen to what I managed to record. I know this isn't going to be good but there's nothing I can do about it now. I press play. He is disappointed, and says so. No matter how harsh he is on me, he can't even come close to how harsh I am on myself.

Harsh
As soon as he leaves the studio, the tears begin rolling down my face. I listen back to the few recordings I eventually managed to gather and try to edit them into something half decent. It might just be due to the disappointment but I'm not sure anymore whether this is what I'd like to do for the rest of my life. If I'm honest, there's another aspect of this role that bothers me. A lot of what we do is repeating news from other sources. As idealistic as it might sound, that's not what I thought journalism would be about nor what I believe it should be. Prior to this experience,

I'd pictured myself creating original content. Sadly, that's not what this job seems to entail.

Job
After a month volunteering at the radio station, it's time to earn a bit of money for the rest of the summer. With some help from Dad, I got a job as Human Resources Assistant at the company where he works. I don't really know what 'Human Resources' mean, let alone what they do. At first, I don't give it much thought – it's just a job. However, by the end of my first day, I have to admit I'm intrigued and keen to learn more. The team is made up of lovely ladies. They are so welcoming, caring and funny. Gossip, jokes and tea are part of the everyday life of the office. It makes the time go by a lot faster. Every day I learn new things, meet new people and begin to understand how things work. It seems odd but somehow I feel like I've done this all before. Perhaps I was some kind of business woman in another life. They say cats have nine lives, maybe humans do as well. Have you ever wondered who or what you might have been in a previous life? Or am I just someone with way too much imagination? Regardless, I'm having a great time here.

Great
Every day I work from 9:00 a.m. until 5:30 p.m. That leaves me with plenty of free time in the evening. After work, I often go for walks in the forest behind our house with Mum, Dad, my sister, or on my own. I find being in nature so relaxing, and walking particularly inspiring. 'All truly great thoughts are conceived by walking' stated Nietzsche[2]. I'm only just starting to agree with

---

[2] Friedrich Wilhelm Nietzsche (1844 – 1900) was a German philosopher. This quote comes from his book *Twilight of the Idols* published in 1889.

him. Ironically, four years ago, I was so upset with my parents for taking me hiking on my birthday. Now I'm the one asking them whether they'd like to join me on a stroll every evening. What a difference a few years make... These newly-established evening walks and the lovely dinners that follow give us a chance to catch up. It feels so wonderful to be back and spend time with my family! Being away from them for a while has made me realise how much they mean to me. Together, we talk for hours about the past, the present, and the future.

Future
As the summer comes to an end, I start to wonder more and more what it is I'd like to do going forward. September will mark the start of my last three years at university. The first one of the three remains fairly general but the following two are the Masters degree and require a specialisation. My original plan was to study journalism, of course, but the last couple of months have thoroughly confused me.

Confused
Journalism is without question what I still dream about. But. There is a but. I also want to travel the world and live in other countries. I wish combining both was a viable option. Sadly, from my experience this summer, my research and the various conversations I've had, it sounds as though what I'm after is somewhat utopian. In France, and probably elsewhere too, you don't just become an international journalist from one day to the next. You can aim to do so but meanwhile, you must expect and accept to work at a local level for a long time. I'm sure some aspects of it would be interesting but, like I said, I can't wait to live abroad. This is going to be a tough choice. I'm torn.

Torn
How could I ever choose between two of the most important items on my 'grown-up' list? I don't want to. I don't want to have to. This feels like an impossible problem to solve. It's not simple maths and doesn't allow for a right or wrong answer. In my head, it seems as though I'm having to choose between two paths that are heading in opposite directions. To add to the confusion, both paths disappear in deep fog after a few metres. Mentally squinting doesn't help, I can only distinguish the beginning of each and neither have signs. Whatever I go for will be based only on pure speculation. After days and nights of going back and forth, of weighing up pros and cons and of listening to conflicting advice, I still can't decide. Hopefully, whichever path I choose won't mean permanently closing the door on the other one.

Path
The summer is coming to an end and soon it will be time to go back to Bordeaux. I'm dreading it. I don't want to be 'the girl who passed out head first in the sand' anymore. It's neither who I feel like I am now nor who I want to be known as. However, I've heard first impressions stick. Will anyone ever consider giving me a second chance?

Chance
When he gives me the news, I can't believe our luck! My boyfriend is coming along for the ride. He applied for an ERASMUS year at Sciences Po Bordeaux and obtained it. I can't wait to jump in his arms, show him around the city and take him to my favourite restaurants. Perhaps this year will turn out better than I expected. His best friend is moving here too,

but only for six months. The plan is for them to live together for half a year and then we'll see.

See

We're so predictable... Thus far my boyfriend has been staying with me day and night. I absolutely love his presence, of course, but I'm struggling with the routine. I don't think I'm ready to settle down like this yet. It's only for a year though so I keep these thoughts to myself. Meanwhile, we focus on making travel plans to escape our cramped daily life and we go out a lot with the other foreign students.

Foreign

Hanging out with them is brilliant. They have no preconception about me, and they make me feel as if I were still abroad. Tonight at dinner we have seven nationalities represented: Norwegian, Swedish, French, German, Slovenian, Slovakian and Irish. The hubbub is getting louder and louder. All the languages merge into one while laughter unifies us all. At one point, I look up and take a deep breath. I feel unbelievably lucky to have met all these incredible people from all over Europe. Looking around the room and taking in the positive vibes, I can't help but wonder: do they feel at home here? Do I? Is France still home for me or could it be more complicated than that?

Complicated

An opportunity has arisen to be a Sales Intern where Dad works. He's put me forward for the role and I'm waiting to hear back. The actual position sounds a bit dull on paper and it has nothing to do with my dream job. However, its location is far from being uninspiring, on the contrary...

Contrary

Just as I was starting to be restless and feel the need to live abroad again, it's official… I'm moving to the Big Apple! Yes, that's right, New York City! Last time I was there; I was seven years old. I don't remember much apart from that giant teddy bear I fell in love with at FAO Schwarz©[3]. Sadly, Mum and Dad refused to buy it back then. Understandably, neither of them were keen to book an extra seat on the plane for it. I'm beyond thrilled about moving to New York! I will miss my boyfriend terribly, but the internship is only for three and a half months. After that I'll head to Norway and spend time with him there. Plus, I'm starting to believe that what's meant to be will be so if we're strong enough, we'll make it through. Before this incredible opportunity becomes a reality though, I have to prepare all the paperwork for my visa.

Paperwork

The whole process is extremely complicated and requires so much information. Everything has to be recorded and cross-checked. I need to prove that I will leave the country even before entering it. What makes a nation so arrogant that they think every visitor wants to overstay their visa at the risk of being deported and blacklisted? This dreadful experience is making me realise how much Mum has done for me over the years and how much she still does now. She helped me study, revise before exams, prepare university applications and is lending a hand with the visa submission as we speak. Despite my short temper, she is always there, firm yet patient. How does she do it? After all the grief I've caused her as a teenager, it's about time I opened

---

[3] FAO Schwarz© is an American toy store located on Fifth Avenue in New-York City.

my eyes. I wish I could find the courage and the right words to tell her how much I appreciate her support. Lacking both, I just hope she can read my mind through my smile.

Smile

I'm so excited about this new adventure that I can't stop smiling. The time has come for another airport goodbye… I hug Mum, my sister, and my boyfriend and wave at them until the last minute before disappearing through security. It's become our ritual. Dad isn't here. That's because he is waiting for me on the other side! He had to fly over to New York a few days ago for meetings. I can't wait to see him and to find out whether this next stop on my journey will feel like home.

CHAPTER 4

Home isn't Here

Sleep
We've finally landed, welcome to New York! Welcome to the city that never sleeps. I guess it's no surprise I didn't manage to get any rest on the flight. I was too impatient and fidgety. In order to pass the time, I watched several silly movies – my usual flight routine. From relaxing to rushing, I'm now power-walking along the never-ending corridors of JFK airport. As quickly as I can, I pass security and grab my suitcase. The large doors open in front of me and through the crowd, I can distinguish Dad's smiling face. It's fantastic to see him here! With a little bit of help from life or luck perhaps, he somehow always seems to manage to be at the right place at the right time in the crucial moments of my life. I don't know how he does it. I just hope that, like Mum, he knows how much I appreciate it. After a long, welcoming hug, he grabs my suitcase and we head to the car.

Car
The office is in Congers. Congers is a small town of less than 10,000 inhabitants located north of New York City and west of the Hudson River. Although it's technically part of New York state – a fact the locals are very proud of – it looks more like the American countryside than the buzzing Big Apple. It's virtually impossible to find somewhere to live that is walking distance from the office so the company provides a car to each of their interns. Very generous of them I think.

Generous
In my head, I picture a small and slightly-dated model. That's all I need and probably all I can manage. I've had my driver's licence for a few years, but I haven't actually driven in several months. Plus, though I like the feeling of freedom I get from it,

being behind the wheel always makes me a bit anxious. Dad tells me the car is of medium size according to American standards. I know that means large according to European standards. I shrug and laugh. I don't believe him. I'm sure he's pulling my leg! He does it all the time. Walking through the car park, he tries to make me guess. "Is it this one? Or this one? Or this one?" All the cars he is pointing at seem gigantic to me. Especially the last one, a red Chevrolet Equinox. He grabs the car keys from his pocket and clicks on the open button. As he does so, the side lights of the Chevrolet turn on and off. No way, I absolutely cannot drive this beast!

Drive

Once I've regained my composure, I open the door and sit in the driver's seat. I'm here now, there's no looking back. The only option is to go ahead and drive. Off we go! Once we've exited the airport car park, the landscape starts to change. Buildings are replaced by trees and streets by fields. We are on our way to Tarrytown. Located on the east bank of the Hudson River, Tarrytown is a small city of just over 10,000 inhabitants. It's a 20-minute drive from Congers, where the office is, and a 35-minute train ride from Manhattan, where the excitement is!

Excitement

We have a couple of apartments to visit. I found them on Craigslist©. Both are shared. Most of my meagre intern wage will have to go towards rent and I should have just enough left for bills and living expenses. We park in front of the first apartment. The location is great, very central, and the building looks modern and inviting. I'm not sure why, but I feel a knot in my stomach. A bit anxious perhaps. "What kind of crazy adventure have I embarked on again?" I ask Dad without expecting any answer.

Answer
A minute after my knock, a young guy opens the door. He looks in a rush. "Hey, have a look around and slam the door behind you. I have to run," he says. Interesting start. The apartment is what I would politely call a 'man cave' – bare, messy, and dirty. I'm not impressed, and neither is Dad. The only positive thing we can think of is that the bedroom is furnished. I really hope the other place is better otherwise I won't have anywhere to stay. The knot in my stomach grows a little tighter. We climb back in the car and drive for a few minutes.

Minutes
The second apartment is located just outside of town. It's not quite as central but the upside is that there is a large car park a few metres away. I pull over in one of its many empty spaces just in front of a restaurant called TGI Fridays©. I've never heard of it, but it seems popular. All the tables outside are taken. People look like they're enjoying the sun with a gigantic burger in their hands. Walking towards the door, I feel as though the knot in my stomach is spreading to my lungs and to my heart. Could this be my new temporary home?

Home
After a couple of knocks, the door opens. Behind it is a short girl or should I say lady. I'm not quite sure how old she is. About 10 years older than me, I would guess. She has long blond hair and a radiant smile that shows off her bright white teeth. "Welcome!" she says cheerfully. Instantly, the knot in my stomach

loosens. This is it. She gives us a short tour of the apartment. It's small, simple, and functional. The front door opens straight into the living room and kitchen. A small corridor then leads to the bathroom and the two bedrooms. The spare bedroom is completely empty. Once the tour is complete, we thank her and head out. She seems lovely.

Lovely

Sitting in the car, Dad and I go through the pros and cons of each apartment. It's a no brainer though, the second one is by far the better option. I'll just have to buy a few cheap pieces of furniture or at least a mattress and bedding. "Let's go to IKEA© then!" Dad says. IKEA©? Here? I had no idea the Swedish company could also be found on the other side of the Atlantic. One of the positive aspects of globalisation, I think to myself pleasantly surprised. I call my new housemate to let her know I'm keen on moving in. She sounds delighted. That night, Dad and I have dinner together and toast to new adventures.

Adventures

I'm quite sure most people wouldn't call a sales internship at a pharmaceutical company an adventure but, as I get ready for my first day, it definitely feels like one to me. I'm wearing the new black and cream skirt I bought before I left. I've matched it with a black top and a cream jacket. "An outfit shouldn't have more than three colours," Granny told me once. I've been following her advice pretty religiously ever since, especially when it comes to office wear. As I apply some eyeliner, I realise my hand is a little shaky. Stress. Make-up, that's something I thought was useless and vulgar when I was younger. It seems like some things do change after all. I'm glad I'm not as judgmental as I once was, although I'm sure there is always room for improvement.

Improvement
It's only been a couple of days, but I'm convinced my driving is getting better. Congers, here I come! To cheer myself on, I turn up the volume of the radio. American rap is blasting through the speakers. I know neither the artist nor the song but I'm moving to the rhythm regardless. The jolting beat fits both the view and my mood perfectly. In the distance, I start to distinguish the metallic structure of Tappan Zee Bridge. The rising sun in the background makes it look even more spectacular. I put on my sunglasses, lower the window and pop my elbow out as I cross the iconic Hudson River. First day, bring it on!

First
The plant is easy to find. As I park in front of the building, the short-lived confidence I'd felt in the car is replaced by shyness. The receptionist welcomes me with a smile and asks me to sit down and wait for a while. After a few minutes sitting on the edge of one of the chairs in reception, my manager appears. She is tall, has short blond hair and wears glasses. Minutes later, sitting in her office, she takes me through the two projects she expects me to work on over the next few months. Honestly, I don't understand the majority of what she is saying. It's all jargon and acronyms. After more than an hour, she stands. It's time to go on a tour of the premises. Everyone she introduces me to seems extremely enthusiastic, especially the American colleagues. The French come across as very reserved in comparison and the Canadians are somewhere in between. What impresses me the most is how the Canadians speak to me: immaculate *Frenglish*.

They start one sentence in French and finish it in English. Sometimes it's just one English word that suddenly pops into a French phrase. I'm a little confused as to which language I'm supposed to respond to them in. After a couple of disastrous attempts at *Frenglish*, I realise it's a lot more difficult than it sounds. I'll stick to English for now, I'm in the US after all!

After

The rest of my first day is pretty non-eventful. I sit at my desk in front of the computer and try to make sense of everything my manager told me this morning. It feels like I have to put together pieces of a puzzle without knowing what the end result is supposed to look like. A challenge. The good news is I love new challenges!

Challenge

Back at the apartment that night, I decide to make spaghetti Bolognese. I've cut the onion, garlic, pepper and tomatoes and I'm just about to stick it all in the pan. The mince will also go in after a few minutes. Meanwhile, the pasta is already cooking away in boiling water. Lost in my thoughts, I don't hear my housemate come back from work. When I turn around, I'm surprised to find her standing just behind me. She is staring at the pan with an inquisitive look on her face.

"What are you making?" she enquires.

Pretty obvious I think to myself though I simply reply, "Spaghetti Bolognese."

"Wow! How do you know how to make it?" she asks.

At first, I think she must be joking. I'm not too familiar with the local sense of humour yet so perhaps that's what it is. I'm about to laugh out loud when I turn towards her and realise that she is being serious. I swallow back my giggles and give her a blank look tainted with disbelief instead.

Not disturbed in the slightest by my lack of response, she continues, "Did you watch a video on YouTube©? Is that how you know what to do?"

I have no clue how to reply to that. She is 29, almost 10 years older than me. She has been living on her own for ages but doesn't know how to cook at all... Not even spaghetti Bolognese! I'm curious as to why?

She explains to me that almost every weekend she drives to her parents' place in Connecticut. She catches up with them and at the same time collects the food her mum has made for her prior to her visit. She either does that or just buys fast food. Dunkin Donuts© is her favourite. I've never heard of it but remain quiet as I don't want her to judge me in return. She carries on talking and confesses that she's never bought fresh vegetables from the supermarket before.

Now it's my turn to say, "Wow," as I'm totally shocked.

Shocked
Six or seven, that's how many times I've been to the US before. Granddad lives in Tennessee and Step-Grandma in Washington. They've encouraged the whole family to visit and have taken us around when we did. I've always had a mix of fascination and affection for this imposing country. Because of it, I somehow thought a little part of me was already American. I'd convinced myself that all it needed was this experience in order to grow. Walking around as if I'm at home, speaking to people as if I knew them and expecting them to react in a predictable way, I slowly realise my naivety. Oblivious to cultural differences, I'd completely forgotten to prepare myself for the shock. It hit me

full force when I least expected it. The extreme enthusiasm and warmth colleagues had shown on my first day quickly faded. Short "How are you doing?" when crossing paths in the corridor replaced both. It took me a couple of times to realise they didn't even expect an answer. Lunch, too, has become a lonely affair. Most days I make a salad at home, bring it to the office and eat it alone in the break room.

Alone
Every evening, my housemate comes up with new questions. It's gone from "Is Paris the capital city of Europe then?" to "France shares a border with Russia, right?" and last night's golden nugget, "Us Americans, we don't like the French very much because of some war I think." She is right this time though. I begin to explain to her the ins and outs of the Iraq war and France's opposition. However, I can tell she isn't interested. So I finish on the fact that George W. Bush subsequently intended to rename French fries 'freedom fries'. That catches her attention. She starts to laugh loudly. Bits of veggie crisps are falling from her mouth onto the sofa. They're so healthy she told me when we went food shopping together. "One of your five a day," she'd said. Right at this moment, I couldn't feel more alone and disconnected.

Disconnected
We're so different. I miss my family and my boyfriend so much. The thought of them so far away suddenly overwhelms me. Tears rush to the corner of my eyes, but I swallow them back. I don't fit in here. I don't belong. I'm not at home. It's as if I was floating above my body and watching my life unfold like a movie. I'm here but not quite here. I'm there but not quite there.

Movie
Despite the way I feel, I keep saying yes to pretty much everything my housemate suggests. I might as well try to make the most of this experience. So when she asks if I want to come to her cousin's BBQ party, I reply, "Yes, of course!" with fake enthusiasm. We drive there together. On the way, passing by hundreds of residential houses, I feel like I'm in a scene of *Desperate Housewives*[1]. Now that we've arrived, it's changed to looking like we're in *American Pie*[2]. All the people standing in the backyard staring at me, the strange foreigner, look as though they could be in that film. I realise it's the cups that triggered my thought. They're all holding these famous goblets: red outside and white inside. I had no idea these existed in real life. I can't believe it! I grab one and pour beer into it. I wish the girls were here to pinch me and turn this into one more of our memorable parties. The cheeky one would make me laugh till my abs ache and the caring one would give me an unbelievably comforting hug. A loud voice in the background interrupts my daydream. "It's beer pong time!" At least, it sounds like I've landed in a comedy rather than in a horror film.

Horror
Running. Faster. Hiding. Better. Sinking. Deeper. Streets of New York. Night time. Not a sound. Only his steps. Don't breathe. Don't cry. Don't think. Give up. Stand up. Run. Further. Fall. Silence. Only his breath. Getting. Closer. Only his hands.

---

[1] *Desperate Housewives* is an American TV series about the lives of a group of women who live on the same residential street. It aired between 2004 and 2012.
[2] *American Pie* is a series of American teen comedy films famous for their provoking sexual humour.

Screaming. Louder. I'm sitting up straight on the bed, sweating and out of breath. I'm absolutely terrified. Frantically, I touch every part of my body to make sure I'm whole and alive. How could it seem so real? It was just a nightmare. "Just a nightmare," I mutter to myself hoping it will dissipate the fear. After a few long minutes, I get out of bed and head to the bathroom. There, I pour some cold water over my face. Having regained my composure somewhat, I look at myself in the mirror. I'm livid. I've heard nightmares are manifestations of the subconscious, something Freudian[3]. Well, I don't know where this one came from, but it was violent. Nothing like this has ever happened to me. That scream, was it part of the dream or did it happen in real life too? I'm not sure. My housemate hasn't budged though so hopefully it was the former... Time to go back to sleep. At least tomorrow is Sunday, so no alarm required.

Alarm

A loud roar wakes me up hours later. It sounds like thunder but judging by the amount of light coming through the blinds, today a sunny day without a storm in sight. The unfamiliar noise is getting louder and louder. What could it be? Curiosity takes over, so I jump out of bed and open the window. As I can't see anything from here, I rush to the living room and open the door. Let's hope no one sees me as I'm still in my pyjamas. Motorbikes! Not one or two, dozens. I close the door, hurry back to my room, throw some clothes on and head out. Approaching the car park, I realise that there's a lot more of them than I originally thought. They've come here by the hundreds. The bikes look different but

---

[3] Sigmund Freud (1856–1939) was an Austrian neurologist. He is considered to be the founder of psychoanalysis. His work around the analysis of dreams and the theory of unconscious are world famous.

have one thing in common: they're all Harley-Davidsons©. I'm not clued up about motorbikes, far from it, but I don't think anyone could remain indifferent to this display of steel and noise. The bikes with long handlebars quickly become my favourite. Shiny and somewhat majestic, they stand out undeniably. Walking around, I can't help but stare at the owners as much as at their bikes. With their long beards and leather overalls, they too look as though they've just come out of a movie set. At the back of the crowd, I see my housemate's long blond hair.

Housemate
She's heading in my direction. She looks astonished. Next thing I know, she is grabbing my arm and whispering in my ear, "Oh my gosh, are you ok?"

"I'm fine thanks, how are you?" I reply calmly.

"You screamed so loudly last night, I thought there was someone in your room either attacking or raping you," she says. "I was terrified so I locked my bedroom door, hid under my bed and waited. After a few minutes of silence, I went back to sleep," she continues unprompted.

Cold shivers make their way down my spine. I'm not sure what distresses me the most: her individualistic reaction or the fact that she's telling me about it without an ounce of remorse in sight. Had someone really been out there hurting me, she would have let it happen and wouldn't even have checked if I was ok. She could have yelled my name through her door but nope. In her own home of all places, she would have let me be attacked, raped or worse, killed. How could anyone be so selfish? Tears of anger and disgust are gathering at the corners of my eyes. I can't swallow them back this time, so I turn around and walk back to the apartment as quickly as I can. I head directly for the shower.

Once in there, under boiling hot water, I cry my heart out... How? HOW? HOW?

How

Finally, Monday morning comes around. I don't think I've ever been so happy to go back to work. At least my internship is going well thus far. I've completed the first project I was assigned to at the start: conducting a market analysis regarding the use of airless devices in the pharmaceutical industry. I'm now focusing on the second project. As part of it, I've learnt how to use one of the company's new systems. The time has now come to pass on my knowledge and support its roll-out. My manager suggests we organise some 'lunch and learn' sessions to do so. Here is how it's going to work: attendees will bring their laptop and I'll walk them through a new scenario every day. For example, I'll show them how to make an order, how to add a supplier or how to record a new product, etc. Today is the first one of these sessions.

Sessions

I'm nervous and excited at the same time. I've been through everything in detail, I've written pages and pages of notes and I've practiced my presentation in front of the mirror. Let's do this! Standing in front of all these Sales Managers and Directors is quite intimidating but I get a thrill from it. I'm enjoying sharing what I've learnt so much, I feel like I could carry on for ages. At the end of the hour, most colleagues come up to me. Some express their appreciation and say they found it really helpful. A few others tell me they're more confident about using the new system now. There are even some who mention they enjoyed my practical teaching approach. I'm on cloud nine. It feels so wonderful to be able to help people. Standing in front of me with a cheerful smile, my manager looks really pleased. After a few more days of these training lunches, my second project is complete. I've only been here three weeks and I'm already done. Two months and a week still to go so… what's next?

Next
Table tennis is the best part of my day. A couple of days ago, I discovered there is a table on the second floor of the building. When I popped by at lunch time, a few guys were playing. They asked me what I was after. "Can I join in?" I replied instead. They looked at each other. I presumed they were trying to find a polite way of declining my request. Taking advantage of their hesitation, I grabbed a spare racket and ball. Standing on the other side of the table from the one who seemed to have the strongest game, I threw the ball high up in the air and served. Back and forth. Back and forth. Back and forth. I lost the point, but I made mine. Without any other words being said, I knew I was in. Playing a game or two during my lunch break has become part of my daily routine. I long for it every morning and reminisce it every afternoon. Now that my projects are complete, I'm beyond bored.

Bored
Every day, I ask my manager and a few colleagues for more work. They all seem terribly busy; some even look pretty overwhelmed. Yet, when I ask, most say there is nothing I can help them with. I wonder why. Being able to delegate tasks you don't like to do or want to do seems like a golden opportunity to me. Perhaps I'm missing a point or there is something I don't know of yet. A few times, colleagues have asked me to make photocopies, scan or bind documents for them. Though I obviously don't learn

much from it, I don't mind as it gives me something to do. One of the directors even requested that I serve him coffee once. Sadly, for him, I don't drink coffee myself and have absolutely no idea how to use the machine, let alone what a decent cup should taste like. Apparently, whatever I made turned out to be utterly disgusting. Everyone around him heard the story and no one asked me to make coffee again. Good! Until today, I thought that was the most frequent and worst possible task in the imaginary book 'Tales of Desperate Interns'.

Desperate
I'm standing inside a freezing-cold walk-in cupboard full of medicine. Wearing a smart and summery little dress, I have goose bumps everywhere. With a sponge in my left hand and a bucket of water and soap in my right, my 'job' is to remove old labels and stickers. I'm scraping until my arms ache. At least this requires no brain power whatsoever, so I have plenty of time to think. If I'm ever in a position to hire interns, this isn't the kind of task I'll ask them to do. I swear to never forget this moment and, no matter what I end up doing in life, I promise to respect every single person I meet along the way.

Single
Geographically single. Being in a long-distance relationship means you get the worst of both worlds. On the one hand, you're committed to someone but can't see them. On the other hand, you're alone but can't make the most of it. American guys are undeniably more forward than I remember Norwegians or French guys ever being. I'm convinced it has a lot to do with the simple fact that I'm French and speak with an accent. Last night in a bar, one of them told me that he found me slim and gorgeous.

Imagine my surprise! I guess over here I'm smaller than average. I'm not going to lie, I love it! I've lost about 10 kilograms since the seventy-six moment. I still think of myself as fat but hearing otherwise from the opposite sex is flattering to my bruised ego. I'm not even remotely interested so I simply savour their words but don't respond favourably to their seduction strategies.

Seduction
'I don't want to waste more time, I'm in a New York state of mind'[4]. The 35-minute journey to Manhattan is becoming more and more familiar. I've spent most of my weekends in the city. Attempting to get lost along its square streets is my favourite hobby. Every single time, I make a point of discovering something new. Central Park, Times Square, the Empire State Building, Rockefeller Center, Wall Street, Brooklyn Bridge, Broadway, Ellis Island, the Statue of Liberty, Fifth Avenue, Grand Central Station, Long Island. The city is absolutely gorgeous and fascinating. It seduces me again and again. Walking around with my head up to contemplate the imposing skyscrapers, I dream of being a New York City-based writer, the French version of Carrie Bradshaw[5]. I would love to live here! If only relocating to Manhattan for the rest of this experience was an option.

Option
To shake things up, this weekend I'm travelling to Philadelphia! Granddad has been invited to speak at an international scientific conference there and Step-Grandma is coming over as well.

---

[4] Quote from 'New York state of mind', a song by Billy Joel released in 1976.
[5] Carrie Bradshaw is the name of the lead character portrayed by actress Sarah Jessica Parker in American Sitcom *Sex and the City*. She is a New York newspaper columnist, freelance writer and later becomes a published author.

More than anything else, I'm looking forward to rediscovering this city. My parents mentioned that we visited it during our very first trip to the US. I was only seven then, so I don't remember it at all. This morning, I take the train from Tarrytown to Grand Central Station, as usual. I was a bit nervous last night, so I checked the different travel options online. Having chosen one, I wrote all the details on the piece of paper I'm now holding tightly in my hand. Train numbers, times, platforms. I'm seriously over prepared. Thankfully, all has gone smoothly thus far. Sitting on the second train heading to Philly, I can finally read and relax.

Philly

A short hour and a half later, I've arrived! I meet Granddad and Step-Grandma at the hotel and we sit down in their room for tea. They're quite busy but they'd like to take me for a tour of the city anyway. Together, we make our way downstairs. In the lobby, a very diverse-looking group of men is heading towards us. They're staring. How odd… Less than a minute later, they're standing right in front of us. They bow at Granddad. "What an honour to meet you, sir," they say, almost in sync. I can't believe it. First of all, he is my Granddad, an old man. Secondly, he is the same person who broke Grandma's heart and who made me feel worthless after I passed my *Baccalauréat*. I can think of a whole list of people who deserve being bowed to and I'm not certain he would make the cut. If he did, he surely wouldn't come on top. I keep all these thoughts to myself. Perhaps there is a side to him they know but I don't. After an abundance of "Thank you!" from both sides, we head into town. There's so much to see and learn here. Out of all the cities I've been to in the US, it's by far the most historic. The cracked Liberty Bell, symbol of the American Independence, particularly impresses me and so does the Rodin Museum. I'm mesmerised by his sculpture *The Cathedral*, which consists of two romantically interlaced hands.

Hands
A few days after returning to Tarrytown, the time has come for me to leave. My housemate gives me a hand with my luggage. Next, I will be travelling to Norway. I can't wait to see my boyfriend again! Thinking of him brings a smile to my face. Our plan is to first spend a week with his family in Nordreisa, and then live in Bergen for a month. There, I'll be working for a company that owns several stores in the famous colourful wooden houses along Bryggen. They sell all sorts of souvenirs from elk magnets to miniature trolls and traditional jewellery. The team is made up of people from all over the world and I've heard that the atmosphere is amazing. I can't wait! It's sad to admit but right now I'm not upset about having to say goodbye to my housemate, her apartment, and this small town.

Goodbye
Somehow, I never truly felt at home here. It was as though I was an outsider, one who didn't belong and couldn't find a way to fit in. Was it me, the place, the timing, or all of the above? I can't be sure. After my experience in Norway, I expected things to be just as blissful and easy. Although they haven't been, I don't regret moving here for one second. I've learnt so much. For instance, I now appreciate how critical it is to prepare yourself for such significant moves and other life changes. I've also grown into a more confident and independent person. Over the last three and a half months, I've realised that I can stand on my own two feet and face challenges head on wherever in the world

I might be. Regardless of what happened, I remain convinced that a life of travelling and living abroad is made for me. Sitting on the plane and reflecting on the last few months, all I hope for is to have the opportunity to come back here one day. That way, I'll be able to give this place a second chance. As the plane takes off, I whisper, "See ya later New York."

CHAPTER 5

Home isn't Home

Back

Guess who's back? It's me again! Mum and Dad are here. I wonder whether these airport reunions are getting repetitive for them. They aren't for me, far from it. All it takes is their embrace so I feel welcomed and safe. Sadly, we don't have much time to catch up. In a few days, I'll be heading back to Bordeaux. If I'm honest, there isn't one ounce of me that wants to go. Despite how much time has passed, I remain convinced that the city still knows the old me, the one I no longer want to be.

Longer

Eighteen months, that's how much time I have left to spend in Bordeaux, the port in the southwest of France known worldwide for its exceptional wine. There's no denying there are much worse places to be but to me it feels so familiar, judgmental and suffocating. Before the summer, we were asked to choose our masters. Studying abroad or changing university wasn't an option. This *Grande Ecole* is five years or nothing, by nothing I mean no degree and potentially having to start from scratch somewhere else. I've considered it but wasn't prepared to study any longer than I had to. I can't wait to be done with it all. I'm ready for a new chapter of my life. Sadly, sometimes you have to take one step back to be able to take two forward, or so I've heard.

Forward

Finally, after a lot of hesitation and sleepless nights, I've selected my top three choices of Masters. The first one is a Masters in Risk Management and International Economy. Out of all the options, it's one of the most selective. Based on my track record, I'm convinced I won't get in.

In

Looking back, I'm not sure why my heart swayed in that direction. To be honest, I think my heart had very little to do with it. My gut too was silenced. I allowed my brain to take over completely. Two main rational thoughts came into play. On the one hand, I believe no TV or radio station in their right mind would be interested in hiring me. On the other hand, I think international business might give me a greater chance to travel and live abroad than my journalism dreams ever could. Predictably, I picked the route that I assumed would be the most likely to take me out of here as early and as fast as possible. 'Follow your brain', isn't that what they say? Or was it 'follow your heart'? The former has been my motto for years though perhaps it shouldn't have been. As it turned out, I did get my first choice this time around.

Out

I often ask myself why I want to travel and live abroad so much. Am I chasing something or trying to escape something else? Perhaps a little bit of both. A couple of days ago, I was having dinner with a few friends when they started talking about an up-and-coming French singer I'd never heard of. When asked, I admitted my ignorance. The look of disbelief and concern they gave me was genuine though somewhat over the top.

"WHAT?! You've never heard of him?" said one of them.

"Are you for real?" shouted another.

"Where have you been?" added the third.

I guess it's in these moments that I feel like a foreigner, an imposter, an outsider in my own country.

Outsider

Everyone else around me seems pretty content with where and who they are. Some friends have mentioned their dreams of finding a stable job and buying a house while all I've wished for are plane rides to new places. Why? Others are constantly talking about weddings and babies while all I think about is my future career. Why? The country I was born and raised in doesn't feel like home to me anymore. Why? I can't help but wonder whether I'll ever find what I'm looking for. Have they? Have you? And what will happen if I don't… will I ever stop wandering?

Wandering

My boyfriend is finishing his studies in Bergen while I'm pursuing mine in Bordeaux. It's horribly tough. Luckily, we have far more options now than our parents and grandparents ever did. Phone apps have replaced letters and we can communicate whenever we want. What a luxury! However, there is nothing like physical intimacy and daily routine to build a long-lasting relationship. Until we have the opportunity to be reunited, we make a point of seeing each other as much as possible. We meet for weekends in Bergen here, weekends in Bordeaux there or catch up elsewhere in Europe. Thus far, we've been to London, Berlin and Sofia together. These weekend escapes are most definitely my favourite as they enable us to combine the pleasure of seeing each other with that of discovering a new city. Looking forward to our next trip helps us get through the days, weeks and months in between.

Between

Routine takes over. After almost three years living in Bordeaux, my friends and I have our little habits. We can't afford to eat out that often but when we do, it's at a handful of restaurants.

We have our favourite Japanese, our favourite Italian, our favourite brunch and afternoon tea places. There is something comforting about being a regular customer and ordering your 'usual' anywhere you go. Sadly, I know I'll probably have to give up on that when I start my life on the road... one more reason to enjoy it now!

Enjoy
These days, I mostly hang out with a couple of girlfriends I've known since the first year at university. Our little trio has carried me through this whole roller coaster of an experience. Judging by our differences, I'm not quite sure how we became such good friends in the first place. Sarcastic girl is studious and has a hilarious dark sense of humour. Confident girl is strong-minded and has an impressive belief in both herself and others. Then there is me. I've always wondered why they keep me around. Four years later, I can't help but ask myself, is our friendship something of the present, of the future, or simply of the past?

Past
We used to be so close. Sarcastic girl and I. Both of us have been through a lot of bullying when we were younger and have lost quite a bit of weight since. She was one of the first people I met after moving to Bordeaux. We lived in the same building during our first year and saw each other all the time. Sadly, lately, something has changed. She has been distant for a while. A few days ago, she just stopped talking to me. It's pretty obvious, as we still see each other every single day on campus or at friend gatherings. I have no idea what happened. "Why?" I keep wondering and end up asking the friends we have in common. They say they don't know but I'm pretty sure they're lying.

Cowardly or wisely, they've decided not to put themselves in the middle. At first, I felt angry. At her. At them. At everyone. However, pretty quickly my anger turned into guilt.

Guilt
I must have done something wrong. It has to be my fault. It wouldn't be a first. I keep looking back through recent events and asking myself: What did I do wrong? How bad is it? What can I do about it now? The whole situation brings me back to primary school. Here is another friendship that seems on its way down the pan. Perhaps I'm simply not meant to have long-term friends. They all seem to get tired of me after a while. I speak too much. I take too much space. I am too much. I know all that though I have no idea what to do about it. On my good days, I manage to be a better version of myself but what's bred in the bone comes out in the flesh. In my desperate and countless attempts at being perfect at everything, friendship is an area where I obviously keep failing.

Failing
After a few weeks of silent treatment, she told me she was ready to talk. I'm on my way to meet her now. My heart is pounding in my chest. I can even feel it in my belly. My palms are unusually sweaty. I feel dizzy. 'You're pathetic!' screams my inner voice repeatedly. We meet up and sit outside a café. It's absolutely freezing or maybe it's just me… I haven't slept properly for days. I'm exhausted. I've also been losing a lot of hair. It reached a point that even I started to get worried. A couple of days ago, I went to see a doctor. She looked at me, her eyes filled with maternal concern, and said that it must be stress related. 'Psychosomatic' was the word she used. I guess that makes a lot

of sense when I'm so torn between the anger I feel towards this 'friend' sitting right in front of me and the hate I feel towards myself.

Hate
Remaining silent, I try to listen to what she has to say but nothing that comes out of her mouth is something that I'd ever want to remember. Apparently, she doesn't hate me. She is indifferent and "That's worse," she adds. Each of her words feels like a dagger through my heart. I try to give her my point of view in a constructive way but, most of all, I do my best not to cry. I cannot give her that satisfaction. I cannot let her see how much her behaviour is affecting me. I cannot be so weak. We talk for what seems like hours. When I finally get a chance to walk away, I head straight to my apartment. As soon as I turn my back to her and leave, the floodgates open, and tears stream down my face. I've lost someone who I thought was a friend for life, and I'm not even sure exactly why. More importantly, I have no clue how I could prevent this from happening again in the future. It's decided, as soon as I can, I will escape. In the process, I will aim to grow a thicker skin and won't let anyone get close enough to ever hurt me like this again. Goodbye weak me.

Goodbye
After months of wishing for it, the end of university is around the corner. The time has come to choose a path – for work and for life. At the end of this year, everyone has to do a six-month internship. Having headed down a very different route than the one I'd originally planned, I feel totally lost. My parents are in Bordeaux for the weekend. As we walk along the city's beautifully-restored docks, I pick their brains. "What should I do with my

life?" I inquire out of the blue, secretly hoping they'll have the perfect answer. Vast question.

Question
In turn, Mum and Dad each come up with different ideas. They ask, they listen, and they reassure. The sun sits high in the sky. Its reflection on the Garonne river makes it almost possible to ignore the repellent brown colour of the water. Though it's not particularly hot, its rays feel warm and comforting on my face. A refreshing breeze catches my long wavy hair and propels it back. I look over at Mum and Dad with a huge smile. I have no idea what I'm doing or what I'm going to do. However, talking to them about it so openly and in such depth makes it seem far less frightening. By the sounds of it, they too didn't have it all figured out when they were my age and they turned out pretty well! I wish I could go back in time and erase some of the things I did and said when I younger. Maybe one day I'll bring myself to say sorry. We keep walking in silence now, taking it all in. Moments like this might be the definition of happiness. Surprisingly, here and now, I oddly feel at home. What if home wasn't a place after all?

Place
When I first started applying for internships six months before the end of term, I was being picky. Asia is where I wanted to go to – a far, different and exciting place – but nothing came up. No answers. No interviews. Nothing but rejections. Day after day, I became increasingly worried. The time had come to extend my search to other parts of the world and even to France. Internships are mandatory, and I can't bear the thought of being unemployed. What would I do all day? When I have free time

and I'm on my own, I have this terrible tendency of watching TV until my eyes hurt. Doing so feels wonderful at first as it allows me to forget about everything and quietens my inner voice. Whether it's with films or a TV series, I tend to identify with one of the characters to an extreme degree and get totally engrossed. At the end of the day, when I finally manage to unglue myself from the screen, it's as if I'd experienced all the emotions the character did. I'm drained. More often than not, that's exactly when I start to feel totally worthless, depressed, empty, and angry. Why did I do this again? How could I waste an entire day doing nothing? What the hell is wrong with me? That's why I need a job! I think for me the most important thing about it is the structure it provides.

Structure
Afraid my miserable alter ego might resurface, it's like I'm possessed. I start frantically applying for everything and anything I can find online. Ten, twenty, forty, eighty internships. I keep track of everything on a spreadsheet which is growing exponentially day by day. I'm approaching one hundred applications when I finally receive a call. It's from a company that makes equipment and systems for aircrafts. They have an intern position in their Paris office. We set up a face-to-face interview in a few days' time. When it rains, it pours. This famous saying seems to apply to jobs too. The following day, a cosmetic company contacts me for an internship at one of their plants a couple of hours drive away from the capital. Both jobs have their advantages and disadvantages, so I've started a mental pros-and-cons table. As I come out of the second interview, I notice a missed call on my phone. I have no idea who it is but luckily, they've left a message.

Message
The caller is the recruitment manager of an environmental company. They are hiring for a two-year *Voluntariat International en Entreprise* (VIE) in Risk Management. To be honest, neither the sector nor the role particularly excite me. But it's a VIE! A VIE is a programme developed by the French Ministry of Foreign Affairs and managed by Business France. It gives the opportunity to young French and European people (18 to 28 years old) to work abroad in a French company. Placements range from six to twenty-four months and the salary, harmonised across all sectors and roles, is far more generous than internships, which are generally unpaid. However, that's not what makes me jump for joy. By far the best part about the job is that it's based in London! That's not in Asia, of course… But it's abroad and that's awesome already. I'm trying to refrain myself from picturing what life in the UK's capital would be like, but I can't help it! On the train to Paris now, I'm preparing myself for the interview. I decided to wear my new suit and lucky shoes. They're turquoise blue with a comfortable square heel; not too high, not too low. Wearing them makes me feel more confident and I'd like to think they give away a bit of my bubbly personality.

Personality
As I approach the company's Paris office, my anxiety is growing exponentially. There is little I wouldn't be prepared to do in order to be able to move to London. I need to show that without sounding needy or desperate. "Welcome," says the recruitment manager as she leads me into the empty interview room. The walls are so white and bare that I feel like I've just entered an operating theatre instead. The first step of the process is a personality test. Having completed it, I wait in the empty room.

The knock is so sudden it makes me jump. As the door opens, the manager comes through.

Manager
She is not what I expected, far from it. In such a male-dominated environment, there is no way she can blend in, I think to myself admiringly. She is absolutely gorgeous, and her outfit is spot on. She is wearing an electric blue skirt matched with a black top, black tights and black shoes with incredibly high heels. How can she walk in these? It's not just about what she is wearing. Though she only looks a few years older than me, she comes across self-assured, composed, and confident. When she starts talking, I can't help but be impressed by her impeccable British accent. She is French, like me, but you can barely hear it. Amazing! If only I could be like her in a few years' time, I pray silently. Perhaps working with her for a while will do the trick. However, saying any of this out loud would come across as pure flattery so I keep my thoughts to myself and do my utmost to answer all her questions. Most of them I'm prepared for and as time passes, the interview turns into more of a two-way conversation. I even manage to crack a few jokes that she laughs at. Good sign! That's when the personality test results come in.

Results
After looking at them in silence for a few minutes, she raises her head, looks straight into my eyes and says that she wants to hire someone who's creative because she believes she isn't. "So, tell me, are you a creative person?" she inquires. Blank. I have no idea what the test says and I'm not sure myself whether I'm creative or not. I definitely was as a child, but that part of my brain hasn't been used for ages. I come up with a textbook answer.

Time is up. As I walk away, I have no idea if I've said and done enough to be offered the job.

Enough
Every time the phone rings, I jump. Every couple of minutes, I refresh my emails. I'm dying to know what will happen. I've been dreaming of Big Ben, Tower Bridge and Piccadilly Circus almost every night since the interview. Over the last few days, I have been offered the other two internships. The topics and sectors are certainly more appealing to me but both positions are based in France and that's not where I want to be. The wait is excruciating. Finally, that's it. I hold on for a few seconds before picking up not to give away my impatience. After all the courteous preamble, the Human Resources manager breaks the news to me. I've been offered the job! I have! I did it! As soon as I hang up, I call my parents. They're in Turkey celebrating Dad's birthday. "One more reason to pop the champagne," Dad says cheerfully. London, here I come. New place, new chapter, new home?

CHAPTER 6

Home is Them

Packing

How can accumulating be so easy when clearing out and packing always seem like such a daunting task? After three years living in the same apartment in Bordeaux, I've amassed so much: books, clothes, and little souvenirs from all my travels. I spend hours and hours sorting through it all. Though I know by now that objects are just material possessions, some feel like they carry greater meaning than others. A few times, I have to take a step back and remind myself that I must be ruthless. I definitely can't bring it all to London. I'm surrounded by growing piles when I come face to face with Boutchou. Patches of fluff are missing from its head and body. It looks old, grey and sad. I grab it and stare into its black plastic eyes. If I didn't know better, I'd swear it's about to talk to me. Suddenly, many deeply buried memories come rushing to my mind.

Memories

The 'grown-up' list is one of them. Surprised to remember it in such detail, I go through it in my head methodically:

#	Item	Status	Comment
1	Travel the world	Work in progress	Can't wait for more exploring!
2	Become fluent in English	Work in progress	Getting there…
3	Never lose Boutchou	Work in progress	Looking right at it!
4	Be skinny and beautiful	Work in progress	Lost 13 kilograms…
5	Be a journalist on TV	On hold	Hoping to get to that later in life…
6	Keep moving	Work in progress	I'm on it!

Do you also go back to your childhood dreams list every now and again? I've never asked anyone. The topic seems far too personal. To be honest, I wouldn't want to share what's on mine with strangers. Plus, though I can't be sure, I assume not many people keep track of their progress in such a systematic way. I have to admit, doing so right now even feels somewhat abnormal to me.

Abnormal

I have to rein in my wandering mind. It's gone as far as wondering if I'll ever reach one of these goals in my lifetime, and if any of them will be mentioned as achievements at my funeral... Sometimes my vivid imagination takes me by surprise. It comes up with unexpected thoughts and takes me to bizarre places. Snapping out of it, I decide that the time has come for a new resolution.

Resolution

Never mind that it's not New Year, this is the start of a new chapter of my life and I'd like to commit to living it to the fullest. If I were to die tomorrow, I don't want to take any regrets to my grave. If, on the other hand, I have the chance of growing old and grey, I wish to become one of those cool grandmas with thousands of stories to tell – stories about other countries, other cultures, and all the wonderful people I will have met along the way.

Way

By the time I break out of my daydream, it's gone from dusk to pitch black outside. Boutchou safely makes it into the KEEP pile and I rush through what's left. Hours later, I lay down on the bed that soon won't be mine and stare at the white ceiling.

Everything is packed. The apartment feels scarily empty. It even echoes. I close my eyes and sleep for a short while.

Short
Early the next morning, everything accelerates. It's time to load the minivan that's taking my belongings back to my parents' house in Louviers. They still live in the same place and I doubt they'll ever move. Once it's all in the van, I can't believe my eyes. I must get better at packing as there won't be a minivan heading to London. I'll be taking the train and all I'll have are my two arms to carry whatever I decide to bring along with me.

Train
Although London is located in a different country, it's actually faster to get there from Paris than it was travelling to Bordeaux. It only takes two hours and fifteen minutes instead of three. That must sound astonishing for people who come from enormous countries. However, it's quite common in Europe where there are even nations that take less than two hours to drive through... Anyway, I'm on the train to London now. The Eurostar© is what it's called. Launched in 1994, this high-speed railway service goes through the mind-blowing 50.5 kilometres long Channel Tunnel built below the waters that separate Britain and France.

Tunnel
We're going through it now. I kind of wish they'd made it transparent. Thinking about it, I picture thousands of colourful fish and mysterious shipwrecks all around us. How awesome would it be to observe the splendour of the sea from a moving train? What I have in mind is a reverse aquarium of sorts, one where marine creatures would be able to move freely while we

observe them confined under thick glass. I wonder whether they didn't opt for glass because there isn't anything worth seeing down here or because the risk of leakage would have been too high. If the latter is accurate, I have to admit I'd much rather have entered into this dark and depressing tube than into an aquarium. Talking about leakage, I really hope these concrete walls actually are waterproof. I've heard there's been fires in here before but floods, I'm not aware of. From one thought to the next, another idea comes to my mind.

Idea

What if they asked artists from all over Europe to decorate the extensive walls of the tunnel? That would make the whole journey far more interesting and uplifting. Sadly, I presume the speed would prevent passengers from appreciating the works of art. Could the designs potentially be adapted to the limitations of the human eye? Good question. One thing is certain, I would have made an appalling engineer. However, it seems like I might be quite creative after all… My daydream is interrupted by a loud voice coming through the speakers.

Voice

"Our train will arrive at London St Pancras in two minutes," the voice declares in English with a thick French accent. Shortly after, our train stops. We've arrived at our destination! I wait until most people have left before stepping onto the platform. I'm travelling with two large suitcases. Dragging them behind reminds me of moving to Norway a few years back. The only difference is that this time I'm on my own. "Everything will be ok," I tell myself quietly. Once on the platform, I look around.

Wow, St Pancras railway station is remarkable! The difference with its French counterpart, Gare du Nord, is striking.

Station
I'm in no rush and the suitcases are as heavy as always, so I take my time and walk slowly along the platform towards the exit. Looking straight ahead, I spot a gigantic statue of two lovers caught in an embrace. Absurdly, I smile at them from ear to ear. I'm so happy to be in London, finally! I wish my boyfriend were here waiting for me at Arrivals. I'll be searching for his familiar face in the middle of all the strangers pass the gate. Even when I know no one will be there, I always look around just in case. Sadly, he definitely won't be able to surprise me as he's in Bergen finishing his studies. He says he'll do his best to move to London as well once he graduates. I hope so as I miss him dearly...

Hope
Behind the lovers of bronze are five giant Olympic rings. Their striking colours – blue, red, yellow, green and black – can't be mistaken for anything else. The games will be held here next year as London won host city over Paris and Madrid. Though I can't be sure, I hope I'll be around then. How amazing would it be to attend one of the events? I'm not an extreme enthusiast but I do really enjoy watching live sports, especially when I'm abroad. Standing in a stadium packed with singing and cheering fans certainly guarantees an immersive and authentic experience. Along with language, food, and art, I believe sport is yet another angle through which one can get to know the local culture better.

Food

There weren't many food options on the train so now that I'm at the station, I start looking for something to eat. There is a French bakery near the exit, perfect! Once at the counter, I politely order a baguette. So cliché, I know. The barista looks at me strangely and asks, "Excuse me, miss, but are you French or American?" He probably has no idea how flattered I am! I've been trying to hide my French accent for years. I'm not sure exactly why... I guess I just really enjoy the idea of being somewhat international and not tied down to any specific country.

Specific

The company has generously offered to put me in a hotel for a few nights. I'm heading there now, dragging my two large suitcases along. Luckily, it's located only a few minutes' walk from the railway station. The bedroom is pretty basic: white walls, white bed sheets, white bathroom but, for now, that's exactly what I need. It gives me time to find an apartment. Based on my research, rent prices are ridiculously high over here, even worse than in Paris. That's why I've decided to look for a flat-share and haven't defined any specific requirements. Mum saw me spending ages looking at options online, so she came up with an idea.

Online

At first, I thought it would be a waste of time, but I kept it to myself. She said I should write on my Facebook© page that I'm moving to London soon and looking for a place to stay. What you have to bear in mind is that I don't think Mum knows what Facebook© is or does. She even called it "Your social media thing, *Focebouque*." In the end, I did as she suggested mainly to prove her wrong.

As it turned out, listening to her was the best thing I could have done. Always follow your mum's advice might be the learning here. Having said that, I'm sure there are plenty of examples of exceptions that would challenge this statement, but this isn't one of them. As soon as I'd updated my status, one of my boyfriend's friends contacted me.

Friends
We all met in Bordeaux a couple of years ago. Since then, he lived in London for a few months before returning to Spain, his home country. By coincidence or fate, the friends he was living with at the time are now looking for someone to replace one of their housemates who has just left the country. What's even more incredible is that the flat is located exactly in the area where I was hoping to live. It's only a 15 to 20-minute walk from the railway station where I'll need to catch the train to Hatfield every morning for work. Plus, the closest underground stop, Manor House, is only about three minutes' walk away. Could it be too good to be true? That's what I wonder on my way over. None of the other people I've reached out to have come back to me yet so all I have is this plan A.

Plan A
I've just arrived at the station now. After walking swiftly up the flights of stairs, I'm outside. The weather is a little cloudy but at least it's not raining. To my left, I spot the fairly large Finsbury Park and to my right a small supermarket and a kebab shop. Following the route on the printout map I've brought with me, I realise the flat is in one of the gigantic buildings straight ahead. Part of a council estate, they are by far the ugliest around. The closer I get, the dodgier the environment becomes. I won't let it get to me though. After only one knock, the door opens.

Behind it are three people. "We were expecting you!" one of them says cheerfully. A tall and slim Danish girl takes the lead and shows me around. As per the floor plan I'd seen previously, the apartment is spread across two small levels. Downstairs are the kitchen, living room and a small balcony. Upstairs are four bedrooms and one bathroom. It's obvious the owner has done all he or she could to maximize the space. One of the bedrooms is so small I reckon it must have been a cupboard in a previous life. The bedroom for rent however is rather nice. It's of a decent size, has a double bed, two cupboards and a small desk and chair. Returning downstairs, I'm surprised not to be as nervous as I thought I would. The three of them are sharing a bottle of wine in the living room. They offer me a glass and invite me to stay.

Stay
We chat for hours. I learn that the other two – a girl and a guy – are both from India, and that the three of them met at university. They've been living together for a few years and get on really well. I don't know whether it's the wine, their vibe or a combination of the two, but I feel totally at ease and relaxed. It's already dark when I check the time; I've been here for ages! As I hug them on my way out – that's how people seem to greet friends over here – I don't say "Goodbye" but "See you tomorrow!"

Tomorrow
In the space of a couple of days, I've moved in and completed most of the necessary admin tasks like opening a bank account, obtaining a local phone, buying an oyster card[1], etc. Tomorrow

---

[1] Oyster card is the name given to the electronic pass used for public transports in London and its surrounding area.

is my first day at work, the first day of my professional career...
I can feel the pressure rising.

Pressure
Walk. Train. Bus. Walk. It's not the easiest journey on paper. I can only imagine what it's going to be like in practice especially for the first time and with my appalling sense of direction. Out of the four housemates, I'm by far the first one up in the morning. On the bright side, it means that I don't have to wait for the shower. After checking endless times that I have everything I need, I leave the flat. Could I be any more anxious? Probably not. I'm not even sure what worries me the most – my first day at the office itself, or just reaching it.

Reaching
The first part of the journey is the easiest: a swift walk through the park. I stand out like a sore thumb though. The benches are all occupied either by homeless folk or youngsters recovering from the night before. Once at Finsbury Park station, I find the platform without too much difficulty and wait for the train. Hatfield is only about 15 minutes away. There, I start searching for the bus that takes employees from the train station to the business park. I'm looking anxiously down at my little printed map and then up at all the signs. That's when I hear a very distinctive voice behind me. Whoever this lady is, I'm absolutely positive that she is French.

French
I can recognise her accent miles away. Hearing it makes me smile. Battling my shyness, I bring myself to ask her, in French, whether she is heading to the same office. Initially taken by

surprise, she stares at me for a few seconds and nods, yes. I instantly notice her sparkling, light blue eyes. Right away, she starts chatting. I can't explain how or why but we click instantly. In contrast to her short and petite physique, her personality is big and bubbly. She tells me that she's only been in the UK for a few months. She followed her husband, a banker, and has since struggled to find a job due to her English which she is really keen on improving. Considering how compassionate she comes across, I'm not surprised when she mentions that she works in Human Resources. The bus journey takes less than 10 minutes but that's all we need to know that we'll become friends. By the time we reach the main reception, we've already arranged a lunch date and 'Friday drinks'.

Friday
That's how I learn about 'Friday drinks'. Apparently, it's somewhat of an institution here. The concept: every Friday, colleagues leave the office together and head to one of the pubs nearby. There, they drink to celebrate the end of the week and the beginning of the weekend. Apparently, more often than not, they get totally drunk. That could not be more different to what I was taught growing up. My parents always emphasised that we shouldn't mix our private and professional lives. Thinking back, I don't remember asking why. I guess it's a bit late for that... Hopefully it won't be too bad if I go by the conveniently adapted phrase: 'When in Britain, do as the Brits do!'

Brits
Despite the company being French, most employees are local Brits. They speak with the same melodious accent my English class cassettes used to have. It's hilarious at first but sometimes

I have to admit that I struggle to understand. Even my manager – who wears a different yet equally amazing outfit every single day – speaks English to me. I've heard colleagues say that it's weird. We're both French so they reckon we should speak French together. I get their point, but I equally understand hers. She says that as I'm in the UK now, I should practice my English as much as I can, even with her. Also, she prefers it as everyone around us can understand what we're discussing. That way they won't assume we're talking behind their backs and, as we're working in an open office, they can chip in whenever they want.

Office
I find it so loud at first. The sound level combined with having to speak English all day and being taught so much, makes me feel like my brain is going to explode. Every evening since I've started, I've come home with a major headache. After a week, I think I'm finally becoming used to it, like everyone else seems to be. Luckily all of my colleagues are considerate and patient. Everyone in the office has been very welcoming, especially the graduates who are only a few years older than me. Actually, especially one of them.

One
Handsome guy is what I call him secretly. He came back from holiday this morning. As our projects overlap, my manager suggested the two of us should go for lunch together. I have to admit, he is definitely easy on the eye. Sitting down at the cafeteria, we end up losing track of time completely. We speak for over three hours about far more than just work. As it turns out, we both love travelling! A few years ago, he even spent five months backpacking around Australia and New Zealand.

While listening to his fascinating life story, I get lost in his mesmerising blue eyes. I have no idea how, but he looks at me in a way no one has ever looked at me before. Under his gaze, I feel absolutely fascinating, intelligent and even beautiful. Of course, it won't go any further. I'm committed and loyal. However, there is no harm in enjoying a bit of flattery, is there?

Flattery

Three and a half years have gone by since the seventy-six moment. I've learnt. I've failed. I've persisted. Depending on the day I hop on the scale, I've lost between 16 and 18 kilograms. I'm finally at a healthy weight with my BMI[2] in the middle of the norm. It's been a long journey… When I was younger I always hoped for a magical cure; a pill I could take or a diet I could go on that would be a quick and easy way to go from chubby to skinny. The reality couldn't be more different. "I'm on a lifelong diet," I have said to friends recently. Having reflected on it, I prefer to answer, "It's not a diet, it's a lifestyle," to those who ask for my secret recipe.

Secret

The truth is there isn't one. Lately, many of my friends and colleagues have mentioned their wish to lose weight, even the slimmest ones. Sadly, I feel as though the perfect woman we all aspire to become continues to shrink. I wonder when it will ever stop. We might have all faded away by then! I'm not going to lie; health had no play in my initial decision to slim down. It was that same perfection I was after. I just wanted to be slimmer so

---

[2] BMI stands for Body Mass Index and is an indicator based on a person's height and weight that is used to determine whether he or she is underweight, 'normal', overweight or obese.

I could look better and thus feel better. Rightly or wrongly, I'd convinced myself that these three things were interconnected. Before I started the process, I had no idea about food. I shoved down my throat whatever I wanted whenever I wanted. Step-by-step, I learnt more about what my body needed. Through a combination of eating healthier, eating less and exercising more, the weight started to fall off slowly but surely.

Surely
The journey hasn't been without hiccups. More than once, I relapsed and ate my feelings away. Usually it happens in the evening, on my own and with tonnes of chocolate. "One day at a time," is what I tell myself to keep going… Having lost this significant amount of weight has undeniably changed my life for the better. Though I haven't been able to completely shake off the image of my old self, I find it easier to travel, be active and be sociable now than ever before.

Sociable
The way people, especially men, look at me is completely different. I've gone from being perceived as the funny, fatty, best friend to a somewhat attractive girl. Most of the time, I don't even realise what's happening. I presume that the majority of women who get men's attention have grown into it gradually from childhood to adulthood. To me, it just feels like I've been dropped into water without knowing how to swim. There is no manual for this, is there? Am I being too available unintentionally? Am I being too awkward? It's fair to say, I have no idea what I'm doing. Instead of trying to make sense of it all, I've decided to simply enjoy the attention. Tonight is time for another 'Friday drinks' session full of innocent flirting opportunities and I, for one, am ready for the weekend!

Weekend

It only takes a few minutes on the Tube to end up in a completely different part of the city. London is a fascinating metropolis that I love exploring. Before I left, so many people told me it was an incredible place. I didn't feel it when I spent a weekend here a year ago, but I do now. Perhaps you have to stay longer or even live in this buzzing city to truly appreciate it. I'm pretty sure that statement applies to everywhere else in the world too. Living somewhere gives you a chance to dive that little bit deeper into the local culture and get under the skin of the place you're in. In fact, a city is much more than just famous sights. It's a vibrant community with its captivating people, and distinct atmosphere. Keen on discovering it all, I first visit the tourist attractions: South Bank, Tower Bridge, Big Ben, Trafalgar Square, Covent Garden, Piccadilly Circus and Leicester Square. Then, I make a point of getting lost off the beaten track. That's how I discover one of London's tiniest streets: Neal's Yard, a small colourful alley off Leicester Square that most people pass without noticing. Tirelessly, every weekend, I head on a different walk and wander along the streets of the capital. The proximity yet contrast between wealthy and rough neighbourhoods keeps surprising me. Not many of the cities I've visited have been so visibly diverse and cosmopolitan.

Cosmopolitan

Since I've arrived, I've met people from all over the world. The house party my housemates organised last night gathered more nationalities than I could account for. It kind of reminded me of that night in Bergen, sitting around our kitchen table.

Kitchen

Like the population, the food is also extremely varied. Dotted around the city are restaurants from all corners of the world. A couple of weeks ago, I went to an Ethiopian eatery for the first time ever. It was absolutely delicious and I couldn't get enough of their *Injera* bread[3]! I'm looking forward to discovering many more cuisines over the next few days, weeks and months. I'm loving it here! Soon I might be calling London home… In the meantime, it feels as if the city and I were on a honeymoon.

Honeymoon

That's what I call this initial period of time after you've arrived in a new city or country. It's when you've just come out of your comfort zone and everything feels both exciting and a little frightening too. I've learnt from my past experiences in Norway and in the US, that it's a phase and sadly doesn't last forever. Soon, your surroundings become familiar and routine settles in. So instead of dwelling on it or worrying about it, I choose to embrace it. When my housemate suggests we go for a walk along the nearby deserted Tube tracks or visit a famous cemetery, I'm up for it. I say "Yes!" to everything and never regret it. If I had to pick three key words to describe my new life here thus far, I'd choose: working, discovering and partying.

Working

I'm really enjoying my job! I learn something new every day and I get on very well with my manager. Today is Friday. As she's out of the office, she's asked me to attend quite a few meetings

---

[3] *Injera* bread is a speciality from Ethiopia, Somalia, Djibouti and Eritrea. Usually made with teff flour, it has a unique texture and taste.

on her behalf. My diary has never been so packed. How does she find time to actually do her work? I guess I'll have to find out sooner rather than later… I'm in the second meeting of the day when my phone rings.

Phone
I'm so glad I remembered to put it on silent mode this morning. That would have been embarrassing… It's Dad. Strange. He doesn't normally call me during work hours. This is an important meeting; several managers and directors are sitting around the table. I need to make sure I can report everything to my manager next week, so I take a lot of notes. I even write down things I don't understand hoping she'll make sense of it later. My phone rings again. It's Dad. Very strange. The meeting should finish in about half an hour, so I'll call him back then. I think it wouldn't look very good if I left the room. My phone rings again. It's Dad. Very, very strange. What if something is wrong? What could it be? What happened?

As discreetly as I can, I text him: 'Is everything ok? I'm in a meeting. I can call you back in 30 minutes. What's going on?'

His response comes a fraction of a second later, 'Call me back as soon as you can'.

Something is definitely wrong.

Wrong
I'm terrified. I have no idea what's being said in this meeting now. My eyes are staring at the black and white clock above the screen. They follow every movement of the hands. Seconds seem to take minutes and minutes, hours. Time is dragging and dragging and dragging. Finally, the most senior person in the room stands up and thanks everyone for their time. I try to hide

my impatience as I politely let my colleagues make their way out of the room first. Once in the corridor, I look for a meeting room. Of course, I'm faced with a classic case of 'meeting jam'. There aren't any available. Never mind, I must call him back now. Whatever is going on, I need to know. My thoughts have gone to all sorts of dark places and considered everyone I care about. I can't deal with the uncertainty any longer. Sitting on the stairs in front of the elevators, I take a long deep breath and dial Dad's phone number.

Dad

He answers very quickly.

"What's going on?" I ask right away.

"It's Grandpa," he says. He lets out a sigh and continues "He passed away last night."

I don't know what to reply.

Grandpa

Grandpa was old, and he hadn't been too well lately, but the doctors said he was on the mend. Somehow, I believed he was invincible. In my eyes, he was the 'Godfather' of our small family. A model of diligence, he'd started working at 14. Without higher education, he managed to climb the ladder and eventually became an engineer. I hope he was proud of himself and his achievements, but I don't know for sure. All his life, he felt like he was being treated differently because he didn't have any degree, so he made it his mission to ensure that his children and grandchildren would be able to achieve what he couldn't, no matter what. I ask Dad questions – when, how, where, what – but I can't really process the answers. All I can think of is that I'll never see him again. Overwhelmed by sadness, I realise I don't have any idea what he'd been through or who he was. I only knew him as Grandpa but not as a man, an individual, a human being. There is so much more I should have asked him and learnt from him before it was too late.

Late
Until today, I'd never been scared of death and its permanence. I'd even wished I'd disappear a few times myself. Now I've realised that it's because I was focusing on my own death rather than that of others. The truth is, I took him and everyone else around me for granted. I thought we had all the time in the world. Why couldn't we? Dad says the funeral will take place in a few days near Paris. It will be on a week day so he asks if I'll be able to come back. The fact that he has to ask makes my heart tighten. I suddenly feel so guilty for not being around. I can't be there for him, Granny and the rest of the family. Grief, anger and guilt are all merging into one. Of course, I want to be there. Sadly, I have a training course that day. The company has paid for it and it wasn't cheap. I need to speak to my manager, but she isn't here and, if I'm honest, I don't really want to talk to anyone right now. I know that if I say the words out loud, it will make it all real.

Real
Still sitting on the stairs, I bid Dad goodbye and call my manager right away. I apologise for disturbing her on her day off and tell her what's going on in as few words as I can. My voice is shaking, and I can feel tears rising to the corners of my eyes. I'm so grateful when she says that family is the most important thing and allows me to postpone the training course. Her reaction teaches me an invaluable lesson: loved ones should always take

precedent over work, wherever in the world you may be. I'll have one day off to go back and forth to France for the funeral. "Thank you," is all I manage to respond. As soon as I hang up, I storm down the stairs. I need to speak to someone. A friendly face. I look for my French colleague, the girl from the train but I can't see her. Hoping to find a place to hide, I rush to the ground floor toilets. There, it all comes out… Floods and floods of tears. Another colleague saw me, she's here now, trying to comfort me. I appreciate her intentions, but I'd rather be alone than with someone I barely know. Hastily, I pull myself together.

Together
I have to sort out everything – buy train tickets, cancel the training course, pack my black clothes, etc. As I head back to my desk, I bump into handsome guy.
 "Are you ok?" he asks.
 "Yes," I reply, looking at my toes.
 "Are you sure you're ok?" he insists.
 A sharp and definite "Yes!" comes out of my mouth this time around. It takes both of us by surprise. I appreciate his concern, I really do. One of his manly hugs would be just what I need right now but I'm sure the floods of tears would come back instantly. Plus, I've only known him for a few weeks; we're at work, he has a girlfriend he lives with and I have a boyfriend. With this in mind, I wish him a good weekend and walk away swiftly.

Walk
That afternoon, I finish my work, skip the usual 'Friday drinks' and take a long walk through Finsbury Park. Striding along its winding paths, I can't help but notice a lot more squirrels than

usual. What if Grandpa had been reincarnated into a squirrel and was coming to tell me everything is going to be ok? Absurd but comforting thought... Perhaps that's what I should believe until I feel better.

Better
A few days later, I'm on the train to Paris. I haven't slept well lately. Thoughts have been racing through my mind day and night. Everything I've been through before – the little grudges, arguments, complaints – have lost all significance. How silly and useless they all seem now. I have a newly found appreciation for this unbelievable life of mine. Grandpa worked in Italy for a few months when Dad was six years old but that's about it. He never had the chance to travel and explore the world. Whatever I'm able to do now is largely thanks to him. He set out a path for his family and I'm so grateful to have been granted the opportunity to expand it internationally. I'm in Paris now.

Paris
Today, like every year on the 21st of June in France, is music festival day. It's normally such a happy day, especially as it's Grandpa's birthday... or should I say *was* Grandpa's birthday. I can't get used to it probably because I don't actually *want* to get used to it. Standing in the metro, I'm surrounded by people who are ready for tonight's celebrations. Drunk, they dance, sing and push everyone around. Seeing them oblivious of pain, sorrow and suffering makes me want to scream. I want to tell them how irrelevant this all is, how death will take us all and how we should stop wasting time getting wasted. Instead, I put my headphones on and close my eyes. What would be the point?

Point
It's cold outside. Dressed in black from head to toe, I walk quickly dragging my little suitcase behind me. Dad is standing in front of the hospital when I arrive. I rush towards him, drop my luggage and run into his arms. This might be the first time I'm hugging him as much as he is hugging me. Without a word, he leads me inside the building. After miles of corridors, we come out of the maze and into a large hall. To the right is a row of small rooms which look like horse boxes. A handful of steps later, we're standing in front of one. I look around and realise that I recognise everyone who is inside. Mum, my sister, my aunt, Granny and in the middle, Grandpa. The coffin is open, which is what Granny wanted. He looks so small and frail lying there with his eyes closed. Nothing to do with the imposing man I remember him to be. Disturbed by the sight, I hadn't realised there was someone else in the little room – a hospital employee by all accounts. He is standing behind the coffin and starts speaking. Listening to him is practically impossible. I'm next to Granny and can't take my eyes off her.

Granny
Elegant and resilient, she has always been short and extremely thin but today she seems even smaller than usual. The shivers that run all over her body are so violent that they are obvious to the naked eye. She looks like she might fall so I grab her. Grateful, she lets go and leans on me fully. I want to support her and perhaps somehow make up for not being around much in the past and, most certainly, in the future. His short speech complete, the man closes the coffin and invites us to leave the room. We all climb into the car and make our way to the cemetery. I'm sitting next to my aunt now.

Aunt
She is quieter than usual though a few odd things come out of her mouth. I wonder if she knows what's happened and understands what's going on now or not. She's suffered from a mental disorder all her adult life. Detected when she was a teenager, it hindered her ability to finish school, find a job, and have relationships. She never had what some may call a 'normal' life. Out of fear and embarrassment linked to her condition, my grandparents cut themselves from the outside world for most of their lives. They never invited anyone over apart from us and went out less and less as the years passed by.

By(e)
I guess that's why we're the only ones here today, bidding him goodbye. Is it better to pass away surrounded by a thousand people who didn't really care or six people who loved you dearly? To each their own. Seeing the coffin lowered into the earth, I gasp for air. That's it, the inevitable outcome of life. Dad makes a poignant speech. I've never heard him talk about his father with such emotion and I'm not sure Grandpa had either. Once we've all said our goodbyes, we walk back to the car. One after the other, I whisper to Mum and then Dad: "If you die, I'll kill you!" It might seem odd but at this moment, I know they can tell that it's my way of saying "I love you."

Love
What we've just been through has shown me how crucial it is to be there for your loved ones, especially when they need you the most. No matter where in the world you end up, always make sure to come back for these defining moments. Whether it's joy or sadness that brings you together, make the most of every second you have with them.

Them

Each of us only have one life. I know it, but sometimes it slips my mind. Is it just me or do you occasionally forget about it as well? France may not have felt like home lately, if ever, but being here right now, absolutely does. After having spent years looking for where I belonged, it finally hits me. The question I should have been asking myself all along wasn't 'Where is home?' but '*What* is home?' Home isn't a place. Home is people. Home is them: Mum, Dad, my sister, and all of my loved ones. It doesn't matter where we are, we can recreate it wherever we go. That's because as long as we're together, we're home.

Home

Since I've moved abroad, people often ask me whether I miss France. Generally, I simply answer "No," but that's only half true. There are two things I miss dearly: my family and food. Actually, they go hand in hand as it's not French cuisine in general I long for but Mum's cooking specifically. When Mum and Dad moved in together, Mum said she would be happy to take care of the cooking if Dad was in charge of the dishes. He accepted and cleverly went out and bought a dishwasher the following day! Mum kept her half of the bargain nonetheless. Working four days a week in the very demanding environment of defence and security, she came home every evening and cooked a delicious meal for the four of us. Since then, when I come back to Louviers, she always puts together a mix of my favourite dishes as well as new creations. What impresses me the most is her ability to make something yummy in no time and out of next to nothing. I can't wait to see what she has in store for our next family gathering.

Next

My manager took me aside today. Odd. As we sat down, away from the rest of the team, she told me she was going to leave the company. I have felt her motivation slow in the last few weeks so I'm not surprised. That's not to say I'm happy though. Quite the opposite. We've been working together for just over six months. She's taught me a lot already but I'm sure there is so much more I need to learn from her. Thanks to her support, I have succeeded with my thesis and completed my masters' degree. I'm finally done with studying – for now. Celebrating success isn't my strong suit so having partied with some champagne and a few good friends, I'm already wondering what's next.

What

I've been considering doing a post graduate certificate in Risk Management. It only takes six months and sounds very practical. Plus, I hope it will increase both my knowledge and credibility. I always feel a bit hesitant having to teach experienced managers and engineers how to identify, prioritise, and mitigate their risks. Standing in a room in front of several of them, I often wonder what they actually gain from my presentations. I believe in the theory behind my job, but the practice doesn't always make obvious sense. At least, knowing my manager had my back made me feel more confident. I have no idea what will happen once she leaves but I'm trying not to let it affect me. Since the day she interviewed me, I've thought that if we didn't work together, we could be really good friends so perhaps this is our chance.

Chance

An email has just come through. The head office in France has decided to sell approximately half of the company's assets in the UK. A lot of change is coming our way. One of the many things living abroad teaches you, often the hard way, is to embrace change, so that's what I decide to do. A few weeks after the announcement, it's become apparent that no one in the business is interested in what I do anymore. Everyone's focus is on this new project. The six-month deadline associated with it is extremely tight. Sitting on the side lines of the action, I'm becoming terribly bored.

Bored
Out of all possible human feelings, boredom is most definitely one of the ones I hate the most. As soon as my days become dull, I start thinking about everything else I could be doing. I begin to wonder if I'm wasting some of the precious time I've been granted on this planet, and become restless.

Restless
A couple of days of boredom later, I choose to follow the phrase: 'If you don't ask, you don't get'. After all, what's the worst that can happen? I'm told no and go back to being bored. At least if I do something and take my future in my own hands, I won't have any regrets! Although that might make me sound extremely brave, that's not how I feel approaching the Chief Operating Officer's desk.

"Hi, may I have a word with you please?" I ask.

He simply nods in agreement.

"I've noticed that a lot of people are extremely busy working on the new project. There must be a lot to do so I'd be delighted to help out." I pause. I rehearsed it so many times in front of the mirror last night that it comes out effortlessly.

Without hesitation, he looks at me, smiles and says, "Sure, you can get involved, starting tomorrow."

Having thanked him politely, I leave the room beyond excited! I hope mergers and acquisitions will be as awesome as it sounds.

Awesome
The first project I get involved in involves a lot of technical work. As you know, I'm no engineer but I'm determined to do a good job so I study, learn and ask thousands of questions. Step-by-step, I begin to gain people's trust and, with their support, deliver substantial results. One project follows the next. I work countless hours and slowly seem to turn into a bit of a workaholic. I don't mind it at all. I'm thrilled to be involved and feel part of a significant milestone in the company's history. Everyone around me is heading in the same direction, with a common goal and as one team. It's exhilarating! Plus, the new project I just started working on is managed by handsome guy and things are starting to get hot...

Hot
Nothing to do with the weather. London is getting colder and colder as we approach the winter. The combination of constant rain and wind is even worse than the cold. No matter what I wear, I end up shivering endlessly as I make my way to the office and back. Autumn, winter and spring merge into one long and grey season after what seemed to have been just a couple of weeks of summer. What a couple of weeks though! As soon as the temperature hits 15 degrees Celsius or more, the locals invade London's beautiful parks and lie down in the sun barely dressed in a desperate attempt to tan. Sadly, those days are behind us... It's now wrapped up in our thick coats, that we all walk around the crowded city carefully avoiding colliding into each other as our paths cross. A part of me may slowly be turning British

judging by the above never-ending monologue about the four seasons. Over here, that's the ultimate topic of conversation. Whether you're stuck in an elevator with your neighbour, you bump into a colleague you don't really like, or you meet friends of friends for the first time, the weather is an ideal ice-breaker: not too vague yet not too personal. Anyway, many apologies for the distraction, I was about to tell you about handsome guy.

Guy
What I believed to be innocent is turning into something else, something I can't rationalise, control or resist. An obsession is in the making. Whenever we're in the same room, bar or restaurant, we end up talking to each other. We're like magnets that attract indefinitely. He broke up with his girlfriend recently. I'm not sure how or why but I can feel it has something to do with me. Unless I'm just imaging things. I don't know what he thinks but, more importantly, I don't know what to do. On the one hand, my boyfriend is smart, caring and supportive. But am I still attracted to him romantically? On the other hand, handsome guy is hot, funny and irresistible. But could it ever lead to anything serious? When I spend a weekend in Norway, I'm convinced that's where my future lies. However, as soon as the distance sets in, I get dangerously close to thinking the opposite. My head says one thing, my gut argues the other, and between the two, my heart is totally confused.

Confused
I don't sleep well anymore. Eating has become a means to an end rather than any form of enjoyment. Exercising seems to be the only thing that keeps me remotely sane. Weekly box exercise classes help me release some of the stress. As a result, I've lost

more weight. Twenty kilograms now. To be honest, I'm pretty pleased about it but that's only a temporary distraction from the critical decision I need to make. After yet another trip to Norway, I'm determined to stay put. What my boyfriend and I have is worth fighting for. This must be one of these tests life throws at you regardless of where you live or who you are. All I can do now is be honest with handsome guy.

Honest
We're in a meeting room at the office, of all places, when I tell him: "Let's be friends." This blunt statement should be closure but it feels nothing like it. It's like I'm an actress in the movie of my life, reciting the lines that I think make sense without fully considering their actual meaning and potential consequences.

Consequences
Lying on my bed that night, my stomach is twisting, turning, and rumbling. Did I make the wrong decision? What am I supposed to do now? Avoiding handsome guy would be ideal but it isn't an option. We work together at the same place, on the same project and for the same boss. Plus, we have so many friends in common and always end up at the same parties. One of those is taking place tonight and I'm dreading it. I've asked a friend to join me. We've only just met so I thought having her around might be a welcome diversion.

Diversion
The evening starts at a pub where we watch a rugby match. Things become extremely awkward as soon as my friend and I arrive. Handsome guy doesn't look at me, muffles a hello and turns back to speak to one of his friends. I wonder whether

everyone else can feel the tension between us. Hoping to suppress my discomfort, I drink one glass after the other. From the pub, we move to a bar. After a few hours, the bar turns into a club.

Club
Commercial pop music is blasting through the speakers, the vibrations hit my body and before I know it, my limbs are moving almost uncontrollably. He catches my hand and we start to dance. We're so close. I can feel his breath on my neck. With each of his exhales, an electric shock ripples down my spine. The initial tension has morphed into one of a completely different nature. But. But. But. I can't.

Can't
I free myself from his arms and rush outside. I need some fresh air and that's exactly what London has to offer. It's absolutely freezing outside. A few minutes pass and I realise that I was hoping he'd followed me out, so I walk back in slowly. From the entrance, our group of friends looks wild. All them are acting as though they own the dance floor. I laugh at the sight until something else catches my eye. The friend I brought along and handsome guy are dancing together. Wait, WHAT?! That's not all, they are kissing too. I can't believe my eyes! Jealousy runs like fire through my veins. I turn around and head straight home. Instantly, I know that my head, my heart, and my gut have aligned. I must take action.

Action
I'm certain that I've finally made the right decision but I'm dreading having to act on it. Although I haven't cheated, I feel as guilty as if I had. My heart has been broken before and I'd

promised never to make anyone feel that pain. I lie down for hours looking at the ceiling and wondering what to say. All of a sudden, I jump out of bed and call my boyfriend. The truth is, it hasn't been smooth sailing lately. What was once passion has slowly turned into friendship. He agrees and says he's been feeling the same way. After talking for ages, we come to the conclusion that it would be better to go our separate ways. I don't tell him about handsome guy. There doesn't seem to be a need to. I hadn't realised that there were enough reasons between the two of us alone to justify splitting up. All I hope is that he never blames himself for what happened. He didn't do or say anything wrong, my heart simply started beating for someone else. I take the time to wish him all the best and I mean it.

Mean
Of course, I can't stop thinking about handsome guy, but I don't want to jump into something new too quickly. It wouldn't be right for anyone involved. So when he tries to kiss me for the first time, I pull away. He must think I'm so mean. Sometimes I wonder why he hasn't given up yet. Hopefully it's because he feels it too, that connection, that bond, that attraction. I've given up trying to explain it, let alone finding a word to accurately describe it. All I hope is that it develops into something even deeper over time.

Time
It's far too early to think about that so I've decided to take a month to be alone and reflect. That was before life reminded me of a basic physics principle… perhaps you've guessed which one already. What happens when you try to pull two magnets apart from each other? Well, as soon as one slips it smashes into

the other full force. A few drinks, that's all it took for me to slip. Once again, we were on the dance floor with our friends. It had been three weeks. Having had a few too many cocktails, I couldn't resist any longer. I saw him leaning on the bar so I walked over, grabbed him by the collar of his purple shirt and kissed him. That was it, an uncontrollable and passionate start to a new chapter of our love life.

Chapter

We can't get enough of each other. We work together, eat together, drink together, travel together and sleep together. Our colleagues don't know, or so we hope. It would be better to keep it this way. We're still involved in the same project and both report to the same boss. Though we agreed to take things slowly, the exact opposite happens. After only three months, I'm already due to meet his parents, two brothers and their girlfriends.

Parents

His dad is having a retirement party and handsome guy has invited me to come along. Although I'm really looking forward to discovering Romsey – his hometown located near Southampton – I'm pretty scared at the idea of meeting his family. What if they don't like me? I'll be the only non-Brit. Will they mind? Will they see me as an intruder? What if I don't understand any of their jokes or say something rude without meaning to? We're in his car now, making our way over. The drive takes just under two hours. Before I know it, we're in front of the door. His family welcomes us with cheerful smiles and big hugs. Instantly, my anxiety dissipates. Over the next couple of days, they teach me countless 'proper' English words as well as the rules of a few traditional board games. His mum even cooks the most delicious roast dinner I've ever eaten. At ease and enjoying my time with them, I realise that with the initial fear gone, I somehow already feel at home.

Fear

Aside from heights, I would say my two biggest fears are boredom and loneliness. Hence why living in a shared flat is, or *was*, ideal. Our lovely Danish housemate left a few weeks ago and has been replaced by one of her friends from university. The new girl is half French and half South African. Bearing in mind our common cultural background and language, I thought we'd get along really well. We did, until it all got out of hand. Every morning on weekdays, I wake around 6:30. Today is no exception. After my alarm rings, I get out of bed and head to the bathroom. As I open my door, still half asleep, I suddenly find myself face to face with a guy I've never met before. Not only is he totally naked, he is also yelling. My body stiffens. My brain freezes. I don't know whether to be scared or amused. There isn't much space between him and the wall of corridor, but my instincts kick in and I take a chance. I storm past him all the way to the bathroom.

Bathroom

Without looking back, I jump in, slam the door behind me and lock it. It all happens so fast. My heart is racing in my chest. My breathing is out of control. My mind is desperately trying to make sense of it all. Who is this guy? What is he doing here? Why is he not wearing any clothes? Why is he screaming at me? I can still hear him. He is asking who I am and what the hell I'm doing here, in his house. Maybe he is insane, a lunatic in our house. What are we going to do? I'm in the bathroom, safe but terrified. I can't reach out to anyone; my phone is in my bedroom.

From this day forward, I must remember to take my phone everywhere I go, even if it's just to the bathroom. It's quiet outside now. I've managed to calm myself down and decide to take a shower. Hopefully, I can still arrive at work on time if I hurry.

Hurry

When I turn off the water minutes later, I hear someone running down the stairs and slamming the front door. Please let it be him, I think to myself. As slowly and quietly as I possibly can, I turn the key into the lock and pull the door open. Behind it is the new girl. She is in floods of tears. In between hiccups she keeps saying "Sorry, sorry, sorry." The whole story comes out of her month in a confused and hysterical blurb. From what I gather, she recently started working as an escort in a club. Her job is to entertain the clients without any obligation to sleep with them. However last night she met this rich guy and really liked him, so she decided to bring him home. As it turns out, he was a cocaine addict. After sniffing some he'd laid out on her breasts, he slept with her and then lost his mind. "He was convinced we were staying at his place and became totally paranoid when he saw you," she continues. My level of shock has gone through the roof. I have no idea how to react. The only thing I can think about is that I have to go to work. My brain is now on autopilot. I must take myself to a safe, stable, and sane environment. After mumbling some dull apologies, I run out to catch my train. The whole day, I feel bad. I should have been there for her. I should have listened. I should have stayed. I text her to let her know I'm thinking of her. It sounds like she is doing better. I'm glad. She says she is going through a rough patch and promises never to let something like this happen again.

Again
Two non-eventful weeks have passed. Though I've never been a fan of routines, for once, I'm glad to see it settling in. The calm after the storm. Or was it before? Today has been a long day at the office. The project I'm working on is taking all my time, my brain power, and my energy. On my way back to the flat, I almost stayed on the train and missed my stop. Lucky I didn't as I'm absolutely starving. Finally, standing in the kitchen, I start to cook a chili con carne, one of my favourite dishes. I'm chopping onions when I hear the front door open. "Hello!" I say cheerfully. What I get as a reply isn't what I expected, to say the least. The new girl storms into the kitchen and throws a whole bunch of cutlery on the floor. Next, she grabs a large knife.

Knife
She is screaming now. "I'm going to kill myself! I'm going to slit my veins, empty myself of all my blood and die!" I try to grab her and take the knife away, but she rushes to the living room yelling the same words again and again. She is getting louder and louder. In the quietest and kindest sounding voice I manage to come up with, considering the circumstances, I try to reason with her and calm her down.

I ask questions, "What happened?", "Do you know where you are?", "Where have you come from?", "Who were you with?", "Are you hurt?"

It's what I was told to do when my former primary school best friend became suicidal at 15 years old. Another long story. I'm sitting on the sofa next to the new girl now. She looks livid. Her black make-up has run down from her eyes all the way to her cheekbones, her dress is ripped in several places and I'm not sure whether she is wearing anything underneath at this point. Not a pretty sight. I'm torn between fear and sadness though the latter is slowly taking over. She's just handed me the knife when the front door opens. I've never been so happy to hear any of my housemates come home.

It's the Indian girl. Right away, she understands something is wrong and we start discreetly talking about what to do. As we turn our backs to the new girl for a few seconds, she jumps to her feet and rushes upstairs. That's when we hear it. *BANG!*

BANG!
My first thought is that she has hit her head somewhere. I don't even take time to breathe. Jumping the steps two by two, I run up shouting her name. There she is, sitting on her bed with my laptop between her legs. It takes me no time to put two and two together.

"What happened to my laptop?" I ask her calmly though I'm furious inside.

"It's not my fault, the wall moved and hit it," she replies smiling from ear to ear.

I know this isn't the right time for an argument. She is way too high. I lean over to grab my computer. She is holding on to it as if it was hers and looks at me with puppy eyes. I don't flinch. My patience has run out. Back in my room, I take a look at the laptop which my parents gave to me for my birthday a few months ago. It's working but the damage to the right side of the keyboard is significant.

Damage
We hear her rattle in her room for a while, take a shower and finally go to bed. After the Indian guy came back, the three of

us kept an ear and eye out to make sure she was ok. The other two feel sad and sorry for her. I, on the other hand, can't help being angry and scared. If this is her today, what will she be like tomorrow? She is completely unpredictable. Though she seems to mainly be a danger to herself right now, we don't know that she couldn't suddenly snap and attempt to hurt us. My housemates say that they know and trust her. Well, I don't and I can't. The next day, she sends me countless messages. She is sorry and says she won't let it happen again. Apparently, she took drugs and lost control. She also admits that she's been using my laptop every single day while I was at work. She never asked me whether she could borrow it, so I had no idea. My privacy has been completely violated. This isn't about the laptop anymore, it's about trust and she has lost mine for good. From that day onwards, I lock my bedroom door. The others ask to speak with me in turn. Apparently, by doing so, I'm the one who's making our flat uncomfortable. I can't believe it! I think the time has come for me to look for a new place to stay.

Place
My list of criteria is quite short: somewhere I feel safe is all I'm asking for. It took me a while and I had to tell the above stories to a few people in order to realise how awful and toxic this environment actually is. How could I have been so oblivious to it all? The fridge is full of rotten food, the ceiling of the bathroom is covered in black mould and the neighbour is a drug dealer. Despite her promises, the new girl has reimbursed me far less than a tenth of the price of the repairs. Fixing my laptop wasn't a cost I'd factored into my budget and it has taken a hit on my savings. However, holding a grudge won't help. Right now, I'd simply like to escape.

Escape
I spend most of the next few weeks staying at handsome guy's place. Any spare minute I have, I use it to hunt through flat-share websites. After responding to quite a few ads, I finally secure a couple of visits. Looking for a new place or searching for a new job, I can't decide which one I dislike the most. Actually, there is something I find particularly awkward about flat hunting: that moment when you enter into someone's own universe although you've never met them before. Despite the explicit invitation, it makes me feel like I'm an intruder invading their personal space. Dirty socks here, open bags of crisps there, suspiciously clean surfaces, etc. Too much information. Within minutes and via a number of vague assumptions, I try to make out who they are and what they would be like to live with. They do the same, I'm sure, although they have a significant disadvantage: my privacy isn't lying in front of their eyes. Like speed dating, first impressions weigh significantly on the outcome.

Outcome
It takes me less than a couple of minutes to know that I wouldn't like living in the first flat I see. A place with seven students equals countless parties... Not a lifestyle that is for me anymore. I hope that doesn't make me sound too boring. I'm approaching the second flat now. After a couple of knocks, the door opens. Behind it are two girls. One is German and works in the film industry; the other is an Irish lawyer. The place is pretty and quaint. What must have been the living room has been turned into a third bedroom, so the only shared area is the kitchen. The available bedroom is fairly large. It has a double bed, two cupboards, a small desk and chair. I like the atmosphere. It's at the top of my budget range but, having just been promoted from my VIE to

a permanent job, I'm prepared to put all of my slight pay rise into rent. Feeling safe is priceless. That, and the need to surround yourself with people who support you, inspire you and pull you up, are the two significant learnings I've taken away from this unfortunate experience.

People
The two girls seem mature yet bubbly and fun. They say six people are visiting the flat today. A one in six chance. That's tough odds to say the least. Once they've met everyone, they'll make a decision. They hope the chosen person will be able to move in right away. I haven't even told the people I live with that I was planning on leaving but there's a girl I don't even know – one of their friends I suppose – who's been crashing on the sofa for weeks. Perhaps she'll want to take over my room. Fingers crossed. I walk around Kentish Town, the local neighbourhood of this potential new home, partly to explore it and partly to avoid going back to my old flat. I've been doing that a lot lately. Sad, isn't it? It's getting dark now, dark and cold. I must head back. I've been clinging onto my phone ever since I left. Finally, it rings.

Rings
It's the German girl and she is giving me great news. They liked me and if I'm interested, I can move in today or tomorrow. I'm more than just interested, I'm over the moon! As soon as I hang up, I jump and let out a cry of joy. Thankfully, I'm the only one walking along the deserted streets of my new neighbourhood. Immediately, I call handsome guy. He agrees to meet me at my old flat with his car. It's decided, I'm moving out this evening! As soon as I get back, I tell my old housemates. They are shocked

and I can read judgment and despise in their eyes. Never mind. On the contrary, the girl who had been sleeping on the tiny sofa for weeks is delighted. She will take over my old room immediately. Though this move is long overdue, everything seems to be working itself out as if it was meant to be. Once my announcement is made, I head to the kitchen and grab a whole roll of large bin bags. As quickly as I can, I stuff everything I own into them. Luckily, I don't have much. A couple of hours later, everything is in the back of handsome guy's car. He kisses me gently. "I'm so happy you've finally left this horrendous place. I was starting to seriously worry about you living there," he says while squeezing my hand. As we drive off, I don't turn back. Instead, I look at him, take a deep breath and smile.

Smile
Handsome guy popped the L word! Of course, I said it back. It felt amazing! Every time I think about him, I can't help but smile from ear to ear. Every time I hang out with him, he comes up with the most random jokes and makes me laugh uncontrollably. Every time I speak to him, I feel like what I say truly matters. We still can't seem to get enough of each other. Every day. Every minute. Every second.

Second
I remember the first time I injured my knee as if it were yesterday. Time heals, or so I've heard. It did. Although it's been bothering me on and off for years, it's finally on the mend. I also remember what I committed to in my 'grown-up' list: keep moving. What better way of doing that than running? I started in the park on weekends. Now, I'm even taking running breaks at lunch time two to three times a week. I managed to convince a few colleagues

to join me. It's more fun to run together! Plus, we motivate one another. When the weather is dreadful outside, it only takes one person to say they are off for a run in order for me to join in. Things would be different on my own, I'm sure I'd come up with all sorts of excuses. At first, we only ran 20 to 30 minutes, but we've upped our game lately.

Upped

It suits me as I'm training for the longest distance I've ever run. Last month, I took part in a 10-kilometres race. Being cheered all the way from start to finish by kind volunteers felt absolutely amazing! London has a lot to offer when it comes to such events. I hadn't heard of anything like this before. What's even better is that each and every one of them is organised for a good cause. It's a win-win-win situation: exercise while having a good time and contributing to making the world a better place. The more I take part, the more I want to take part. With every race, I hope to increase the distance. I'm starting to dream big. One day, I'd like to complete a marathon. It will take time and a lot of training, I know, but it would be both an incredible achievement and a sweet revenge over the snowboarding accident I had all these years ago and the dodgy knee I've been dragging around ever since. From knee injury to marathon finisher. It sounds unbelievable when I say it in my head. I'd love to be a living proof that when you put your mind to something, you can achieve it. Today I'm taking part in the Ricky Road Run with several colleagues. It's just over 16 kilometres (10 miles). That's one step closer to the half marathon and a couple of steps away from the full. I can't wait!

Wait

Handsome guy is volunteering and will cheer us on. I would love to impress him, not with my slow running but with my dedication. Each time I take part in such an event, I feel a pinch of anxiety rising from the pit of my stomach to my heart when I stand along the starting line waiting for the pistol to kick things off. It's really cold today. I tried stretching and warming up my muscles, but it only took a minute standing still for them to tighten up again. "Four degrees," someone says behind me. The simple sound of it sends shivers down my spine. There is no going back though. It's time to shine, or at least time to make it to the finish line! Left, right, left, right, left, right. That's what I tell myself to keep going. Even if I'm running, I don't seem to be able to get warm, but I've got to keep going nonetheless. Left, right, left, right, left, right. This will be nothing when I run a marathon, not even half way. Left, right, left, right, left, right. My knee hurts. "Don't stop, it's all in your head!" I whisper stubbornly to myself. Left, right, left, right, left, right. I've just passed the eight-mile mark. I'm almost there. Only two miles to go. Left, right, left, right, left, right. My knee hurts. It really does now. I must finish no matter what. For myself.

Matter

My rambling mind doesn't even see it coming. One second I'm up and literally running. The next, I'm lying on the ground stunned. What happened? I'm not sure. But it hurts and I'm freezing. A couple of volunteers come rushing towards me.

"The medics are on their way, just relax," one of them says.

I can't relax, I want to complete what I've started. I must. "No, no, no, I have to keep going," is all I manage to mumble through the tears.

Shock, pain and anger have become one numbing feeling. My mind won't give up on something my body obviously can't deliver. The medics arrive and take extremely good care of me. Minutes later, I'm sitting in an ambulance. It's this way, embarrassed and disappointed in myself, that I cross the finish line. Luckily, the injury isn't as serious as I first feared. It's just a strain to the muscle above my bad knee and should take anytime from two to four weeks to heal. Handsome guy and I are going to Bucharest next weekend, so the timing isn't great... Such is life, I suppose. He was terrified when he heard the news, but he couldn't show it. We're still hiding our relationship from our colleagues. It's exhilarating at the best of times but far from ideal in worst case scenarios, like this one. Although I can't predict the future, I have a feeling that today marks the end of my short and appalling running career. It's time to find a new sport to stay fit.

Sport
London 2012. The city is hosting the Olympic and Paralympic games. There are posters and decorations everywhere. I'm so lucky to be living here at such an exciting time! Sadly, I wasn't quick enough, so I don't have tickets for any of the events. It doesn't make me look forward to it any less though. The atmosphere promises to be vibrant all over town. Plus, handsome guy asked me to book a day off in the middle of that period. Hopefully we'll go to a nice pub or venue where we can watch some of the action. I keep asking him what we'll be doing. I can't help it; no one has ever surprised me before.

Surprised
Having thought about it, I can't even make up my mind as to whether I like surprises or not. The mysterious day is around the

corner and I'm determined to find out what he has in store for us. Half-jokingly, I ask him which Olympic sport we'll be watching together. I catch a glimpse of shock in his eyes.

"WHAT?!" I scream. Bending under pressure, he spills it all out. We're going to see a day of men's handball. I couldn't be more delighted! Handball is one of the sports I grew up watching. Dad loves it and my sister even used to play. It's so wonderful and generous of him! Jumping for joy, I suddenly realise that he has gone very quiet.

"What's wrong?" I enquire.

"I'm so upset I didn't manage to surprise you," he replies.

If only he knew how little it matters. This is one of the most amazing gifts ever, a once in a lifetime opportunity. In my mind, the Olympic and Paralympic games are so much more than just about sport. They are events that bring nations from all over the world together and spread a message of peace and tolerance.

Tolerance

Travelling and living abroad has taught me so much and still continues to. It's a learning journey that will never end. Perhaps one day I'll have enough material to write a book called 'The School of Living Abroad' or something along these lines. I've thought about it quite a lot lately and one word stands out: Tolerance[4], the first step towards acceptance. It is, without a shadow of a doubt, a value that I hope to transmit throughout my life, however long or short it might be. But what does it mean exactly?

1. A fair, objective, and permissive attitude toward those whose opinions, practices, race, religion, nationality, etc., differ from one's own.

---

[4] This definition can be found in the online dictionary WordReference©.

2. Interest in and concern for ideas, opinions, practices, etc., foreign to one's own.
3. The act of enduring or capacity to endure.

Naturally, some life experiences reinforce our values while others challenge them.

Challenge

This family holiday is triggering the latter. Though it might sound surprising at my age, I still love going on holiday with my parents and my sister. This summer, we're travelling to Asia again. Two years ago, we went to Indonesia and had a fabulous time! We fell in love with the place, the people, the culture and the food. So it's full of enthusiasm that we're flying over to China for a couple of weeks. We're starting our trip in Beijing, the capital and will soon be visiting Chengde, Shaolin, Luoyang, Pingyao, Longmen, Datong, Xian as well as a few other places I've already forgotten the names of. As soon as we land, the culture shock hits us.

Culture

All over the world, countries, regions, and even cities all have their own unique culture. Accepting and embracing these individualities is something living abroad and meeting people from all over the world teaches you. Sometimes it seems easy and you might even adopt a few of the practices you come across without even realising it. Other times, like here here and now, it feels like a rather tough process. On the one hand, Chinese history and culture fascinates me. On the other hand, there is so much that shocks and baffles me. While I do my best to prevent it, I can't help but cast a judgmental eye on some of what I witness. Judgment isn't helpful though as it undeniably hinders our ability to be open-minded and compassionate.

Open-minded
Confident girl, my friend from university, has moved to Shanghai. Her plan is to work there for a couple of years. What an ideal opportunity for me to travel to China again! I believe visiting friends who are from or live in other countries gives you a different perspective. It's a chance to see beyond the main tourist spots and dive one step deeper into the local culture and lifestyle. It may also mean free accommodation, a perk one can't ignore. I'm really looking forward to exploring 'her Shanghai' but first we've decided to meet in Sanya. Southernmost city of the island of Hainan, Sanya, also known as 'China's Florida', is famous for its white sand and surfing beaches.

Beaches
Who knew China had beaches? The few days we spend there together fly by. We hike in the jungle, chill by the beach and drink litres of coconut water. Most tourists are either Chinese or Russian. Looking at us, people assume we're the latter. At bars and restaurants, they greet us in Russian and hand us menus we can't make any sense of. Feeling audacious, we order blindly from one of them. My friend speaks Chinese, but we thought it'd be funnier this way. The first two dishes turn out to be potatoes and vegetables, which are nice enough. We've already started eating them when the third, and last one, comes out. Our wide smiles turn into a frown as the waiter lowers the plate onto the table. What on earth is that?

That
It looks like the bottom part of birds' legs. There must be a mistake. We would never order this! Looking across the table, it seems as though both of us are just as shocked. "These are chicken claws,"

she says. Damn! Do people actually eat these? Not only does it look revolting, I can't believe there's much meat around such scrawny feet. She tries to argue with the waiter but it's pointless. We did order this dish unknowingly. It seems like we might not have been ready for the full blown culinary adventure we were embarking on. Local food is a window into a country's culture, one that I'm always keen on jumping through but everyone has their limits I suppose…

Limits
When I travelled to China with my family, every single one of us lost weight. We couldn't get used to the food and struggled to find anything that would satisfy our taste buds. Some days, all we ate was steamed rice, some kind of sweet bread, and bananas. That's why, coming back to China this time around, food is one of my main concerns. According to confident girl, things are different in Shanghai. To my greatest surprise, she ends up being absolutely right. Thanks to her guidance and mind-blowing language skills, I discover plenty of delicious dishes and realise how diverse Chinese food actually is. Tonight is my last evening in town and she is taking me to a Mongolian place. I can't wait! It will be great to catch up with her after a day of exploring on my own.

Exploring
I never thought I'd actually enjoy walking around by myself but the sense of freedom it provides is growing on me. Today, I've planned a trip to the city's famous traditional gardens known as Yu Garden. I'm travelling there by metro which already seems like a crazy adventure. Coming out of the station, I expect to enter a haven of peace. Instead, I'm overwhelmed by the heat

and the number of people crawling in all directions. Unexpectedly, I've ended up in a buzzing tourist market. There are people everywhere, pushing, rushing and stopping. Some stare at me. Others take pictures of me. When I finally reach the garden, it's with great relief that I walk along its small alleys, marvel at its ponds full of brightly coloured fish and stare at its centenary trees. After taking my time to explore this relaxing maze, I sit down on a bench and relax. A few minutes later, I decide to head out. Making my way through the tourist market as quickly as I can, I eventually reach the main street. It is here, as I slow down to find my way, that an incongruous thought hits me.

Thought
I will live here one day. For some unexplainable reason, I'm sure of it. It's irrational, I know, but I can't ignore this overpowering feeling somewhere in my gut. Some might call it a premonition, others a fantasy. My mind starts to wander. I picture myself moving to Shanghai and strolling along these streets that would have gone from being foreign to feeling familiar. Doing so, I lose track of time and space. Everything looks the same in this neighbourhood. Where am I? Lost.

Lost
I eventually find my way back to the main road. That night, I have a wonderful time with confident girl. As always, she is full of great advice and honest opinions. There is something particularly charismatic about her. However, worried she'd judge me; I don't tell her about my premonition. I simply choose to enjoy her delightful presence. At the end of yet another delicious meal, I wish I could stay here longer. Sadly, the time has come for me to head back to London's reality.

Reality

My phone rings. It's one of my old housemates – the Indian girl I used to live with. She says a letter came through the post for me. It's from the city council and isn't the first one. She ignored the others, but apparently this one looks different.

"There is red all over it," she explains.

I can't actually see it but distinguishing a hint of fear in her voice, it doesn't take much for me to predict she isn't bearing good news.

"It states that they will take you to court if you don't pay your council taxes immediately," she continues.

I'm confused. My mind starts racing. I'm panicking. We had a chat about council taxes with my old housemates previously and my understanding was that we didn't have to pay any. Since moving out, I've been paying these taxes diligently on a monthly basis but before that, I genuinely thought I didn't have to. Knowing how much they're charging me now, thinking about how long I've lived in the old place for and adding the penalties the letter refers to, this isn't going to be cheap. How could I be so gullible? Why didn't I double check?

Check

Suddenly, a wave of anger crashes over me. It's directed at myself. Those are always the strongest. As soon as I hang up, I call the council. After a mix of apologies, explanations, discussions and emotions, the result isn't quite as bad as I'd feared. Still, this is a costly error that could have easily been avoided. I've always been a bit naïve and forgetful when it comes to these admin things… It's the only aspect of moving abroad I dislike. No matter how much I try to plan, I inevitably end up lost somewhere in the middle of what I call the 'admin maze'. Determined to avoid

it next time, I add taxes to the bottom of my list of top relocation topics which I thought I'd share. Who knows, it might come in handy for you too.
- Visa
- Bank
- Phone
- Insurance
- National Insurance number or equivalent
- Embassy registration
- Taxes

While I'm at it, I write it on my spreadsheet template, the one I use for every single international move. Perhaps the project management qualification I've just completed is rubbing off on my personal life. It would be about time! As it turns out, people who are the most organised at the office can easily be the least structured outside of it.

Organised

I'm so bored again. It's not that I don't have anything to do, it's that what I have to do is extremely dull. The promotion they gave me was supposed to be this extremely exciting opportunity. It felt like it for a while but after just a couple months, I'm pretty sure I already know all I need to. Everything has become repetitive. Plus, water and waste have never been my dream industries to work in. Not that I really know what my dream is anymore. Whatever was on the 'grown-up' list seems irrelevant, outdated, and unrealistic. All I'm certain of is that what I'm doing right now has no place on it. I've spoken with my manager and asked for new projects but that's not the way he sees things.

Manager
He is a 50-something expert in insurance who just sits and waits for people to come to him for advice. His ideal day is one during which he does the bare minimum, enjoys a nice pub lunch, and leaves on time. All this while giving everyone else – especially his boss – the impression he is working extremely hard and is overwhelmingly busy. My requests and enthusiasm are disruptive to the order of things he's established and cultivated for years. It's pretty clear there's nothing more for me to learn here apart from more to add to my 'not to do as a manager' list. Yes, I have one of those too. Hopefully it will come in handy sooner rather than later. At the moment, I only have one direct report.

Report
Being able to learn from others and with others is what managing people means to me. Right now, that's actually the only part of my job I enjoy. Our relationship started on the wrong foot. He'd applied for the job I stepped into... Being older and having more seniority than I did, he assumed he would get it. During the first one-on-one meeting we had, I asked him what his career aspirations were. He simply answered, "You're the boss, you tell me what to do and I'll do it." I wasn't prepared to hear that. He left me baffled and struggling for words. Step-by-step, things improved. When, after a few months, I open up to him subtly about how bored I am, he does the same in return. Surprised, we realise we share identical views. We jokingly say that we should set-up fake meetings so we can apply for new jobs.

Apply
At first, I was really picky. For a few months, I only applied for a handful of jobs I thought sounded amazing. Tired of what I was doing, I hoped to change both industry and role. From water

and waste to anything else, and from risk to project management. A friend told me that out of the three pillars of a job – location, industry, and role – it's really difficult, if not impossible, to change more than one at a time. "Well, here are two of my favourite things: take on a challenge and prove people wrong," is what I answered. This unexpected burst of confidence from the rebellious little girl buried within me quickly faded as I received rejection after rejection. In a flash of despair, I ended up applying for about 50 jobs last weekend. I barely looked at the descriptions and hoped that fate would play its part. Days passed, nothing happened. I guess I approached this incorrectly… Anyway, next week, I'll be in Scotland with my manager visiting some waste treatment plants. A welcome distraction.

Scotland
Traditional Scottish weather – meaning wind, rain, and freezing temperatures – welcomes us. Outside, it only takes a couple of minutes for me to shiver relentlessly. However, being inside isn't any better. Escaping the overpowering smell that comes out of the impressive mountains of rotting rubbish is an impossible task. During my presentation, I'm forced to breathe through my mouth in order to make sure I don't gag. Halfway through, we take a break. I really wish there was somewhere I could go for fresh air. Looking around the table, I realise I'm not just the only woman, I'm also by far the youngest. It has caused me to face a lot of sexism and ageism over the course of my short career but nothing yet quite as bad as some of the stories I've heard from other female friends and colleagues. A buzz in my jacket pocket brings me back to reality. My phone is ringing. Unknown number. I wonder who it could be…

Who

The recruitment manager of a travel company is who called! This whole chain of events started a few weeks ago. After a successful phone interview with her, I was selected for the second round of the process: face-to-face. When I arrived at the company's offices, I was so nervous. Travel? I love travel! How amazing would it be to work in an industry you were absolutely passionate about! I put on my high heels in front of the building and headed in. My stomach was churning and my heart racing as I gave my name to the friendly receptionist. Behind her desk, I noticed there were about 15 to 20 people waiting. All men. All much older than me.

"Are we all here for the same job?" I asked hoping she wouldn't detect the tremor in my voice.

"Yes, sure," she'd replied with a polite smile.

There is no way I'm going to secure this job, is the first thought that crossed my mind. These men clearly have far more experience than I do. Looking around as we all sat at the impressive boardroom table, I decided to take a more positive outlook on the situation. At least, no matter how little I said or did during the interviews, I naturally stood out.

Interviews

The selection process began with speed dating-style interviews. I found some of the questions surprisingly personal.

Answering "What is your biggest regret?" in 45 seconds was particularly tough.

Honest, I said, "I wish I had travelled even more."

Next step was a group exercise and presentation followed by a one-on-one interview with the Chief Executive Officer's right-hand lady. How inspiring yet intimidating it was meeting such a successful woman in person. Even if nothing else came out of it, I was grateful for the insightful conversation we'd had.

Conversation
To my greatest surprise, I was asked to come back for the final round of the selection process: a one-on-one with the future manager. I thought it went pretty well but I knew there were still quite a few candidates being considered so I tried not to get my hopes up too high. Why would they choose me over all these senior men? On the positive side, this experience had given me the push I needed to apply for more roles. However, it seems that was unnecessary after all. Hiding at the end of the corridor of one of Scotland's waste treatment plants and surrounded by that dreadful smell, I listen to the recruitment manager. "Congratulations! We would like to offer you the job!" she says joyfully. I can't believe my ears! I feel like jumping, screaming, dancing! Instead, I make my way back to the meeting room slowly and pretend that nothing happened, for now.

Pretend
I am – have always have been – a terrible liar. As a teenager, I tried countless times to fool my parents by telling one of them that the other had already agreed for me to go out. It never worked so I gave up and started living by the motto 'Honesty is the *only* policy'. Though it has sometimes put me in rather awkward situations, it's now part of who I am: an open book, a truth teller. That's why keeping this new job a secret is so tough. I can't wait to resign and start a new chapter of my career.

Resign
As I hand the letter to my manager and talk him through what it means – trying hard not to smile – I can read shock in his eyes.

He didn't see it coming. That's strange, as I thought my boredom and frustration were obvious. Next, I have a one-on-one with my direct report.

Direct

His reaction couldn't be more different. He's really happy for me and confesses that he has also received a job offer and will be resigning soon. I'm so pleased for him!

"Thank you!" he says "Your borderline insane drive and enthusiasm have shown me that I'm in charge of my own life and inspired me to finally make the changes I've been thinking about and sitting on for ages."

Wow! From f*** you to thank you! He has made a complete 180-degree turn and given me the most incredible compliment of my short career to date. I'm so humbled and feel my cheeks turning bright red. From him, I've learnt how important it is to stay calm and grounded both in business and in life. I thank him sincerely and say: "You will never regret stepping out of your comfort zone and following your dreams. Some of the most amazing things in your life will happen as soon as you go through with it."

Moments like this are exactly why I do my utmost to do what I do the way I do it, I think to myself.

Utmost

Fast forward a month of draining handover, tomorrow is my first day in the new job. I can't decide what to wear. I've lost 20 kilograms now. I never thought I'd make it this far. I was certain that being chubby was part of me. On the one hand, I can't deny that I look and feel very different. On the other, I haven't been able to shake the image of myself as a whale, which I've carried for all these years. Sadly, sometimes I relapse into bad eating habits, especially when I'm anxious – like tonight. Anyway, the point is that my suit is too big for me, so I don't know what to put on. Outfit and weight are the only two things I have direct control over right now. I'm sure that's why my mind holds onto them in moments of stress like this. Damn, I won't be rested tomorrow.

Rested
The first couple of days go by in a blur. There is so much to do and even more to learn. Each company has its acronyms, its ways of working, and its more or less mysterious internal politics. I've been trying to find my way through the maze. Thus far, the most fascinating person to observe has been the company's Chief Executive Officer.

Chief
A strong-minded woman that was brought in to transform and restructure the business, she is inspiring in some ways and frightening in others. Standing in front of her, I often have the impression that I'm a four year old who's done something wrong. Is that how a leader should make you feel? I wonder. She is adamant that all meetings must start and end on time. With this in mind, she introduced a 'bell system'.

Bell
One ring of the bell warns presenters they only have two minutes left. Two rings of the bell indicate their time is up. At that point, if they don't stop talking, she interrupts. As the youngest and most junior woman in the room, the tedious and embarrassing task of ringing the bell often ends up with me. Sitting in the meeting room, waiting for her to arrive, we all lift our heads at

the sound of her killer heels against the floor. Impeccably dressed from head to toe, she fills the room with her perfume as she enters. A cup of green tea, which has been prepared by one of her three assistants and placed precisely in front of her seat, is steaming away, ready to be drunk. After greeting everyone firmly, she looks at the bell then at me in turn. With a smile that couldn't be more fake, she declares, "We all have to start somewhere." I can barely contain my anger. It's as though my life had suddenly turned into a scene from *The Devil Wears Prada*[5]. Jumping out of my seat and throwing the bell in her face is so tempting. Instead, I smile politely and say, "Sure." Best birthday treatment ever...

Birthday
I haven't told anyone as I've only been working here for three days but today is my birthday. After such a dreadful start to the festivities, I can't wait to meet handsome guy tonight. He said he would cook dinner for me.

Dinner
Late and drained is a good description of how I feel when I arrive at his place. Step-by-step, I make my way up the stairs. I need to rant about it all so badly. Hastily, I push the door of the living room which is oddly closed. That's when I see him and his lovely little set-up. Candles on the table are lit and presented in a heart shape. A homemade salmon quiche and side salad are waiting to be eaten. My mood lifts and so do both corners of my mouth turning it into a wide smile. After we demolish the main course, he says he's bought a carrot cake and some champagne. My favourite combination! We talk about

---

[5] *The Devil Wears Prada* is an American comedy drama movie released in 2006 and staring Meryl Streep and Anne Hathaway.

our upcoming travel plans to Thailand, Switzerland, and Slovenia; about our hopes and dreams for the future and then eventually about everything and nothing. It seems like we might be ready for the next step.

Next
According to handsome guy, what we are about to do is a huge deal. I agree that it will be one of the milestones of our relationship, but we've been spending pretty much every night together, either at my place or at his, so I don't think moving in together will be so different. Plus, I'm really excited about it! No more packing every night, forgetting things here and there and deciding when and where to meet. We'll have our own place, somewhere we can call home. Home, not because it's a place but because it's where the two of us will live. He certainly feels home to me. I keep those thoughts to myself though as I think they'd freak him out. After weeks of painful flat hunting, we finally find one we really like. I can't wait to make it our own.

Own
I've always enjoyed decorating new places. One day, I'd love to either buy or build a house and do it up integrating artefacts from all over the world. Each continent would have its own room. I can actually picture it when I close my eyes. However, that's in complete contradiction with my dream of travelling and moving from place to place, city to city, country to country for the rest of my life. Building a house or exploring the world – a choice must be made.

World
Routine has settled in. Some aspects are wonderful, like the simple fact of coming home to handsome guy, cooking together,

and watching a movie nestled up in our comfy sofa. Other times, I can hear the outside world calling. Luckily, work allows me to travel to various European countries and the intensity of the job gives me very little spare time to think. Still, my feet are becoming more and more itchy. I miss exploring. I dream of new places. I wish I could hop on a plane with him not even knowing where it takes us. Every time I fly for work, I stare at the board for a few minutes and look through all the destinations we could be heading. In my head, I make a top three out of them and keep on daydreaming all the way to the gate.

Daydreaming
One of handsome guy's best friends has just quit his job and moved to Rio with his Brazilian girlfriend. To me, that sounds as amazing as it sounds insane! I admire their courage and have given them the nickname of the nomadic couple. I don't think I could quit everything and just move away… My career is more important to me than I thought it would be. It's not just about ambition, it's also about structure. When I have a day off, I'm often tempted not to do anything at all. Imagine if every single day was like that… No time to get up by, no place to go, nobody to report to. I'm pretty sure I would end up watching TV for hours, eating tonnes of chocolate, and feeling depressed. When I last spoke to the nomadic couple though, this seemed to be the least of their worries. I can't wait to find out how things are going with them when we see each other in Brazil. I hope this trip will calm my inner voice endlessly begging me for new adventures.

Brazil
We land in Rio and in no time, I fall in love with this unbelievable city! For starters, it's got the beach right in the middle of it. How cool is that? And it doesn't stop there. Nature surrounds the city and we spend every afternoon completing a different hike: Sugar Loaf, Christ the Redeemer and the Two Brothers, to name a few. Once again, we're making the most of being shown around by locals. They invite us to a football match at the gigantic and iconic Maracanã stadium, and take us to all of their favourite local bars and restaurants. As we also wanted to have some time to ourselves, we've decided to go to Iguaçu for a few days just the two of us.

Iguaçu
There, at the border between Paraguay, Argentina and Brazil, is where you find some of the largest waterfalls in the world. Iguaçu is one of these places that's been on my list for ages. We flew from Rio to Foz de Iguaçu in the afternoon and are now relaxing at the hostel. After a few drinks and some dinner, we head to bed. I often wake up in the middle of the night to go to the bathroom. Tonight, for some inexplicable reason, instinct perhaps, I take this opportunity to check my phone.

Instinct
I've received a new email from Mum. She's been in the US visiting Granddad at the hospital for the past few days. He's been unwell, something to do with his lungs. The after-effects of polio – which he suffered from when he was 20 years old – is making him weaker and weaker. I've been thinking about him a lot although I've also tried to have a good time here; especially as a couple of days ago the doctors said he was on the mend. With

that in mind, Mum flew back to France yesterday. I'm about to open her email now. She called it 'Bad News'.

Bad
My blood freezes and my heart tightens as I click on it. Next to me, handsome guy is sleeping deeply. I close my eyes and take a few slow, silent, breaths. Once opened, I skim through the words as fast as I can. A gasp of surprise escapes me. Granddad passed away. I don't know how to feel about it. On the one hand, his words dramatically damaged my confidence all those years ago. On the other hand, the desire to prove him wrong motivated me to always aim high and constantly improve myself. I guess I owe him that. I never had the chance to ask if he meant the things he said in the past. Was I still a disappointment, a failure, an embarrassment in his eyes? Or, had I managed to change his mind? Sadly, now I'll never be able to find out.

Out
Mum says the whole family is holding a gathering in Paris tonight. There will be about 30 people. The only one missing is me. There it is again, the guilt of not being there for your family and loved ones because you live abroad. Most of the time, the pros of this lifestyle outweigh the cons but in situations like this, it all comes back full force and hits you right in the face. I should be home with Mum and everyone else. Frenetically, I check various flight options on my phone.

Flight
The Internet is terrible so it takes ages. With the page finally up, I realise that there is no way I could afford these last-minute deals. Plus, due to the distance and time difference, I would never make

it back in time for the family reunion. In her message, Mum tells me to stay put and make the most of my trip. She insists that I might not have the chance to return to Brazil and that anyway, nothing will happen for a while. The plan is to cremate his body in the US, leave half of the ashes there and bring the other half back to France. Step-Grandma will fly with the urn. Is that what happens when you lead an international life? Your body ends up being split across different countries… I can't decide whether I find the idea poetic or horrific. Either way, it means I'll be able to attend the funeral in France upon my return. After reading her email, there is nothing else I can focus on throughout the rest of the trip.

Trip
It's like my body is in Brazil and my eyes see everything that's around me but my mind has wandered elsewhere temporarily. Handsome guy doesn't seem to understand what I'm going through so we argue constantly. Our friends also have something else in mind, understandably. All three of them are here to party. I do my best to pretend that everything is ok and follow them around. One night, we go out to this amazing samba school off the beaten track and drink delicious *caipirinhas*[6]. The colours are beautiful and so are the dancers' outfits. I let the music carry me and resonate through my limbs. The sound combined with the alcohol has a deliciously numbing effect on me. Intoxicated, I feel as though I'm in a haze, floating above reality. Next, we're off to Paraty, a small town a few hours' drive from Rio. There, we stay at an eco-lodge and cook an incredible barbecue.

---

[6] *Caipirinha* is a cocktail made with an alcohol called cachaça as well as sugar, lime, and crushed ice. It is often referred to as Brazil's national drink.

Objectively, I see how amazing this whole experience is, but my brain can't process it so I isolate myself, hide and disappear. All I can think about is the upcoming funeral.

Funeral
Granddad is – or *was* – famous. In his field, chromatography, everyone knows him and his work. Over the course of his career, he published several books and thousands of articles. His funeral promises to be very different to Grandpa's. Not that these things ought to be compared. There's already been a ceremony in his honour in the US. The next one will be held in France and split in two events. The first part will take place in Niort, over his parents' tomb, where his ashes will be placed. Only close family will be present. The second part will be held in Paris at Ecole Polytechnique, which is one of the most prestigious public institutions of higher education and research in France. Granddad studied and even taught there at the beginning of his career. Mum said they're expecting 70 to 80 people from all over Europe to attend. That's why they need someone to be the English-speaking master of ceremony.

Ceremony
Although flattered to be asked, I consider declining the offer. After reflecting on it deeply, I accept. I know it means a lot to Mum and I've had time to think a few things through. Perhaps Granddad's disappointment is something I built up in my head. Plus, regardless of past events, I've learnt a lot from him. The power of diligence, the combination of work and passion and the love of travel are what I believe he stood for and transmitted to us all – his children and grandchildren. Thanks to him, my cousins and I spent time together every year in Corsica. While we may not be as

close today as we were then, I've kept fond memories of these trips. As I prepare my speech carefully, I consider quoting Mum who's been telling me for years that nothing is ever all black or all white and that I should introduce more grey into my way of thinking.

Grey
That's the colour of the sky every Monday morning at 4:30 – that awkward time between night and day. I've taken on a new job – same company but different place and different boss. I now commute to Frankfurt every Monday and work there till Thursday. At first, it was great fun! It gave me a chance to practice my rusty German, learn something new, progress my career and most importantly fulfil my burning desire for travel and exploration. But after two or three times, travelling back and forth started to become repetitive and absolutely exhausting. The offices aren't even in Frankfurt – a lovely city by all accounts – but in the business park of Oberursel.

Oberursel
There is absolutely nothing to do around here. The hotel I stay in is across the road from the office so all I do is walk a few hundred metres back and forth between the two. For dinner, I order a tomato soup from room service and put on the French channel TV5 Monde in the background as I carry on working, mainly to keep myself busy.

Busy
I can't believe that the guy I report to now is in such a position. Not only does he spend more time pretending to work than actually working, he doesn't even respect the people around him. I constantly feel the need to apologise to other colleagues for his behaviour, his requests, and his nonsense. In meetings,

I can't stop my eyes from rolling and my smile from turning into a frown as soon as he opens his mouth. There's nothing he's tasked me with that's worthwhile either for me or for the company and I'm sick and tired of his borderline harassing comments about the way I speak or dress. How can he get away with it? It only took me a few weeks to realise this wasn't going to work, but changing roles internally twice so quickly isn't an option. The only thing that's keeping me here, for now, is that I've been selected to take part in the company's leadership development course for high potential individuals. It's called the 'Navigator programme' and starts tomorrow.

Navigator
The course is divided into four parts and will take a year to complete. The first module, which starts today in Tenerife, is about personal development as a basis for leadership. There are 18 of us in the group, most of whom I've never met before. Petite, blond and full of energy, one girl stands out to me. As we start chatting, we hit it off immediately and decide to team up for the next exercise.

Exercise
The facilitators have asked us to draw a timeline of our life from birth up until now. At the top, we have to write all the events we deem positive and, at the bottom, all the ones we perceive as negative. Once complete, we're supposed to talk our partner through it in detail. Listening to her, I'm reminded of the fact that you should never judge a person by his or her appearance. Everyone has a story that has the power to surprise, shock, and move you. Hers is one of courage, persistence, and positivity. From a promising young jockey to a dramatic horse riding accident which left her in hospital for months… And, all the

way to, step-by-step, becoming one of the company's heads of marketing. What an inspiration! I can't believe my ears when she says she feels insecure because she didn't go to university and doesn't have a degree. It's nonsense. What she has been through has taught her far more than any diploma could have. I would know…

Know
Talking her through my timeline, I'm puzzled by her reaction. What I thought was simply the story of my life, comes across to her as an unbelievably impressive list of achievements. My reaction to it is quite different. It's with great astonishment that I realise something I hadn't before. Everything positive, above the line, has to do with school and work. Everything negative or challenging, below the line, are names of people. Have I favoured my academic life and professional career at the expense of my relationships for the last 27 years? Unsure of the answer or perhaps unwilling to face it, I let the question linger in my head.

Question
A few days ago, the company I work for signed a commercial agreement with a Chinese partner. This simple news revived my memory of the feeling I had walking along the streets of Shanghai a couple of years ago. Yesterday, I overheard my former boss speaking about the deal with other colleagues so I approached him later and asked a few questions. He must have perceived my interest as he suggested that I speak to the company's Chief Financial Officer who sponsors the project. WHAT?! was my initial reaction. I barely know the man and find him extremely intimidating. Me, talking to him? No, no, no.

No

A few days pass and remind me how unhappy I am in my current role. What do I have to lose? Nothing. What's the worst thing that can happen? He laughs in my face and says, "No," or just ignores me. I can survive any of these scenarios. Once again, I remind myself that 'if you don't ask, you don't get', and I just go for it.

Go

The next day, I walk up to his assistant's desk and ask her if I can have 10 minutes with him. She says he is leaving for the airport soon and won't be back for a couple of weeks. Damn. As I thank her, he appears behind me. His assistant tells him I was looking for him. "Fine, she can follow me to the elevator," he replies. Very familiar with the layout of the office, I know that this gives me about 30 seconds of his time. An elevator pitch on speed.

Pitch

"I've heard about the agreement with our new Chinese partner," I start. "So I'd like to express my interest to move to China and help set-up the company there if…"

As I speak out the well-rehearsed words, he turns to me looking beyond surprised and interrupts. "Oh, ok," is all that comes out of his mouth before the elevator doors shut on him.

However ridiculous that sounds, my hands are shaking and small drops of sweat are rolling down my forehead as I walk back to my desk. I haven't told anyone about this, neither handsome guy nor my parents. Considering how it went, I guess nothing will come out of it anyway. Plus, there must be so many people who've expressed the same interest. How fantastic would it be to move to China though? If only…

Only
Two long months later, when I least expect it, my phone rings. I hope it's not my boss… I've become terrible at hiding the disdain I have for him. I pick up the phone hastily. It's someone else on the other side of the line: the project leader for the future China operations. I can't believe it! After all this time, I'd practically forgotten about the opportunity. I'd even convinced myself that it'd be better if things stayed the way they were anyway. I love living with handsome guy in London. The project leader interviews me on the spot. Our call lasts just over an hour. By the end of it, I still have no idea what will happen, but things seem to be slowly moving from dream to possibility. Meanwhile, I decide to keep it all to myself.

Myself
Another internal conflict has started. It's consuming my whole being – my mind, my body and my heart. Once again, I have a choice to make. On the one hand, there is London, the place I've called home for the last four and a half years, somewhere cosy and familiar. On the other hand, there is Shanghai, the city I somehow felt I'd end up living in one day, somewhere new and exciting. If it were just me, it would be a no-brainer but it's not just me anymore. There's two of us, a tight team growing closer every day. Am I about to favour my career at the expense of my relationship once again? If I don't, how could I not regret it? Is it one of these life-changing crossroads people talk about?

Crossroads
The advantage in any decision, at least, is that you never know what you might have missed out on should you have taken the other route. I met with the project leader today. He said that he

is planning on moving over to Shanghai with his wife and children. My initial impression of him hasn't been very favourable and his reputation in the business isn't great but I doubt he could be any worse than my current boss. A few days after the interview, he told me I had the job! I felt like breaking into a victory dance, but it might not have gone down very well in the middle of the office. Plus, I still haven't told anyone about this yet. Does that make me a terrible person? What should I do now? I think I know, but can I bear the consequences of my decision? That is the question.

Consequences
I'm off to Crete on a business trip. After my meetings, my parents and handsome guy will join me for a long weekend. Just the four of us. I've been looking forward to it for weeks but now that I have this major announcement to make, dread has replaced eagerness. The meetings couldn't go any slower. I can't wait to be involved in something actually meaningful: setting up a business from scratch in a new market full of potential and promises. I haven't felt so excited about something in a while! My parents arrive first.

Parents
They take it very well and say that they are looking forward to visiting me in China. I wonder how they can remain so relaxed as I move further and further away. Perhaps they've always known that I would travel and live abroad. If so, when did they realise it and how do they feel about it? They never said anything, never judged, and never tried to stop me. At first, I thought it was because they might want me gone. However, now, seeing how difficult it is for friends who've chosen a similar lifestyle

without the support of their family, I simply feel grateful. I'll have to bring myself to ask them one day. Tomorrow, handsome guy will arrive. That's when the conversation I'm terrified to have will start.

Conversation
He has just landed. Mum, Dad, and I pick him up from the airport. Together, we head to the centre of Heraklion. The town has a lovely harbour with small cafes and restaurants dotted around. The weather is sunny and warm. It's a perfect day for a stroll followed by a cold drink. My parents pretend to have some shopping to do and leave us behind. We start walking along the docks. He is cheerful and chatty while I remain silent and distant. After a few minutes, I decide to speak out.

Speak
Now it's his turn to be silent and distant. I wish I knew what he was thinking. I feel so guilty for having accepted the job without consulting him first. If only I could go back in time and speak to him about it earlier. In my humble defence, I just didn't think anything was going to come out of this process. We're home to each other and we can still be if he agrees to move to China with me. I'd really like him to come. A new adventure for the two of us, something crazy we would never forget. After a few minutes of awkward silence, it's his turn to speak.

Turn
I'm holding my breath. Don't interrupt. Don't beg. Don't cry. He expresses his surprise though he says he knew I wouldn't stay in the UK forever. "You should definitely take it, it's an opportunity you can't miss out on," he states. As I open my

mouth to express my fears and concerns, he carries on by saying that he'll join me if he can find a job there. I can't believe my ears! This couldn't have gone any better. We have about four months before I leave, he should be able to find a job in that time. Fingers crossed. If not by then, I bet he'll secure something within six months give or take. I'm positive. This feels like it's meant to be. We join my parents for lunch at the terrace of a nice little Greek restaurant. I have a huge smile on my face and can't wait to celebrate with a glass of bubbly. My itchy feet are ready to carry me all the way to China!

CHAPTER 7

Home is Me

Again

Handsome guy and I have just come back to London after a two-week holiday in Guatemala and Belize. We had a blast! Together, we climbed an active volcano, saw a gorgeous sunset from the Mayan ruins of Yaxha, ate loads of delicious food, held a tarantula, hugged a shark and more. Randomly, when queuing for the toilet in Tikal, I met a French girl who lives in Shanghai. It's amazing how small the world gets when you start to travel and live abroad.

Abroad

Living overseas is amazing! For some reason, it's hard for me to find the right words to describe why. That might be because it has nothing to do with facts. It's all about feelings. Living abroad to me means being free. It gives me a chance to discover the world, one place at a time. It allows me to fully immerse myself in a different culture. It enables me to meet incredibly inspiring people. With each place, I have the option to reinvent myself completely or to simply change, evolve, adjust. Taking in my surroundings and observing the locals, I learn and pick-up tastes and behaviours, which I then add to my own individual culture combination. Over time, I become a blend of all the places I've lived in or travelled to. In other words, I'm the canvas and the world is the artist. Under its brush, I turn into an expanding cultural patchwork of all the places that have influenced me. From here, from there, from everywhere. Step-by-step, chapter by chapter, year by year, I aspire to become a modern voyager. To echo the admirable Wilfred Thesiger[1], I hope to be one of the many explorers of the tradition of the future.

---

[1] Wilfred Thesiger (1910–2003) was an English explorer and travel writer. His exact words were 'I was perhaps the last explorer in the tradition of the past'.

Future
I still hate packing just as much as I always have. What makes it even more difficult is seeing our apartment being emptied of my presence. I'm pretty sure most people around us, friends and family, thought that our natural next step would be to settle down, buy a place and so on. But I'm not ready for it and I don't think he is either. I only have 48 hours to sort out everything and I'm struggling to even start. Handsome guy hasn't found a job in China yet. We both know how my previous long-distance relationship ended and neither of us have heard an example of one that's worked. Why am I doing this? My move is undeniably selfish. Once again, I'm putting my career aspirations ahead of my personal life. However, that doesn't reflect the way I feel about him, about us, and about our future. I tell him. Lying on our backs next to each other with our hands tightly interlaced, we cry together. Tomorrow, it'll be time to go.

Go
Our goodbyes are harrowing. I don't want to talk about it and I try my hardest not to think about it. Otherwise floods of tears come rushing forth, which is quite embarrassing in the queue for airport security. A few more steps and I'll be on the plane watching a silly movie to take me far away from reality. The last four and a half years in London have been so wonderful. Well, to be honest, they've been full of ups and downs, highs and lows, laughter, smiles, and tears. Looking back on all that's happened, I feel immensely sad and nostalgic as I leave this amazing city. I fell in love here… with my career, with the place, with my friends and with handsome guy. Walking away from it all feels immensely difficult and somewhat absurd but as a 'serial mover', this is what I do. China will be the fifth country

I live in and I'm convinced it won't be the last. If I can, I'd like to keep moving from country to country for the rest of my life.

Life
What is life all about? Amongst the billions of other people on this planet, do I matter? Don't I? Can I make a difference? Can't I? Will I be remembered? Won't I? What is my purpose? What will I regret? Am I making a terrible mistake?

Mistake
I've prepared myself for the wide range of struggles related to the relocation process: the language barrier, work, food, meeting new people, and more. I've studied. I've read. I've listened. However, I expect this experience to be even more of a shock than whatever I might have anticipated. The time I've already spent living abroad has taught me that the theory and the practice can be miles apart. Also, my last holiday in China gave me an idea of the challenges I could be about to face. All I hope right now is that I won't make any major cultural *faux pas* and will manage to find my way through the admin maze. Moving to a new country is always tough, even more so if you don't speak the language. Simple things like opening a bank account or obtaining a local phone number become next to impossible when you can't communicate at all.

Communicate
Luckily, I'm moving here with work, so they've appointed a relocation agency to help me find an apartment and settle in. Thus far, I've been living in a hotel across the street from the office. I'm a big fan of their decoration style and delicious breakfasts but I'm slowly beginning to tire of living out of a suitcase and not being able to cook for myself. I've had a few

email exchanges with the agent and she is picking me up very shortly to visit a selection of apartments. When she arrives, her appearance surprises me. From the sound and tone of her voice, I pictured someone quite strong and senior. On the contrary, she is a tiny, youthful-looking Chinese lady who has so much energy. After showing me seven properties, she accompanies me to the bank and to the phone store. No one speaks English in either of these places. Not a single word. There is no way someone who can neither speak nor read Mandarin would understand the different options available to them. Even accompanied by a local who is fluent in English, I feel pretty lost. This move is most definitely putting both my communication and organisational skills to the test... I'm working through so many to-do lists, it's insane. Anyway, the good news is that I've chosen an apartment! In 10 days, I'll be moving into my new temporary home.

Temporary
Everything around me feels temporary: the hotel I'm staying at, the empty office I work in, and the route I take between the two. It's not only temporary, it's lonely. I've come over to Shanghai to set-up the Chinese operations of the company. What that means is there is nothing in place thus far. The office itself is brand new and earlier today I inaugurated it... by myself. The general manager, the finance director, who is also my boss, and my one and only local Chinese colleague aren't here at the moment. They won't actually be around for another couple of weeks.

Weeks
Alone in the office. Alone at home. Alone. I miss handsome guy. I miss my parents. I miss my sister. I miss my grandmas. I miss my friends. What have I done?

Done

To keep my head and morale up, I decide to focus on settling in. I'm on a mission that consists of ticking off all the items on my relocation list. Once again, having moved to a new place, the time has come for one of my trips to IKEA©. I couldn't believe it either, but it turns out they have a presence in China too, which is brilliant. I choose to head there by metro. Weirdly enough, it ends up being a lot easier than I thought it would. Firstly, I manage to buy a pass using body language only. It feels like one of those disproportionately satisfying little victories. Then, I realise that the stop names are all written both in characters and in our alphabet. That makes the journey a lot less stressful than I had anticipated.

Anticipated

Amongst a long list of other websites and apps, Google© is blocked here so I don't have Google maps© to keep me on the right track. I've heard that you could gain access to all these through a VPN[2]. Sadly, I'm pretty much as unskilled with technology as I am with directions, so I haven't looked into it in great detail. Plus, I've downloaded WeChat©, which is China's ultimate social media platform, a combination of all we know overseas and more. Apparently, you can even pay your bills, restaurants, and taxis through it. Wow! I haven't tried those functionalities yet but what I've already noticed is that you couldn't possibly do business or make friends without it. One of the first questions new Chinese acquaintances ask me is whether I have WeChat© or not. They seem so happy when I answer positively. I'm not sure how to use

---

[2] VPN stands for Virtual Private Network. It allows users to connect to overseas networks and thus access a variety of mobile applications otherwise blocked in China.

it for directions though, so it's following a good old offline map that I find my way to IKEA©.

IKEA©

Moving to China, I knew that everything would be different. However, I didn't expect to experience a small culture shock at IKEA©, of all places. It seems like what I perceive to be a simple furniture store, the locals think of as more of a theme park. People come here for hours, sometimes even the whole day. Some lie down in the beds to take a nap. Others sit on the sofas with their friends and chat over a cup of take-away coffee. They come here for the atmosphere, the entertainment and the food rather than to actually buy anything. I'm totally baffled by what I observe. Out of all of the IKEA© stores I've been to in the world, I've never seen such a large empty-handed crowd. It takes me a long time to bypass the hordes of people chilling and chatting everywhere just so I can grab what I'm after. I get there eventually and by the end of this tedious process, I'm really happy with what's in my trolley. Next step is to ask for it to be delivered to my new apartment. I hoped they would speak a little English at the till, but not at all. After about half an hour of trying to explain myself in body language, I'm starting to get quite frustrated. I give it one last shot and miraculously, they seem to finally understand me, or so I hope. I'm really looking forward to making my new place a bit cosier, not just for me but for handsome guy too. Fingers crossed he finds a job here soon.

Finds

Yesterday, I explored my new neighbourhood. I walked everywhere and got lost amongst the identical-looking alleys of Shanghai's Former French Concession. It was fantastic! The area has a lovely vibe to it with loads of enticing restaurants, bars and shops dotted around. From 1849 until 1943, it was actually French, hence the name it still holds today. The facades of some of the buildings, the large plane trees and the winding streets are subtle testimonies of that era. Not only does this gigantic 25-million inhabitants' metropolis fascinates me with its history, its architecture and culture also amaze me. East meets west. Does it truly though? Or, is it just an impression on the surface? I wonder. Looking up, down and around me, I do my best to take it all in – the sights, the sounds, the smells. Everything is so different and captivating here.

Captivating
Hoping to make my daily life easier, I've started taking Mandarin Chinese lessons. I find this language incredibly challenging though equally intriguing. Speaking it requires mastering four different tones. This means that one syllable can be pronounced four different ways and thus refer to four completely different things. For example, *ma* can either stand for mother or horse depending on how you say it. And that's only valid for speaking. Learning how to write is a whole different task. Sometimes I feel like I'm having to learn two languages in one. Each character has its individual meaning and design. Combining them seems to open a world of endless possibilities. Some, such as hand, moon or even people, more or less look like what they mean. Others come across as totally cryptic. My teacher says I'll need to know between three and four thousand of them to be able to read the newspaper. Thus far, I think I've mastered ten or so. Let's be honest, I have a long way to go and it's unlikely I'll be able to get there in the next two to three years, but I'd like to keep trying nonetheless.

Nonetheless

My previous experiences abroad have shown me that language is one of the keys to understanding a culture and I'm really interested in that of China. I'll probably barely get the chance to scratch its surface in my time here but I'm keen on giving it a go. To find out more, I ask my teacher and local colleagues a lot of questions. The team in the office is growing, which is wonderful to see.

Growing

We're recruiting new people every week, if not every day. Thus far, all of them are locals and, surprisingly, most of them are female. Finding the right people for the roles has been a challenge to say the least. The other day, we interviewed a guy who decided that it would be appropriate to pick up his phone in front of us and have a chat for 10 minutes with whomever was on the line. I suppose that's how things are in a country where unemployment is particularly low. China currently being a hiring market with high turnover means that it's fairly easy for people to find a new job. The opposite is true where I'm from. There, it's more common to see thousands of overqualified candidates fight over one underpaying job. I'm not sure my new colleagues realise how lucky they are in comparison. Despite a few such hiccups, we've managed to hire a team of motivated and promising talents.

Promising

At lunch time, we all walk to one of the few local restaurants nearby the office. My colleagues enjoy encouraging me to try new, and often strange dishes. I don't mind as my curiosity takes over. Today, I'm having to wear plastic gloves, grab what I believe to be pork elbow and dig my teeth into it. There is even a straw on the side for the bone marrow. Moments like this are when I have to remind myself that I'm here to experience new things and must keep an open mind. To my surprise, the meat is absolutely delicious. Although the bone marrow isn't something I'll have again, I'm glad I 'manned up' and tasted it anyway. In between bites and under their inquisitive stares, I ask them countless questions about Chinese culture, their families, habits, views, hopes and dreams.

Views

What I find remarkable is noticing that though certain aspects are completely different, others are fully aligned. The latter is key. Those similarities are the things that make us human. In fact, all of us around the table share a deep desire to make sure our family and friends are safe, healthy, and happy. We also aspire to make ourselves and those around us proud. It's not just about our wishes, it's also feelings that link us. Happiness, sadness, laughter, tears, joy, despair, we go through them all. The way we express them might differ, but the raw emotions are identical. These thoughts lead me to wonder: how much of who we are is determined by our humanity versus by our nationality or the place where we were born and raised? Are we spending too much time focusing on observing and analysing our differences rather than cherishing our similarities?

Differences

Since I've moved to China, friends often ask me what I think are the main cultural differences between here and where I'm from. In other words, they would like to know what has shocked me the most thus far. Putting aside some of the strange food items I've tried, my answer would be: relationships and marriage. To me, this beautiful commitment two people make to each other is about love and partnership. However, it seems to be more of a business deal here. The other day, I stumbled upon the wedding market at People Square. There, family members or individuals themselves leave small cards with their basic information. These include things like height, weight, salary, car and property ownership. A lot of people then skim through the thousands of cards looking for their or their children's perfect match. The pressure on young people, especially women, to get married is tremendous. If they haven't committed before the age of 30, they're called 'leftovers'. Charming isn't it? The situation for men is far from being better, especially in Shanghai and its surrounding area.

Men

In order to find a wife, men must own a car and a property. Only then do they become eligible. Once married, many of them are forced to hand over everything to their wife, even their monthly salary. She is the one who then controls the couple's finances and gives her husband pocket money on a weekly or sometimes daily basis. I had no idea about this before moving here. For a split second it pleased my feminist side, but rather quickly I went back on my judgment. It's equality I'm a defender of and this arrangement has nothing to do with it, to say the least. However, being judgmental isn't helpful when learning about a different culture so I try my best to park these thoughts. I have so much to discover from such a historically-rich country that is growing and developing at an unbelievable pace. At the end of the day, I'm just a humble visitor here and my eyes and ears are wide open.

Visitor
Every single time you enter China, regardless of the purpose of your visit, you must declare yourself to the police. Most tourists aren't aware of that fact as the hotel declares their arrival to the authorities on their behalf. However, when you move into your own place, you're the one responsible for presenting yourself at the station. This is a task that once again requires either a good command of the language or a kind local friend. The next step for all resident permit and working visa holders is a full blown medical examination.

Examination
Getting there by public transport was already a mission! Now that I've arrived, I have no clue what to expect. Using hand signals and without a shadow of a smile, the nurse ushers me towards the changing rooms. It seems as though she is asking me to take off all my clothes and put on a hospital dressing gown instead. A few minutes later, it's feeling naked and uncomfortable that I step back out into the corridor. There, I'm far from alone. There are lots of other expatriates going through the same process – men, women, and children. It's freezing. As we wait, some of us start chatting hoping to shake off the awkwardness. Every few minutes, a nurse pops her head out and screams a number as she looks at one of us. Whoever has been summoned then disappears into one of the consultation rooms. X-rays. Blood test. Ultra-sound. It feels like we're animals. If I didn't know better, I'd wonder what happens at the end. Instead, I can't help but ask myself what they do with those who don't pass the medical tests and which criteria this is all based on. At least the process is extremely efficient. I'm in and out of there in no time and with no information whatsoever. Apparently, that will come through later, along with my Alien Employment Licence.

Alien
I can't believe that's what they actually call it. Interesting choice of words. I may be one myself, but thus far it's the environment around me that seems rather alien. I've just entered into what's commonly referred to as 'the honeymoon phase'. Everything feels different and exciting! I've been through this phase every time I've moved to a new city or country. From experience, I know that it doesn't last very long so, once again, I embrace it. Shanghai looks absolutely majestic when the sky is this blue. Keen on exploring this giant metropolis, I've returned to all the tourist sites I'd been to the first time I visited – Yu Garden, The Bund, the Former French Concession, Lujiazui – and have now set out to find those that are off the beaten track. The Propaganda Art Centre is amongst them.

Centre
It's not far from my apartment so I've decided to walk there. After about 10 minutes, I'm standing in front of what looks like a residential compound. It's got three imposing towers of at least 20 floors each. According to the map, this is it. It can't be... I look around for clues, signs, anything. Suddenly, someone taps on my shoulder. He looks like one of the guards. Without a word, he hands me a small map of the area. On it, a red line traces the way to the entrance of the museum, which seems to be in the basement of one of the big towers. For a minute, I wonder whether it's a dangerous scam or whether this man is being genuinely helpful. I look up but he has already disappeared, so I can't ask. Anyway, I wouldn't have any idea how to. Hesitantly, I start to follow the small map. It takes me down some dodgy-looking stairs and through a tiny corridor. A few more steps later, I begin to see a couple of frames dotted on the white walls. Good sign.

Though the location seems odd at first, I think it's actually the perfect place to host this unique collection. The posters are impressive. Their colours are striking. They go from varied in the 1930s to mostly red in the 1960s. From my perspective, the power of the exhibition lies in that it shows posters both as a form of political engagement and expression as well as a form of art. Of course, walking through the rooms with my cultural background raises a lot of questions and alarm bells in my head but I'm sticking to my approach of observing with an open mind.

Open
It's with this outlook that I explore the city and start to settle in. Before I know it, I've already developed a little routine. I've figured out the quickest way to walk from the tube station to the office. I've picked out my favourite dish on the menu at our lunch canteen. I've even found a lovely bakery near my apartment for when I miss French bread. It still amazes me how adaptable we humans can be and how quickly we're able to recreate a familiar environment in an unfamiliar setting.

Familiar
This week has been very tough. All I do here is work. I've stopped counting my hours but if I did, I think it would add up to anywhere between 70 and 80 a week. I start at about 8:30 in the morning. Later, around 7:30 p.m., I go home, have some dinner and start working again until midnight. Even weekends are filled with work. Why? Somehow, I feel emotionally connected to this start-up business. Despite the complete lack of recognition I receive from my boss, I keep going because I honestly believe that what I'm involved in is so meaningful, so tangible and so exciting! The other reason is far less upbeat. Truth is, I haven't

found anything better to do. I miss the life I had back in London, the people who surrounded me then and the ease with which everything unfolded. Here, struggles are a daily affair and even making friends has proven a challenging task. Meeting people isn't an issue but connecting with them on a deeper level just hasn't happened for me yet. I find the social scene particularly superficial. It seems to be all about appearances and very little about thoughts. So, more often than not, I prefer to stay home on my own and work. Sad? Maybe.

Maybe

Last night, I watched my favourite episode of *Sex and the City*. It's the one during which Carrie moves to Paris with her Russian boyfriend. She goes there full of enthusiasm and naivety. At the beginning, everything is new and exciting but very quickly reality catches up with her. She then struggles to adapt to her new environment and its foreign language, culture, and habits. What's even harder for her is to cope with though, is the loneliness. She misses her New-York life, her friends, her apartment and her job. Watching it made me feel so emotional. Alone in my apartment, I started crying uncontrollably. I'm going through exactly the same roller coaster of emotions as she is but in real life. What I hope will differ, is the outcome. She ends up moving back to the US. Regardless of how tough it feels being here now, I still wish to stay. I hope to be able to push through and find a way of making the most of this incredible opportunity.

Incredible

The Chairman of the Chinese partner company we work with has disappeared. He is one of the richest and most famous business men in the country. There are all sorts of speculative rumours going around internally as well as in both the local and international press. He is said to have been arrested by the police as part of a corruption case. Whether he is being accused of something or is a simple witness, no one seems to know. Information is scarce but spreading very quickly. Before I know it, I receive several emails from my colleagues in China and in Europe asking me what's going on and what it might mean for the company. Some of them are quite blunt and even ask whether I still have a job. They have a point. A start-up business that's barely begun can disappear anytime. This is an uncertainty many would find unbearable. I don't mind it though. One of the things living abroad teaches you is adaptability. Over the years, I've grown to embrace and even chase change while always believing that what is meant to be, will be. Plus, thus far, nothing has changed in our day-to-day workload and office routine. So, "Let's not freak out and just keep going," is what I preach to the team.

Team
Dad will be my first visitor and I can't wait to welcome him! By chance, or fate, he's been asked to lead a project that should bring him to China several times over the next 12 to 18 months. Amazing! I've left work early to make sure I'm at home when he arrives. Sitting at the dining table with my laptop, I'm trying to finish off a few emails but I can't focus. My legs are shaking with impatience and excitement. When I finally hear his knock on the door, my heart lifts. Welcome to my place on the other side of the world! He's only going to stay in Shanghai for a couple of days before heading to Suzhou where he'll be working for a week. Two days isn't much time but we both want to make the most of it, so I take him to all the tourist sites and beyond. I've even

booked a guided tour of the city's art district, M50, a hidden gem many visitors miss out on. We walk everywhere, and we talk so much. At one point, I realise that something about our relationship has changed. We no longer speak to each other purely as father and daughter but as equals. Two adults on the same team. Of course, I still come to him for advice and moral support. Anyway, I think a significant part of me will never stop seeing him as an invincible super hero. Hence my initial surprise when he shared with me some of his work-related matters and even asked for my opinion. I'm not sure my recommendations were of any help, but I really appreciated having such an open conversation; one that made me feel respected and trusted as an adult, no longer a child.

Respected
After a weekend in what felt like a protective and positive cocoon, it's time to get back to work's madness. Speculations about the chairman haven't stopped. On the contrary, our local partner company's shares were suspended and countless internal meetings were held. It's without any official news that their annual conference begins. Looking around, I think there must be about 450 attendees in the room. Saying that not many of those are from overseas would be an understatement. Being one of the few, I've been given a simultaneous translation device. Its appearance is the same as that of an old Walkman© device, just like those we used to listen to back in the day. As the master of ceremony begins to speak in Mandarin, so does the first translator in approximate English. His voice comes bursting through the headphones. He sounds like a football commentator. Loud, enthusiastic, over-the-top. I can't contain a burst of laughter, which draws the attention of the people around me. The two in front even turn around with a disapproving stare. The fun of it

all doesn't last long anyway. Pretty quickly a major headache kicks in. It's only been a few minutes and I'm already wondering how I'm going to make it through the day without falling asleep in my chair. Having turned the volume of the device way down, I'm contemplating various escape strategies when the master of ceremony ends his introduction by dropping a bombshell. He's just invited all of us to welcome onto the stage a special guest. The Chairman. As he walks in, everyone around the room stands up as one and claps loudly.

Chairman
I can feel the energy and emotion travelling through the audience. A standing ovation for a man who's just come out of prison. I can't help but wonder what's behind each individual's reaction. Is it respect, admiration, relief, fear or something else? The chairman's speech lasts for an hour. To my surprise, it doesn't include a word about what happened to him over the past four days. Not a word. My Chinese colleagues say it's normal. They apparently don't even feel the need to know. Maybe I'm too curious for my own good.

Curious
That trail of thoughts leads me to wonder where I'd be if it wasn't for my endless curiosity. Not here today, that's for certain. The following presentations go ahead one after the other. Long, vague, and unclear. That's how I'd describe them. Translator or presenter issue, both perhaps… who knows?

Knows
Some days, I feel like I simply don't know anything. There is so much for me to learn about this country, its culture and its people. We have just over 10 employees in the company now, but there

is enough work for a team of two to three times that size. I'm in charge of so many projects. Although I really enjoy the diversity, it's impossible for one person to take on so many things at once, certainly not without sufficient resources and support from above. Being one of the only two people from the London office who relocated to China, I thought that the other person, who also happens to be my boss, and I would work closely together. Naïve, I assumed that he'd want to help me both settle in and eventually improve my career and skills. Instead, his lack of trust and constant judgment have made me question my abilities and have had a major impact on my already lagging self-worth. To my surprise, I've found myself far more integrated with the local colleagues. Together, we've prepared our first ever holiday packages, which will go on sale later this week.

Sale

Three holiday packages for the Chinese market made up of two lovely hotels in Phuket, Thailand, is what we started with. We put them on sale earlier this week and secured our first booking yesterday! When we heard the news, the whole team spontaneously began to high five and hug each other. That's what I love about working in a start-up. It's like being part of a family with the business as our baby. This first sale feels like a toddler's first steps. From here, there is only one way to go: onwards and upwards.

Upwards

Once again, I'm sitting on a plane waiting for it to take off. Strangely, time appears to have flown by but slowed right down at the same time. Until now. It took quite a lot to convince my boss to allow me to go back to Europe for Christmas. I'll have to work while I'm there and won't be allowed to take time off over Chinese New Year. Those were his conditions. Fine by me.

Staying in Shanghai on my own over the holiday season was simply not an option. Christmas means a lot to me, though it doesn't have much significance here. Retailers and online shops use it as a commercial opportunity and there are a few decorations around town but that's about it. I've asked around and none of my colleagues have any celebrations planned. Most of them will actually be working over this period. They'd much rather keep their very few days of annual leave for Chinese New Year, which takes place late-January or early-February, depending on the lunar calendar. So, no Christmas spirit in the air, just pollution.

Pollution

Winter is usually the worst time of year. The sky can easily remain brown or grey for days. Recently, I've had problems breathing and frequent headaches. My throat has been very dry and itchy. To prevent it, I've started wearing a mask when I go out for more than 30 to 45 minutes. I'm not sure whether it helps that much but it can't hurt right? When I return from Europe, I'll need to get an air purifier for my apartment. I've grown tired of reading the shock in people's eyes when I say I don't have one yet. Air quality is definitely one of Shanghai's expatriates' favourite conservation bit. Everyone has a pollution forecast app on their phone and most even check it more often than the weather equivalent. Rightly or wrongly, resigned to the fact that there's nothing immediate I can do about it, I've taken a pretty chilled approach. I have to admit though that a breath of fresh air is very high up on my Christmas list. It comes just after seeing handsome guy and my family. It's on a massive high and filled with extreme tiredness that I'm flying to Europe right now.

High
My head is full of excitement tainted by a pinch of anxiety and guilt. I feel like I'm leaving the team behind somewhat unfairly. I'm obviously finding it very hard to switch off from work. Also, I'm slightly worried about the disconnection there might be between who I am here in China and the person those people I love in Europe, know me as. How do I explain what I'm up to and how it feels without sounding like I'm totally up myself? Will they judge me for having turned into somewhat of a terribly sad workaholic? Have I changed too much?

Changed
Three days… It's already been three days. How time flies when you're living in the moment and are in brilliant company! If anything, these few days have further deepened my belief that home is where you and your loved ones are.

Anything
This morning, I had my hair cut. There aren't many things that I haven't done while living abroad. Having a haircut is one of them. Even after about eight years on the road, there's only one hairdresser I go to. I've gone there since I was a child and sometimes wait more than a year to see her. It's all about trust. She's seen how my hair has been affected by some of the stressful episodes of my life and knows exactly who I am and what I'm after. Perhaps it's a way of keeping some form of solidity and permanence in my life. A steady anchor. Do we ever stop needing a degree of consistency?

Consistency

The sound of the doorbell snaps me out of my deep thoughts. I turn to Mum and enquire whether we're expecting someone for lunch. "Just go and open the door," she yells from the kitchen. Fine. Without giving it further consideration, I get on with it. "WHAT?! HOW?! WHAT?! HOW?! WHAT?! HOW?!" is all I manage to say staring at my high school friends in absolute shock. My parents have never surprised me before. This is unbelievable! They're all laughing at my reaction as they jump into my open arms. The five of us haven't been reunited for over 10 years. I can't believe it! I'm dying to hear from every single one of them. Our conversations are punctuated by my recurring exclamations of surprise and gratitude. They ask me about my new life half way across the world. I wonder if they know how tough it is to answer general questions such as "How is China?" So incredibly vast. Where do you start: the country, travel, work, apartment, friends, language, or…? Sometimes I simply answer, "It's both wonderful and extremely challenging," hoping that more precise interrogations will follow. Today they do. Bouncing off of each other's stories, we can't stop talking. If only I could take them back to Shanghai.

Take

I've always said that New Year resolutions are pointless because nobody ever keeps them anyway, but this year feels different. Having taken some time out of my incredibly fast-paced Shanghai routine has made me realise I must make certain changes. Otherwise, it's without a shadow of a doubt, that I'll burn myself out and end up crippled with regrets. I've decided to keep my list short, realistic, and achievable. Thus far it reads:

1. Look after myself better
2. Explore China, Asia, and further afield
3. Come up with a business idea

The third one is something I've been thinking quite a lot about lately. I do feel like taking a big jump and starting my own adventure sometime in the future, hopefully sooner rather than later. All I need now, of course, is a viable idea. Not an easy task to say the least. I'd like it to have something to do with travel, my passion. It should also have a positive, constructive and generous outcome. Ideally, it would open the world of travel and exploration to more and more people. That's as far as it goes, for now. I truly hope this experience in China will help me figure out what this could be, and give me a chance to develop the skill-set and network needed to succeed.

Succeed

After such an amazing break, the time has already come to head back to Shanghai. They say goodbyes should get easier. They don't. Hugging handsome guy at the airport, I'm in tears. I feel as though I'm back to square one, wondering why I'm doing this. All I hope is that he will be able to find a job and join me soon. In the meantime, as always, I've planned to watch a silly movie in order to take my mind away from it all. Sitting on the plane, I put on the film *The Intern*[3]. It's about a young woman entrepreneur who started and now runs her own online retail fashion store. Following the recommendation of one of her employees, she hires

---

[3] *The Intern* is an American comedy which was written, produced and directed by Nancy Meyers. It was released in 2015 and stars, amongst others, Robert De Niro as an intern and Anne Hathaway as the entrepreneur and Chief Executive Officer.

a senior intern, a 70-ish retired man. Watching it reminds me that, at the moment, I treat the company I work for as if it were my own. Illogically, I put in as many hours and as much effort as I can into something that ultimately isn't mine and where my power of decision is pretty insignificant. As time passes, I begin to completely identify with the main character of the film. I realise that, just like her, I aspire to be able to do it all and turn into a superwoman – perfect in every way.

Superwoman
The more I do, the more I want to do. The more I achieve, the more I want to achieve. The more I succeed, the more I want to succeed. A never-ending cycle. Of course, I know that perfection isn't an option but for some reason I can't help hoping that perhaps I could be an exception.

Exception
For many, adventure goes hand-in-hand with extreme sports. For me, heading on an adventure simply means getting out of your comfort zone. It could translate into anything from just leaving the house on a tough day all the way to jumping out of an airplane, and everything in between. Take this business trip for example. I'm on my way to Thailand where I will be overseeing the filming of two promotional videos in VR. VR stands for Virtual Reality. In other words, these videos will be watched in 360 degrees using a mobile phone and a special headset. Not only does the technology itself remain quite new, the techniques we're about to use are very innovative. Over the next few days, we will film static, underwater and drone shots, all in three dimensions. Seeing the equipment for the first time, I can't contain my excitement! I'm so happy to be involved in this project.

Project

As the days go by, my role widens. I'm as keen to help as I am to find out how everything works in front of and behind the camera. What better place to do this in than Phuket with its stunning, endless, white sandy beaches? We explore the whole island and even go to Phang Nga Bay, famous for being the set of a James Bond movie[4]. In such an incredible setting, my dreams come back to me with full force. I hadn't thought about the 'grown-up' list in a long time. Walking along the beach after a long day of shooting, I start wondering whether my current job actually fulfils me, or whether I'm fooling myself into believing it is. Speaking to the founders of the VR company is absolutely inspiring. They've both worked in start-up companies for years and ended up creating their own business. One of them – cool guy – is British and has an acting background. The other is Belgian and has endless stories to tell about both the successes and failures of his business ventures. At one point, he even went bankrupt, which he says taught him a lot. Listening to them convinces me even more that starting my own thing, whatever it may be, is the way to go. However, my fear of failure remains and paralyses me. I wish there was a simple pill of courage I could take.

Pill

There are so many other things I wish someone could find a cure for. One of them would really help me. Over the past two years, I've been suffering on and off from skin rashes, stomach problems, and even bleeding from somewhere you don't want to hear about.

---

[4] Phang Nga Bay and its iconic limestone rocks appeared in the James Bond movie *The Man with the Golden Gun* in 1974. From them on, it began to be referred to as 'James Bond Island', even in guide books.

After a traumatising trip to the hospital on my own back in London a year ago, I ended up being referred to a specialist for a colonoscopy. Not very common at my age but the doctor wanted to start by ruling out all terrifying suppositions. As it turned out, something up there was torn, hence the bleeding. I couldn't believe my ears when I woke from the general aesthetic to hear the surgeon say that he'd fixed it with Botox. Sadly, I was too disorientated to ask whether he'd saved some for my face. Jokes aside, that was a painful experience I would have loved to do without. Thereafter, I tried everything I could to figure out the causes of what the doctor had diagnosed as IBS which stands for Irritable Bowel Syndrome.

IBS
One-by-one, I stopped eating gluten, only ate cooked food and started to drink all sorts of random plant-based teas deemed to be good for the digestive system. Nothing worked. After just a few days, I was back to square one again. Clueless, exhausted, embarrassed and desperate is how this whole thing makes me feel. When Mum came across a food intolerance test, she suggested I take it over Christmas. As strange as it might sound, I couldn't have wished for a better present.

Present
A few weeks later, the results have just come in. According to the test, I'm intolerant to 13 different food items. These include cow and goat milk in all their forms, eggs, coffee, and leek. Some are easy to avoid; others are extremely challenging. I have to stop eating cheese, butter, cream, pizza, cake, ice cream and my absolute favourite… milk chocolate. I'm so upset. What am I going to cook? Having been raised in Normandy, I've grown-up eating cheese at almost every meal. What if I'd already eaten

my lifetime quota of dairy? Maybe that's what it is. Interrupting this spontaneous pity party, I reflect on how brilliant it is to finally shed some light on what might have caused my endless stomach problems. Hopefully, this new diet will put an end to the struggle.

Struggle

Feeling empowered and determined, I spend most of my first weekend back in Shanghai cooking meals for the following week. Hopefully, that will prevent me from focusing on what I can no longer eat. My main concern now is how this new regime might affect my future travels. From experience, many countries including France, aren't very considerate when it comes to food allergies and intolerances. In China, I reckon this will somehow be both easier and harder to deal with. Easier, on the one hand, because very few local dishes are made with dairy. Harder, on the other hand, because of the language barrier. Firstly, I have no idea how to explain this in Mandarin. Secondly, all food labels are written in characters, so I won't be able to check what packaged products actually include. Thirdly, dairy or egg-free items don't seem to be as commonly found here as in other countries such as the UK, Germany, or Scandinavia. This is for me a reminder of all the many barriers people might face when wanting to travel.

Barriers

Reflecting on it, I suddenly feel a surge of gratitude and humility. I have been so lucky to be able to travel and live abroad for as long and as far as I have. The more I think about it, the more I'd like to find ways of encouraging and supporting people to do the same or something similar. There you have it, my mission: inspire others to step and look outside of the borders of their box.

Box
'Don't put people in boxes'. A pretty common English saying that means that one shouldn't judge and categorise others. As it turns out, people ought not to be put in boxes in China either, but for a different reason. Working with a colleague on the design of a holiday voucher, I suggested that we draw a simple box around the general manager's signature. My words were met with a shocked and frightened stare. Curious, I asked what was wrong. Patiently, she explained that here, putting people's names in boxes indicates that they are dead and buried. When you think about it pictorially for a second, it actually makes sense. Accidentally, I've made a clumsy cultural *faux pas*. Embarrassing, one may think, but interesting is how I prefer to see it. Making mistakes, as long as they aren't deliberately offensive of course, is one of the best ways of learning more about a country, its unique culture and way of life.

Mistakes
I can't sleep these days. It's my own fault. In the evenings, I work while watching TV and eating when I should be in bed sleeping instead. I can't help it. I feel caught in a downhill spiral that's gaining speed each time it completes a turn. I'm exercising less and a couple of nights ago, I binge ate again. It was like I couldn't stop stuffing my face with whatever was around. My brain tuned out and my body gave up on sending signals of being full, so I kept on eating and eating and eating for hours. Having swallowed every single sweet item available – vegan chocolate, cookies, fresh and dried fruit – I even ended up munching on cereal directly from the box. Disgusting. That's how I felt when I woke this morning. Why do I keep doing this to myself? These are all signs that something is wrong. With the greatest scorn, I'm witnessing

and acknowledging the consequences of my actions but for some inexplicable reason, I don't do anything about it. If only someone could shake me so hard I'd snap out of it but everywhere around me is empty. There is no one I can turn to. I'm totally alone. Alone. Do other people feel this way? If so, what do they do about it? How does one survive in complete loneliness?

Survive

My boss had insisted that if I went back to Europe for Christmas, I wouldn't get any time off during Chinese New Year. I'd mentioned in vain that most, if not all, companies in the country close over that period. Predictably, it was only three weeks prior to the holidays that he realised our whole building would indeed be shut. With a fake smile and an ironic tone, he told me earlier today that I'd better start planning something quickly. How thoughtful. Not. There are two main weeks of annual leave in China: October Golden Week and Chinese New Year. As shocking as it sounds, everyone in the country gets a week off at the same time. That means up to 1.3 billion people could be travelling nationally and internationally all at once. Natural consequence of this phenomenon, prices to most destinations skyrocket around these dates. Last-minute planning isn't really an option, but it will have to do. Considering how I've been feeling lately, I need a change of scenery.

Scenery

As soon as I get back to my apartment that evening, I begin searching for destinations I can afford to travel to. It's going to have to be something off the beaten track. Looking at a map of Asia and letting my mind wander for a few minutes, a country unexpectedly catches my attention. Sharing borders with China in the north and India in the south, east, and west, this landlocked territory is home to the highest mountains on earth. Another interesting fact, it's the only nation in the world that doesn't have a rectangular or square flag. Mysterious... Nepal.

Nepal
I don't know much about Nepal but the idea of trekking up a mountain in the hope of leaving all my worries and doubts behind sounds perfect to me. What an incredible challenge that would be! A new adventure. After extensive research, I come to the realisation that February will be too cold to reach Everest Base Camp but hiking up to Annapurna Base Camp remains an option. Leaving myself no chance to change my mind, I contact a local travel agent right away. I hope I'll survive the cold and the physical intensity. I've done no training whatsoever. All I know is that right now, this is exactly what I need.

Need
My best friend and I have spent over an hour on the phone already. How things change! Five years ago, she was my manager back in London. Do you remember her? Yes, the elegant lady who hired me just after I'd finished university. Well, once she left the company, we stayed in touch. The more we caught-up, the more we realised how much we had in common. With time, we grew closer and closer. Since I've moved to China, she is the friend I've spoken to the most and, over time, she has become my best friend. Chatting with her feels so good. There is no need to hide, no need to lie, no need to pretend. We talk for hours at a time about absolutely everything. Tonight, I tell her about my upcoming crazy hiking holiday to Nepal. She thinks it's a brilliant idea and says that it's also exactly what she needs. I'm

not sure what she means by that but I invite her to come with me. The trip is two weeks away, she lives in London and is pretty risk adverse as far as I know. Convinced she won't come; I try to persuade her anyway. We chat hypothetically for ages and make overly-ambitious plans before bidding each other good night and hanging up.

Plans
In 12 days, I'll be in a totally different country, surrounded by nature. My itinerary is finalised, and I've booked everything: flights, accommodation, a mountain guide, a Sherpa and even paragliding in Pokhara. I'm as ready as I could be, though I still haven't done any training. Days go by quickly as work is as busy as ever. I barely have time to think. Sitting in the company's endless and useless weekly management meeting, my phone buzzes. Seeing her name come up on the screen makes me smile instantly. Her message is short and sweet. She is coming to Nepal with me! Her flights are booked! How unbelievable is that?!

Unbelievable
As I make my way through check-in, customs and security at Shanghai Pudong airport, my best friend is doing exactly the same at London Heathrow. We're in total sync. I can't wait to see her in Kathmandu and embark together on a life-changing experience. We haven't even started yet but I'm convinced that's what it will be. Our first mission is to reach our destination. I'm flying from Shanghai to Chengdu then Lhasa and finally Kathmandu. In China, flight delays are very common so I'm not surprised when we take off two hours later than scheduled. It's already one o'clock at night when I land in Chengdu. Dark and cold. According to the website of the Airport International

Hotel I've booked, guests can call on arrival to arrange for a shuttle service to pick them up, but when I contact them, no one there speaks English. Ironic hotel name, I think to myself. The receptionist keeps using an automated translation machine. Its loud and mechanical voice comes through the phone. "Where are you?", "Do you speak Chinese?", "Is there a Chinese-speaking person around you?" I reply but she doesn't understand a word of what I'm saying. This nonsense is making me lose patience. After about an hour of getting harassed by dubious taxi drivers and looking for an English-speaking person in vain, I'm desperate. What am I going to do? As I start to panic, I look up and spot another hotel in the distance. It seems fancy. Carrying my two heavy bags on my back, it takes me about 15 minutes to walk there. Luckily, the receptionist speaks a little bit of English and is able to call my hotel and ask them to pick me up. Once there, I only have three hours left to sleep. Perhaps I should have stayed in the airport overnight instead, but I was worried it might close. Oh well, things should be better in the morning. Fingers crossed.

Morning

Different receptionist. Similar story. I ask her about the transfer bus to the airport in any way I can think of. She tells me to wait. That's probably the only English word she knows so I miss the shuttle. Anger takes over and I completely lose it this time. I start screaming at her. Not being understood is tiring enough but what makes it worse is when you feel as though the person in front of you isn't even trying to help whatsoever.

Trying
Luckily, in the process, I meet a random young Chinese guy who can speak some English. He kindly offers to give me a lift to the airport. I'm not sure he realises it, but he possibly just saved my entire trip. I hope life, karma, or whatever you'd like to call it will give him back the assistance he gave me a hundredfold. A few hours later, I land in Lhasa. According to my itinerary, this was supposed to be a touch-down and head-out kind of stop but we've been asked to get off the aircraft and are now waiting at the airport. I've spotted a couple of people who were on the previous flight with me and really hope they're also heading to Kathmandu. There are no screens in the room and, once again, no one speaks a word of English, not even a member of staff. I have no idea if I'm in the right place and what's going on. A wave of despair crashes over me and I start to wonder if I'll ever reach Nepal.

Reach
I made it! Forget about the journey, what counts this time is the outcome. The customs officer at Kathmandu airport greets me with a smile from ear to ear and wishes me a warm welcome in English after saying, "*Namaste*." How kind and polite of him! Finally, I can breathe both literally and figuratively. A short while later, my best friend arrives. We jump into each other's arms then rush towards our flight to Pokhara, which is due to leave in 20 minutes from another terminal. Covered in sweat, we make it just before the door closes. The plane is so tiny. It only has 10 seats. How cool!

Cool
And so the adventure begins… Upon our arrival, we meet our mountain guide and our Sherpa. They both look so young and

tiny. I suppose it makes sense when you know they climb mountains for a living. Together, the four of us head to their favourite local restaurant where we tuck into our first Dhal Bat. The place is so small that there are only two tables and eight seats. We pick the one really close to the kitchen so that we can see how the locals cook. Everything is made from scratch with fresh veggies and meat. The process is fascinating to observe. Once served, the plates look gorgeous and the food so appetising. Little bowls with curry, dhal, vegetables and pickles surround a generous serving of rice. This is exactly the fuel we need for our upcoming challenge.

Challenge
We drive to the start of the trek. Along the way, the consequences of last year's earthquake are heart breaking to see. Staring out of the window, I take it all in and try not to let it get to me. After a quick lunch, we start walking. Wow, it's steep! I'm finding it tough already. It would have definitely been worth doing some training. There is nothing I can do about it now though, so I push through going slow and steady, one step at a time. We walk past little villages where goats bleat, spices are laid out to dry, and people get on with their daily lives. I'm so impressed by our Sherpa. He is carrying both of our large backpacks as well as his small bag. It must be so heavy. I don't think I could even lift it, let alone hike with it. The four of us walk for hours past beautiful waterfalls, over wiggly bridges and up thousands of steps.

Steps
One area has so many of them that I decide to call it 'death by steps'. Fun thoughts like these distract me and keep me going. Every day, we reach new heights. The landscape changes, green

fields and villages are replaced by rocks and snow-covered paths. Soon, we lose phone reception, showers are no longer an option and accommodation becomes more and more basic. We don't mind. On the contrary, we both find it relaxing and inspiring to lead a simpler life. The gorgeous views are an absolute pleasure to focus on. Plus, it feels so good to be physically rather than mentally tired. I sleep so much better these days. Work matters suddenly seem so pointless and insignificant. Tomorrow, after four intense days, we will finally reach our goal.

Goal
Annapurna Base Camp lies in front of us -4,130 metres above sea level. Looking at the snow-capped peaks, I feel so small, irrelevant, and yet so alive. The altitude makes it tough to breathe so I walk extremely slowly and take in the beauty of the surrounding mountains. The weather is splendid. Rays of sun highlight the brightness of the untouched snow. When, four exhausting hours later, we finally reach the colourful sign that welcomes us to Annapurna Base Camp, I sigh deeply. A tear of pride and joy rolls down my face. We hug each other. We made it! I feel immensely happy and equally stunned. Looking back at the girl I was growing up, I never thought that I would be doing something like this, not in a million years. That night, we celebrate by eating delicious vegetarian *momos*[5] and drinking cups of hot lemon.

---

[5] *Momos* are Tibetan dumplings. Only vegetarian food is served at Base Camp because the surrounding region doesn't allow any slaughter or consumption of animals on its territory.

Hot
On the contrary, it's absolutely freezing here… Somewhere between -10 and -15 degrees Celsius. There is no heating so everyone sits near the stove of the kitchen. With our guide, our Sherpa, and one of their friends, we play Dombal – a Nepali card game – until the sun goes down. It's great fun! When the time comes to go to bed, I wrap myself up in all my clothes, eight layers on top and three at the bottom. I'll be sleeping with my woolly hat, scarf and gloves on, that's for sure. The following day, we wake up ridiculously early to watch the sunrise.

Sunrise
Surprisingly, when you're standing at Annapurna Base Camp, you're not at the top but at the bottom of the mountain as taller peaks surround you. The sun rises behind them turning the snow from pure white to yellow, then orange and even red. It's absolutely breathtaking. I don't want to leave this place. Not only have I surpassed my own expectations, I've seen extraordinary things and feel closer to my best friend than ever before.

Before
She's told me that she's met a guy at work and is torn between her existing relationship and this growing attraction. That's what she came on this trip to reflect upon. One thing is for certain, I can relate to her situation so we talk about it for hours. We could probably keep going endlessly but the time has come to walk back down.

Down
At first, walking down is fast and fun but it doesn't take long for my bad knee to start hurting. It's the same one I damaged all

those years ago. Overly optimistic or utterly idiotic, I thought it would be fine and didn't take anything with me. I have no strap, no cream, no medication, nothing at all. It's using two poles as crutches that I walk slowly down the mountain. The pain throbs but I know I have no choice. There is only one way and it's down. To distract myself, I try to focus on the beautiful landscape around me but at one point, I crumble. I start crying uncontrollably. I'm not sure what triggered it. A mix of frustration, sadness and anger I guess. Why do I still need to carry around this dodgy leg attached to my now willing and driven body? Every single step is an excruciating reminder of how unhealthy I used to be. Luckily, my best friend is far ahead so she doesn't catch a glimpse of my meltdown. Our guide is lovely and shares with me his own and far more significant difficulties, which eventually takes my mind off mine.

Eventually
Several unbearable hours later, it's with great relief that we finally return to where we started our ascent six days ago. This incredible trip has shown me how much better I need to become at looking after myself and how little my current job actually matters in the grand scheme of things. All in all, this was one of the hardest and most rewarding experiences I've ever been through and most likely will ever go through in my lifetime. That afternoon, we head back to our hotel where we take a revivifying hot shower. The first one in days. Lying in bed, we reflect on how amazing this whole trip has been. I'm incredibly happy and grateful she came, and she says she's glad I convinced her to join me. It's now time to mentally prepare ourselves for our paragliding jump tomorrow. I'm terrified of heights, but I can't wait to see the Himalayas from the sky!

Sky

Fast forward from one flight to the next, I'm off to Thailand again! This time it's to coordinate the filming of a Chinese reality TV show at one of the company's hotels. The crew is enormous – about 60 people in total including the two main stars. Apparently, they're both pretty famous in China but I've never heard of them. The show is called *We are in love* and is based on a concept from South Korea. The principle is that two celebrities pretend they are in love and undertake romantic activities together. As my colleague explains it to me, I can't quite grasp what makes it so incredibly popular. Nonetheless, the programme is a massive success. The online version of the first season has been watched 850 million times.

Watched

Everything about the filming of this show is very last minute and extremely disorganised. I take advantage of my poor Mandarin language abilities to stand back and observe. When I end up on camera, I find it exhilarating! This fun claim to fame is the highlight of my trip and revives the dreams I had of working as a TV presenter. I can't help but wonder what my life would be like now if I'd pursued a career in media and what it would be like if I did so from this day forward. Maybe I would be going through the same questions I am now or maybe not. I'm pretty sure I have a romanticised image of the industry. In the end, there is only one way of finding out: giving it a go. But how? I ask myself as I make my way back to grey and cold Shanghai.

Grey

People walk backwards. Well, mostly elderly people. I see them doing so in the park every morning while others are practicing

Tai Chi or dancing. Curious, I ask one of my colleagues what it's all about. He says they do so because they believe that walking backwards helps with their balance. I see. "Don't do it though, it's an old people thing," he continues. His comment makes me think about how significant the generation gap seems to be here. Old men play *mahjong*[6]. Old ladies dance together on the pavement and in parks. In the meantime, what do young people do? They spend their day glued to their smartphone. Is this specific to China or does a worldwide generation divide actually exist? Has technology made it wider faster? Will any traditions forever remain?

Traditions
Today is Qingming festival, also known in English as Tomb Sweeping Day. Everyone around me who is able to do so, is going to their ancestors' graves to tidy them up, pray and make wishes. I find such a custom particularly endearing and wish I could visit Granddad and Grandpa's tombs. Meanwhile, I hope to travel to places my ancestors couldn't reach and bring back stories and souvenirs to the ones who are still here and keen to hear them.

Ones
My family came to visit. We went to the Yellow Mountains and had a wonderful time. That place is absolutely stunning! I understand why it inspired so many talented Chinese artists over the years. Time flew by so quickly though. Too quickly. Their departure has left me feeling upset and empty…

---

[6] *Mahjong* is a popular traditional Chinese tile-based game usually played by four participants.

Upset
To be honest, I can't come to terms with something I picked up on during our trip. Countless people pointed their finger at us and called us "*lao wai*", "*lao wai*", "*lao wai*."[7] Sometimes I wonder whether having no command of Chinese isn't a blessing in disguise. Foreigner. What if I pointed my finger at Asian people in Europe and called them foreigners? I wonder what would happen then. I guess they would sue me for racism or something along these lines and so they should. How could one ever feel at home in a country where people constantly refer to him or her as a foreigner?

Foreigner
Someone who isn't welcome. Someone who doesn't understand. Someone who doesn't belong. I've been here for seven months and it seems like the honeymoon phase has just come to a tragic end. Recently, I've sadly realised that I've become more and more intolerant towards certain behaviours such as staring, pushing, spitting, screaming, etc. Some say the advantages of living here take over again with time. Others argue that it's impossible to stay here longer than two years. I'm not sure what the answer will be for me yet but to be honest it largely depends on what handsome guy ends up deciding. He isn't here yet and it doesn't look as though he'll ever be. It's strange to admit that your destiny no longer lies solely in your hands, but only with him do I feel complete, calm, and safe.

Safe
Shanghai is one of the, if not *the* safest city I've ever lived in. Physically that is. Emotionally it's a different story… I might have

---
[7] '*Lao wai*' in Chinese means 'foreigner' in English.

just hit rock bottom. I feel terribly depressed, lonely and worthless. I can't be bothered to go out and meet up with people. I don't have the courage to exercise. I don't speak much to handsome guy, or my friends and family. I don't sleep a lot. and when I do, I sleep terribly. I'm overeating dramatically. Vicious cycle of self-destruction. Dark and familiar. Small victories all seem to be followed by bigger falls. This endless downward spiral is sucking me in a little further every second, every minute and every day. Worried, I decide to consult a professional.

According to her, I'm suffering from 'adaptation disorder'.

"Sure," I said, convinced that my issues are far deeper.

Deeper

What I'm doing now – working myself into the ground and feeling lonelier than ever – has nothing to do with my 'grown-up' list…

What happened to my dreams?

Life. Fear of failure. Lack of confidence.

What now?

Successful career. Expat contract. Travel.

What next?

I have no idea…

Idea

Almost every day in Shanghai I meet people who started their own business, built something out of nothing and never gave up. It's so inspiring. Looking at myself, it's the opposite I see. I'm working for someone else's cause, one that I used to believe in but can't anymore. The company is going through a change of management, focus, and values. Knowing what this will bring, I can't help but wonder if my place is elsewhere.

Wonder
In times like this, I often ask myself whether people that surround me – colleagues and acquaintances – are genuinely unaware or purposefully oblivious to the emotional roller coaster I'm on. Does anyone around me or anywhere in the world feel the same way – lost, unsure and crippled with self-doubt? These thoughts are so overpowering. They leave no space to connect with others and thus deepen my loneliness.

Loneliness
People often ask me how things are going in China. The truth is that living here right now is extremely difficult. Hearing such an answer might make them think it's got something to do with the culture, the behaviours, the food or the environment but they would be mistaken. This is a wonderful place I truly appreciate. I've embraced it all, even its sometime rude people, smelly food, dirty roads and terribly polluted air because they too make this place unique, buzzing, diverse, fascinating and simply unforgettable. The struggles I have aren't with China; they are within me. My shortcomings. They are the difficulties I have being on my own, my constant self-doubt and the hole in my heart only others seem to be able to fill.

Self-doubt
If you've read this far, there a few favours I'd kindly ask of you.
Please don't judge me too harshly. I'm only human.
Please don't pity me. I'm lucky.
Please don't rule me out. I must fix myself.
Please bear with me. I will.

Will

"Will you EVER come over?" I scream at handsome guy. He's visiting me in Shanghai. Though it might seem unfair, I've wanted to ask him the question for weeks. It didn't feel right to speak about this over the phone, so I waited for us to be face-to-face. His chilled demeanour and detached attitude are driving me absolutely insane right now. We need a plan. Or perhaps, I'm the only one who needs a plan. Either way, I must know when we'll be together again. The long distance is driving me crazy. I miss him too much! This isn't right! It doesn't make sense and isn't worth it! After hours of pushing and pulling, he admits that he won't relocate to China and says he has no idea about the future. He promises to take some time to think about what he wishes to do.

Wishes

With travel comes humility, with humility comes appreciation, with appreciation comes serenity. I've just spent a wonderful weekend in Tokyo with a new friend. She is Taiwanese, grew up in Australia, and has plenty of stories to tell. Together, we visited amazing places, ate delicious food and spoke to extraordinarily kind and polite people. A special mention to the local toilets too. Unbelievable! Some of them, in public places even, have integrated heated seats. Who knew a warm butt and a warm heart could go hand in hand? At the Sensoji temple, she insisted that we made a donation so we could make a wish and receive a prediction. Mine was number 10 and called 'Best Fortune'. It reads:

> *Bad old things will turn into happiness.*
> *New hope appearing, you will get treasures.*
> *You can hope on the cloud in the sky.*

Just like dead trees bloom flowers when spring comes.
Everything will be prosperous. Your wishes will be realised.
A sick person will recover. The lost article will be found.
The person you are waiting for will come.

Though I don't really believe in prophecies, I do hope this card contains some form of truth. I'm finally starting to look forward to finding out what the future holds again. This trip was the breath of fresh air I needed. It got me thinking that perhaps travelling more would help but could I do it on my own? In Asia maybe but in China, without speaking Mandarin very well, I'm not sure I could ever find the confidence.

Confidence
'Life goes on' as they say... Mine seems to be flashing past at the moment. I have a long list of trips ahead of me. The beauty in this madness is that it leaves me with very little time to overthink. My travels start in South East Asia. Handsome guy and I meet in Malaysia for a week of holiday. We begin our trip in Kuala Lumpur and then visit Cameron Highlands, Penang and George Town. It's humbling to see how different cultures, religions, and origins live together without apparent divergence or conflict. Reflecting on what I've witnessed makes me wish that other parts of the world could learn from this unified and harmonious country. Once again, I'm reminded to be grateful that, through travel, I'm able to discover other ways of life and philosophies. If travel is the teacher at a school that's the world, then every trip is a lesson that has the power to open our minds a little wider.

Trip
A few days after my return, a couple of colleagues and I head off to Beijing for business. In between meetings, we make it to the Great Wall. What an incredible sight! As soon as we reach it, I separate myself from the group slightly and start to walk along its waving spine. Emotions rise as I remember the first time I was here with my family. The wall is as majestic as ever. It hasn't changed but I certainly have, so much has happened in the last six years. Letting my thoughts linger along the wall, I wish that one day I could come back and stay longer. A colleague catches up with me.

Colleague
We've grown quite close over the last few weeks. She is Chinese, but others call her a 'banana'. What the term is meant to describe is someone who has a Chinese appearance, hence the yellow, but with a foreign mind-set, hence the white. The opposite is referred to as an 'egg'. Though I find the terminology dreadful, the people it describes are fascinating characters. They embody a combination of Oriental and Occidental cultures. Their identity has become far more complex, diverse, and intertwined than the nationality on their passport might suggest.

Intertwined
Hong-Kong, where I travel to next, is a city that illustrates this perfectly. A long weekend there leaves me with the feeling that I, too, am the combination of all the places I've lived in and travelled to. My next destination will be Sri Lanka for a family holiday. I can't wait but before that, it's time for football.

Football

The company is receiving a group of about 120 people over 10 days and across three cities. It's not any group though, it's actually Borussia Dortmund, the iconic German football club which ranks amongst the best in Europe. Originally, I wasn't very keen on being involved in the logistics of their trip. I couldn't help asking myself: considering my education, my status and expertise, why should I be wiping these famous people's asses? But unexpectedly, I ended up absolutely loving it! First off, we didn't actually have to wipe anybody's backside – though I wouldn't be that surprised if I heard it had happened. Secondly, everyone in the group – players included – were all extremely kind and grateful. There is something absolutely thrilling about rubbing shoulders with celebrities! Thirdly, everyone in our team worked so well together. Every day, regardless of the stress levels and extreme sleep deprivation, we operated as one gang, one crew, one force. To each problem, we found a solution. In front of each hurdle, we gathered. At the end of each challenge, we took a second to laugh. This project brought a different light onto my experience in China and I can genuinely say that I will never forget about it.

Forget

Defining moments. They are the ones you know you will remember forever. No matter what happened before or what happens next. Sometimes they are out of the ordinary, other times, they are simply the first. First win. First drink. First love. Working for a start-up business often feels like going through defining moment after defining moment. Most of what I'm doing, I've never done before or, if I have, it was in a totally different country and context. The upcoming milestone of my career has been in the making for over half a year. Tomorrow, it will come to life. It's the official launch of the company in China.

Launch
I've been in charge of all the preparations and now of the delivery. The company has grown a lot lately and internal politics have reached a new high. In fact, one colleague seems determined to make me fail but I'm doing my best not to let it get to me. If anything, it fuels my will to surpass myself and wow the 140 attendees we're expecting. Together with the team, we spend the night transforming the venue. The next morning, it's not only stunning; it's also branded. The view of the old and new Shanghai from the balcony is outstanding. Staring at it as the sun rises gives me the warmth and comfort I need to carry on. Determined and unstoppable, I ignore my boss's relentless texts asking whether I'm going to burn out or not, I give the team a pep talk and off we go.

Go
What a day! The pressure was mind-blowing. The energy was extraordinary. The event unfolded extremely quickly. And suddenly it's all over. Another one of those pinch-me moments. Of course, all I can focus on right now are all the little things that went wrong but the feedback from the attendees and colleagues eventually starts to register. The local media coverage is plentifully and positive and the share price of the company even rises on the day. Never in my wildest dreams had I thought that could happen.

Happen
Hello London! It's so wonderful to be back! Somehow, it feels as though everything is new yet familiar. I can't stop smiling at random people, appreciating the beauty all around me and absorbing every sensation and emotion. I'm only here for a weeklong business trip and plan on making the most of it. I'll be meeting all my friends, popping over to Paris to see my family and of course spending as much time as I can with handsome guy. We have a lot to talk about. He's made up his mind. Finally, we have a plan, which I genuinely hope will work out. Australia, that's where he said he'd like to move next. I've never been but I should be living there soon. Crazy, I know! In a couple of weeks, he'll apply for a working holiday visa. If he gets it, he'll quit his job and move out there to look for a new one. I'll then follow the same process and join him 'Down Under'! Things will get in motion once I complete my two-year assignment. That's a year away… A lot can happen in that time so let's see.

See
In the meantime, I really need to think about what the next step of my career will be. I'm about to follow my heart fully, which is leaving my mind screaming and rambling. The company doesn't have any offices in Australia, so I'll have to quit my job. It's like I'm standing in front of a blank piece of paper. I've lived abroad before, but this is different. In the past, I always had studies or a job to go to. When I left, I had a solid plan with its foundations laid out in front of me. This time around, I'll be giving up a promising career for love. I'm pretty sure that's what I'd rationally advise any of my friends not to do, if they ever contemplated the idea. I'm worried. Every single one of my nights is filled with relentless nightmares. The 'grown-up' list

has come back to me again and my head is full of unanswered questions. Do I look for a similar role in the travel industry? Do I pursue my dream of working in media? Do I start my own business? Or do I do something completely different?

Different
Busy knocked on the door.
I invited it in,
Said I was having dinner with lazy.
They started arguing.
That left stuck and I alone,
At each other staring.
I'm back in Shanghai now, struggling to re-adjust. I'm trying to find an outlet. Here it is… The idea. The project. The aspiration. Sadly, it comes with other things too… The fear. The self-doubt. The disbelief.

Aspiration
I'd like to find a way to inspire other people to travel and live abroad. Why? Because I believe that the more people do so, the smaller the world will get. Eventually, borders will become redundant and tolerance, acceptance, and peace will be the norm rather than the exception. The world I dream of is one where saying "world citizen" out loud does not sound utopian but inspirational. It's one where, when people meet for the first time, the question they ask after "What's your name?" isn't "Where are you from?" but "Who are you and what's your story?" Right now, I don't have much more than a name for this idea: Be Beyond Borders. What's next?

Next
After insisting that I should stick to a specific job for the next three years at least, my boss has just asked me to get involved in a new project. It's one that will require a full-time commitment, I know it even before I start. Once more, he ignores my input. Instead of pushing back, I take this as a new challenge and decide to try to do both my current job and the new project at the same time, which turns out to be absolutely exhausting…

Exhausting
Quickly, I realise that nothing has been communicated internally so several people are working on the same topic in parallel. That's his style: create confusion and competition between team members. It's an 'interesting' leadership approach, one that doesn't make sense to me whatsoever. All it adds up to is frustration. No one is working in the same direction and everyone is criticising each other in the process. A lot of this negativity ends up my way daily, but I already know that I'll be gone soon so I do my best to ignore it. In the meantime, I focus on my new task: building a new stream for the business.

Building
The goal is to provide travel services and experiences for foreigners who live in China and wish to travel within China as well as to Asia, and beyond. Everything has to be developed from scratch. Starting with a strategy and a detailed plan, I'll then need to cover all areas from product development to website, social media, marketing, sales and operations. For the first time in my career, I'll be leading a team that is accountable for bringing in revenue to the company. One more string to my bow. Fingers crossed it succeeds before I leave.

More

Still absurdly trying to do both my job and the new project at the same time, I'm working myself into the ground. It's beyond exhausted that I get ready to receive an official delegation of 200 people over the next three days. Then, the day after they leave, I'll be heading to Europe for Christmas. Something to look forward to. This literally feels like the ultimate stretch before a vital break. The large group arrived last night, and this evening they're having a dinner party on a boat. Having seen them off earlier, my colleagues and I are now waiting at the harbour for them to return.

Harbour

I've never been here before. This isn't somewhere tourists would venture. It's far from being a pleasant place, to say the least. My colleagues and I have some dinner in a local restaurant nearby, from where we can monitor the arrival of the delegation. As the boat approaches a few hours later, we split up. We previously agreed that one of them would be waiting on the dock, the other in front of the bus and that I'd be standing in the hangar in between. Once I'm in position, the lights go off. I try to ask one of the caretakers why but can't quite make sense of the answer. All I gather is that he wants me to leave as quickly as possible, so I rush outside.

Rush

I don't want any of the attendees to get lost because I wasn't standing at the right place. Putting two and two together quickly, I realise that they'll have to come through a small dark alley. That's the only available path between the dock and our bus which will drive them back to their hotel. I can see the boat mooring, so I pick up the pace. I'm walking as fast as I can now. There are a few locals selling random items on the right-hand side. What brings them here at this time of night, I will never know. I'm quite certain they won't sell anything to the people in our group. As soon as they see me, they start shouting "*lao wai*", "*lao wai*", "*lao wai*." I ignore their voices, stick to the left-hand side and keep going. One of them, I presume in an attempt to showcase his merchandise, has put little wheels under his shoes, the ones that flash in different colours. He is rolling my way now, approaching me from the right. Hoping my body language will speak louder than words, I accelerate. I'm past him now.

Past

Or so I thought. My back foot catches his pointy toes. I fall. It only takes a split second for my whole body to hit the floor. My knees didn't have time to bend. It's like I turned into a collapsed pancake: flat from head to toe. I'm stunned. Violent shivers spread up and down my spine. Tears of anger and shock fall down my cheeks. Next, the pain kicks in. Thanks to some obscure yet brilliant reflex, I folded my left arm in front of my face in the process. That's the only reason why my nose and teeth are intact. However, now isn't the time to marvel at the brilliance of the human brain. Two hundred people will be coming off that boat in a matter of minutes. They can't see me with my head in the dirt. Getting back up as swiftly as I can, I realise that all the local sellers have gathered around me. None of them offers a helping hand. Instead, the one who caused the accident screams at me, in Mandarin of course. I have no idea what he is saying. Anyway, I have no time for it. As quickly as I can, I stand up, dust off my coat and head towards one of my colleagues.

Stand

Her eyes are filled with concern when she sees me. I tell her what happened briefly, wipe my tears away and head back into position. Within the seconds it takes me to return, all the local sellers have disappeared. At least they won't be disturbing our guests... The pain in my left arm is throbbing now. I can feel my heart beating through it. I'm so cold. I can't stop shaking. Carefully, I put my left hand into my coat pocket. As the group disembarks, I show them the way by extending my right arm. Ironically, I'm now grateful for the darkness in which I can partially hide. I'm sure the tears have made me look like a sad panda because of my running make-up. Once the whole delegation has left, my colleagues and I jump on the last bus. We make our way back to the hotel to ensure everything is in order there before calling it a day. The pain has now reached a whole new level.

Pain

Sitting on the bus, I can no longer stop the tears from coming down my cheeks. It hurts so badly. My colleagues are telling me not to worry. Apparently, they're sure that I'm fine though they have absolutely no medical knowledge whatsoever. I'm convinced they even think I'm dramatising. But I know something is wrong. Three weeks ago, handsome guy and I met for a long weekend in Abu-Dhabi – as you do. There, I had a quad biking accident in the middle of the desert. I suffered a serious injury to the back of my right leg. Bruising and ripped skin was the emergency doctor's diagnosis. That was painful, but this is a whole different level of suffering. I can't even straighten my pinkie. I'm left handed, of course. What am I going to do? Could it be broken? What if I can't write and type? There is no way around this, I have to go to the hospital. In China. In the middle of the night.

Night
Back at the hotel, I tell the team leader what happened and request to go see a doctor. He agrees, though he doesn't seem to care much about the situation. Too preoccupied by the delegations' thousands of requests. Understandable? Most definitely. Acceptable? I'm not so sure. Luckily, a colleague offers to come along. A few weeks ago, someone told me a hospital story from which I picked up the name of an English speaking 24/7 emergency facility in Shanghai. I have no idea why or how I remember it – fate perhaps. Once I've arrived, there is only one doctor on duty. Three patients require his attention. The other two are showing signs of a heart attack so, logically, my injury isn't a priority. By now, my hand looks like an egg has grown under my skin. It hurts just the same though the ice and the morphine are starting to help. It's just gone past midnight when I tell my colleague to go home. Chatting to my family and handsome guy on WeChat© makes me feel less alone as I wait for the verdict. After a series of x-rays and a couple more hours of waiting, the doctor tells me that my hand is broken. The fifth metacarpal is split. It's a misplaced fracture which means that the bone is no longer aligned. He puts my whole forearm into a heavy plaster cast and gives me more morphine to take back to my apartment. Frustratingly, I'll have to return to the hospital in order to see a specialist in a couple of days.

Days
I have a newly-found understanding and respect for people who only have the use of one of their arms. Everything takes me so

much longer... I'm having to slow right down. It might not be such a bad thing if my hand wasn't aching this much. The morphine the doctor had prescribed makes me ill. Sitting on the sofa, I'm shaking and sweating uncontrollably. After less than a day, I decide to stop using it. The nights are the longest. The cast is so heavy and uncomfortable that I'm having to place my forearm on a pillow. When the pain strikes, I squeeze Boutchou in my right hand. Lying on my back, I wait and hope that I'll manage to fall asleep eventually. In the meantime, I can't help but wonder how high Boutchou would rank in the list of cuddly toys who've travelled the most in the world. It has followed me pretty much everywhere since I was one. Sadly, the years haven't been very kind to it. Despite its gloomy appearance, it somehow still manages to help me through the tough times.

Tough

In the morning, I make my way to the hospital for my appointment with the orthopaedist. After another series of x-rays, he invites me into his office. His diagnosis is clear: the fracture is significant and indeed misplaced. He proposes to operate on me tomorrow and insert a small metal plate and two screws to align the bone. I haven't slept properly in a couple days, which makes me an emotional wreck. Ironically, the first thing that comes to my mind is the fear that I'll always beep when going through airport security... A split second later, feeling overwhelmed and paralysed, I realise that I'm totally alone. I'm supposed to be flying back to Europe for Christmas tomorrow morning. I don't know what to do. I politely request that the doctor gives me a few minutes of privacy. He agrees and as soon as he has left the room, I call handsome guy and my parents crying my eyes out. "Come home as fast as you can," is their advice so when the doctor returns, I refuse the surgery. Instead, I ask him for a smaller cast and a letter for the airline to make sure they'll allow me to fly in my condition.

Condition

After the appointment, I walk past a few shops. My cast doesn't fit in most of my clothes and it's freezing outside. As quickly as I can, I find a couple of large jumpers and a poncho coat. They make me look silly but at least I won't catch a cold on top of all this! Then, having returned to my apartment, I start packing. What I would normally do in about an hour, ends up taking three. I'm exhausted. This prompts me to put my ego aside and ask for help. I separately message two friends asking if either of them could accompany me to the airport the following morning. Sadly, there is no way I can manoeuvre my luggage on my own. It's a weekend so I'm hoping they'll be available. A few hours later, one replies saying he's going out tonight and will be moving house tomorrow so he can't make it. No news at all from the other. It's official, I'm totally and utterly alone. How could a place where you have no one to count on ever feel like home? If home is them – your loved ones – then what is home when they're not there? Perhaps the question I should have been asking myself all along wasn't 'Where is home?' or 'What is home?' but '*Who* is home?' I interrupt my reflections to focus on finding a solution to the problem at hand.

Solution

In the end, I kindly ask a colleague to help me book a taxi and request that the driver carry my suitcase all the way to the check-in counter. I'll tip him for it, no problem. With that sorted, I phone the airline to see whether they can arrange for someone to help me with my luggage when I arrive. Surprisingly, the operator says they don't provide any assistance for people who can walk. Thanks for that. Needless to say the trip ends up being one of the most challenging, if not *the* most challenging, I've ever taken. When I finally reach London, I see handsome guy in the crowd. He's been waiting for me at the airport. As I fall into the comfort of his strong embrace, I feel so relieved. Being with someone you can lean on and who cares about you is priceless.

Priceless

The next morning, I have a breakfast date with my best friend. I've only seen her once since Nepal and I can't wait to catch up. Last time we spoke, she'd told me she'd just left her long-term partner and started dating the colleague she had a crush on. Big news! I wonder what she might have in store for me this time… Minutes after we sit down in a warm and cosy little café, she tells me she has an announcement to make. Bigger news! I can't believe it. It's crazy how quickly things change when you live half way across the world. A few months back, a doctor told her she had little chance for it to happen but for some reason I'm sure that it has… I'm right, she is pregnant! My heart lifts at the news. I'm so happy for her! And it gets better. Her partner is Australian and soon he'll have to move back to Brisbane. She plans on relocating there with him. That means we'll be living in the same country again in a few months. I can't wait. "Everything happens for a reason," she says as we bid each other goodbye. Her words resonate with me during the whole train journey from London to Paris.

Train

The good thing about having a broken hand is that people tend to be more considerate towards you. They let you through, smile at you, and sometimes even speak to you. When they do, they often start by asking how it happened. I've thought about pretending it was a Kung Fu accident but haven't dared yet. It would be a far better – and shorter – story to tell. Once that initial question answered, some people then tell you about their own broken bones experiences. The most compassionate, even offer their help. Due to an accident on the rails, the train journey takes a lot longer than usual, but I don't mind as I'm chatting with the girl next to me for most of the journey. It helps me ignore the growing pain. The flight has caused my hand to swell even more which is making the plaster cast feel tighter and tighter. By the time I finally reach Paris, my fingers are all blue and I can barely move them. As soon as I meet my parents and my sister, they drive me to the emergency room.

Emergency

Thereafter, I spend four days in and out of various hospitals. The confusion as to whether I require surgery or not turns into a never-ending story. Eventually, the hand specialist realigns my bone under local anaesthetic without having to resort to an invasive procedure. Good news. Also, the international insurance agrees to cover the costs. Good news times two. I'm relieved as the bill would have been almost as painful as the fracture itself. Exhausted by the whole experience and still physically impaired, I ask my boss for a week of sick leave. I can't see myself returning to China on my own just yet. I wouldn't be able to work properly with one hand anyway. Plus, it's so wonderful to be back in Louviers with my family and handsome guy.

Louviers

Whether this place is or isn't actually home, all that matters is that, right here right now, surrounded by the people I love the most, I feel at home. I'm unbelievably lucky and eternally grateful for the way they look after me.

Grateful

Three weeks in Europe go by so fast. After just over 10 days in France, handsome guy and I travel back to the UK and spend time with his family in Romsey. They, too, are welcoming and caring. I wish I could stay on this side of the world for longer, but the time has come to return to China. If anything, this broken hand has taught me to slow down and reminded me to look after myself better – work less, enjoy life, and travel more.

Enjoy

I've made a list of the places I'd like to visit before I leave China. I'm ready to make the most of my last 10 months in Shanghai while preparing for our upcoming move to Australia!

Australia

Chinese New Year is only about a month after Christmas this year. Before moving 'Down Under', I've decided to take advantage of this bank holiday week to check it out. There are two main reasons for my trip. Firstly, I want to make sure I'll like it there. Secondly, I find it a lot easier to picture myself living somewhere if I've visited before. My hand is still broken but my cast is far smaller now and the level of pain is decreasing every day. I've packed as lightly as I can: one piece of hand luggage for 10 days. It'll be easier for me to manage. My right arm and hand have become stronger with time. I can now even write with my weak hand. It takes a lot longer but definitely helps, especially when it comes to filling in immigration documents. Once in Australia, the plan is for me to stay a few days in Melbourne with our friends, the nomadic couple. What a small world! I haven't seen them since Brazil and I'm really looking forward to catching up. After that, I'll travel to Sydney on my own. That way, I can get a sense of both of the cities where we're most likely to live.

Likely

The trip goes so quickly. Australia is amazing! Everyone is so friendly and kind. Food is delicious with plenty of options for those, like me, suffering with allergies and intolerances. The weather is beautiful as it's summer at the moment. Landscapes are splendid and animals adorable. I've seen a cute koala but no kangaroos yet. I guess I'll have to come back. Oh wait, I will! I can definitely see myself living here, even more so because our friends – the nomadic couple – are around. They're planning on leaving before I'm due to arrive, but I hope they change their mind. Fingers crossed. Not only does this brief visit make me want to relocate even more, it also shows me that travelling solo absolutely is an option. I'd never thought it would be something I'd enjoy. The loneliness had always scared me but, with this trip, I realise how fantastic exploring on your own actually is. When you're by yourself, you can do whatever you wish whenever you wish and, if you don't want to be alone, you can always talk to random people. All the unexpected discussions you have and friends you make along the way are brilliant. It's decided, I'm going to stop waiting for other people to make up their mind, and start exploring the world solo. If I can do it with a broken hand, it can't be that difficult to do it without. New horizons, here I come!

Horizons

Keen to start sharing my travel experiences more as I keep exploring, I take up photography. They say pictures speak a thousand words, I couldn't agree more. I love capturing everything that's around me. I take my newly-acquired camera everywhere, starting with a family weekend in Macao. What a surprising city that is. The Portuguese and Chinese architectures and cultures blend in seamlessly. One minute, we feel as though we're sitting at a café in Lisbon. The next, we have the impression of being at a traditional restaurant somewhere in Beijing.

Restaurant

Back in Shanghai, I'm off on a dumpling-making tour. Food was one of the things I dreaded the most before moving here. Thankfully, my worries proved to be unfounded. Through this experience, I've realised how diverse Chinese food actually is. I've been able to learn what I like and what I don't. Dumplings fall into the first category. I find them absolutely delicious! Whether they are served in soup, boiled, steamed or fried, and filled with vegetables, meat or shrimp, they delight my taste buds. That's why I'm so keen on learning how to make them today. The chef is great fun and teaches us how to cook steamed shrimp dumplings in a few simple steps. Watching him is fascinating. As it turns out, the process requires serious skills. My version of this Cantonese speciality looks quite awful but tastes good nonetheless.

Cantonese

The time has come for my best friend to move to Australia after having lived in the UK for the past 11 years. She is five months pregnant. On her way to Brisbane, the place she will soon call her new home, she is stopping over in Hong Kong for about 24 hours. I wouldn't miss this opportunity to see her so I'm on a plane heading south. Spending time with her, as always, is wonderful. She is really showing now and looks absolutely gorgeous. I feel just as happy about her news now than when she first told me. Back in Nepal, she mentioned she would like to travel the world like I do but felt unable to. At the time, she had just bought a house in the UK and wanted to start a family. How life sometimes changes in ways you could never predict. Just over a year later, she's on her way to the other side of the world where she will give birth to an international baby. Our time together passes by so quickly. We explore the city and talk, talk, talk, every step of the way. I can't wait to join her 'Down Under'.

Join
Before breaking my hand, my main source of exercise was body pump which consists of lifting weights to music. After the accident, I'm trying to find something else to keep moving and stay fit. It has to be fairly gentle so I won't risk hurting myself again before the bone has fully recovered. The Chinese doctor who is following my progress says that will take at least six months, if not a whole year. Seeing him causes me grief every single time. His manner is rude, abrupt and hurtful. I'm impatient and can't wait to be done with him and the whole hand situation. In the meantime, I thought I'd try yoga.

Yoga
I never particularly liked yoga. Truth be told, I've always thought exercise should make you sweat buckets and I know for a fact that this won't. In French, we say, 'Only idiots don't change their

mind'[8], so here I am, attending my first class. The instructor is a young French girl who completed her training in India and has just started teaching in the spare bedroom of her apartment. In the room, the atmosphere is warm and cosy. The slow pace of movement, the importance of the breath and the spirituality behind it all suddenly speak to me. After each class, I feel more relaxed, centred, and ready to face the day ahead. When I finally decide to purchase a 10 class-subscription, she hands me her card. Her last name looks familiar. It's the same name as a girl I went to university with. Not realising it, I share my thoughts out loud. "Really?" she says. "That's my cousin you're talking about," she continues. Once again, I'm reminded of how small the world is. The further through life I go, the more convinced I am that we're all interconnected. We might not instantly manage to figure out how, through what or why, but we are. This unexpected link between us, however small and perhaps irrelevant, is enough to convince me to give yoga a proper go. There is something here for me to learn. I'm not sure what it is yet or if I'll ever find it but I, for one, am always up for some exploration.

Exploration
It's not often that I visit the same place twice. Doing so gives me a feeling of *déjà vu* that doesn't sit well with my burning desire to explore the world. But to every rule, there is an exception. Brazil is this exceptional exception. What brings me there once more is the wedding of the nomadic couple. I'm super excited! Flying over from Shanghai is an absolute mission but missing their big day would never cross my mind. Plus, I have the opportunity to

---

[8] The French phrase *'Il n'y a que les imbéciles qui ne changent pas d'avis'*, has here been translated to 'Only idiots don't change their mind'.

stop in Paris half way, which means I'll see my family and will even be in town for my sister's birthday. I haven't managed to be with her on the day for several years, so I have some making up to do. The two of us have grown closer with time. Our personalities are quite different, but our core values are the same. Through the years, our relationship has evolved into one of mutual respect. Though it's hard for me not to see her as a baby I need to protect anymore, I'm trying my best to get there. She is doing really well in Paris. A qualified biomedical engineer, she has a job she likes and lives with her boyfriend. She tells me she is really happy how things are and doesn't feel any urge to travel, move, or change. Sometimes I wonder how she can have it all figured out when I still feel lost at the best of times.

Best
Having spent a lovely few days with her and the rest of my family, I'm now on my way to Rio. There, handsome guy is waiting for me. Many of his friends have arrived too. A flat with eight guys plus me that should be… great fun! A few of us are keen on exploring. We hike in the surrounding mountains and walk around the city. It's wonderful to be in Brazil again and have the chance to create new and happier memories over some of the previous ones tainted by Granddad's passing. The wedding comes around quickly and is absolutely gorgeous.

Gorgeous
The venue offers stunning views of the entire city, the ceremony – emotional and unique – reflects the nomadic couple's personality perfectly and the guests from all over the world, are fascinating. Talking to a few of them makes me realise that I'm not the only one reflecting on the topics of home, borders, and identity. I wonder whether there might be even more of us in the world.

Perhaps you, too, are asking yourself the same or similar existential questions? Looking at the nomadic couple having a blast on the dance floor as my thoughts unfold, I feel extremely honoured to be part of their big day. Knowing they will be in Australia too makes me even more excited about moving there! They've postponed their departure so we should be able to spend some time together after I arrive. We've even talked about all four of us living in the same place for a while. Perhaps we'll end up taking over their flat and car in Melbourne, who knows? Stealing their life, in a good way.

Stealing

As I expected, the new project has turned into a full-time job. Slowly but surely, I've moved away from what I was previously doing and have started my own little team. Thus far, I've recruited two ladies. One is an American-born Chinese from New-York City and has lived in China for 13 years. The other is from Malawi and has lived in China for about 6 years. They say managers hire people who are similar to them. I don't know whether this is the case. One thing is certain though, we all get along really well. Having them around has made coming to work far more enjoyable, which has subsequently made being back in Shanghai a little easier. Together, we're organising a big family fun event. Around 100 to 150 attendees are expected. Caught up in the preparation, I haven't had time to come up with my master of ceremony speech yet. It's about 9:30 the night before when I leave the office thinking I'll head home and finally write it. I'm starving so on my way I decide to stop by a little shop and buy a couple of *bao zi*[9]. Having paid for them, I make my way to

---

[9] *Bao zi* are Chinese steamed and filled buns.

the metro station. The sidewalk is crowded tonight. Elderly men and women are dancing to loud, traditional music. My bag is open as I grab bits of food from it while power-walking. As usual, I catch the metro and then walk home from the station. Back at my apartment, I take out my laptop and papers to work on my speech. That's when I notice that something is missing. I can't believe it at first... My wallet. No way, it's gone.

Gone

Without taking the time to think, I rush out. I retrace my steps all the way to the little shop where I bought the food. Nearby, I speak to the police. Between my broken Mandarin and their broken English, we barely manage to understand each other. No one has seen anything. Damn. I know it's just a material possession and such things don't matter. Nevertheless, I can't help but be extremely upset. It feels as though bad luck is following me. Why does this keep happening? What have I done? Is this karma? I wonder. It's well past midnight when I come back to my apartment.

Back

There is so much I need to do, cancel my bank cards, order new versions of everything that was in my wallet, make a police declaration and more. Luckily, I have a couple of friends who started their own company helping lost foreigners like me. They're the loveliest couple ever. I'll get in touch with them as soon as possible, but it will have to wait until after tomorrow's crucial event. Confident girl used to say that I'm lucky with the big things in life but extremely unlucky with the little ones. It's unquestionably better this way but some days, like today, it's hard to remain positive. Shanghai is meant to be one of the safest cities in the world, and I still believe it is. I was probably just at the wrong place at the wrong time. What was I thinking, eating with my bag open? It wasn't the first time but it's definitely the last. At least I don't keep my passport in my wallet, so I can still travel...

Travel
We have a bank holiday coming up. What better opportunity to go on a solo trip? Still a bit anxious about travelling in China by myself due to the language barrier, I've decided to pay a visit to South Korea's capital: Seoul. I'm staying in the spare bedroom of a lovely couple. He is Turkish and she is South Korean. A few years ago, she quit her job and wrote a book that is now being used as an educational tool in various schools all over the country. I'm impressed and inspired!

Inspired
After a long conversation with her, I head out to explore the city. I walk everywhere and take great pleasure in getting lost along the capital's streets. Every shrine I see, I visit. Every park I pass by, I enter. Every sight I spot, I photograph. These precious moments on my own bring me peace of mind and give me space to think. Sitting down on a bench, it suddenly hits me. I know what I'd like to become. A storyteller.

Storyteller
Talking. Writing.
For others. For me.
About love. About the world.
A passion. A dream.
That's all well and good. But what would I say? Could it ever be interesting enough to be read? And how would I make a living? Plus, it sounds like a solitary affair.

Solitary
The time has come for my first solo trip in China. I've made it easy for myself. I'm going to be spending a weekend in Nanjing which is located an hour and a half away from Shanghai by train. I've booked one night in a decent hotel where someone at reception should speak a bit of English, hopefully. I've also printed countless pages of maps just in case my newly downloaded VPN stops working and I lose access to Google maps©. My colleagues made fun of my thorough planning but better safe and relaxed than sorry, right? Once in the city, I walk everywhere. Thousands and thousands of steps. I find the purple mountains green and serene, the history behind the Ming Tomb and Sun Yat-sen mausoleum fascinating, and the atmosphere in the old town buzzing. However, the place that makes the strongest impression on me is the Nanjing Massacre Memorial Hall. It reminds me of the Caen Memorial museum, not far from Louviers. I had never quite realised World War II affected China. It's astounding how much our countries and people have in common. During my visit, a thought comes to my mind… We need to stop letting history repeat itself. Love must win over hatred. What if travel could help with that?

Could
Through travel, one becomes more open-minded and less likely to fear or judge others. What if inspiring more and more people to travel the world could make it a safer and more united place? Perhaps contributing to this could be the life purpose I've been searching for all along. Exploring a place alone might seem lonely but every time I do so, my mind broadens somehow. The silence around me provides space for inspiration and every step I take allows my thoughts to reach depths I didn't know they could.

Time after time, I feel more in line with myself than ever before. It's as if I was finally creating a home for myself within me, somewhere I would always be welcomed and respected. The starting point of self-sufficiency and independence. I'm already looking forward to my next solo trip to Guilin, Yangshuo, and Longsheng in the south of China. My newly-found appreciation for travelling by myself doesn't mean I no longer need to be around others though. On the contrary, it makes me more open to their stories and more accepting of whoever they might be. Friend or foe.

Friend
Wise guy and I first met on that famous business trip to Crete. It seems ages ago now! With hindsight, the memory of telling handsome guy I was moving to China hurts just as much now as it did then. That, combined with the recollection of the job and boss I had at the time, isn't something I particularly like to be reminded of. I do my best to put all these thoughts aside when I speak to wise guy on the phone. Ironic how life sometimes turns the tables… Just over a year ago, I was presenting the most useless numbers in front of a room filled with people far more senior than me, him included. Now, I'm in charge of doing the first screening of interviews for a role he's applied for. I guess you never know what's around the corner, and better treat others fairly. "Don't burn a bridge you might have to cross," is how he wisely puts it. He's been in charge of contracting hotels in Greece for many years and would, without a shadow of a doubt, add tremendous value to the company here. That's what I report back to my boss when asked for what I think of him.

Him

Eventually, he is appointed to the position and relocates to China. Looking at us, I bet most people would say we have nothing to do with each other. Here is yet another one of the great things about living abroad: unexpected friendships. Two people who might have never interacted where they're from, suddenly have something fundamental in common: they've both ended up in the same foreign environment. More likely than not, they will face similar challenges and frustrations. Helping each other overcome these hurdles will become the foundations of such unexpected friendships. Over the years, these are something I've grown to cherish and, thus far, there isn't anyone I've met along the way that I haven't learnt something from. Wise guy is no exception.

Wise

This new and unexpected friend is keen on making me slow down and look after myself better. Though still a bit reluctant, I appreciate his efforts and advice. He's got a point. As for me, I hope to help him settle in Shanghai, get him out of his comfort zone and become more active. Day after day, we spend more time together. We go for spontaneous walks at the weekend, catch up over weekly lunch meetings and even take a trip to Zhangjiajie. This incredible place was the inspiration behind the scenery of the movie *Avatar*[10]. It's home to stunning limestone rock formations, lush nature and roaring waterfalls. However, what most people come here to see these days is the breathtaking longest and highest glass bridge in the world. Standing on top

---

[10] *Avatar* is an American science fiction film set on an imaginary planet and featuring blue hybrid human-aliens. It is the creation of James Cameron and was released in 2009.

of its glass panels revives my fear of heights. With a bit of persistence, I hope to conquer it one day. Joking around and chatting about everything and anything from work to life makes this trip all the more enjoyable. I'd almost forgotten how lovely it was to be around someone I can trust, talk to and hang out with.

Trust

A lot of people ask me how I can possibly trust handsome guy. Thousands of kilometres and seven to eight hours of time difference stand between us. I have no idea what he is up to and vice versa. Long distance brings a great deal of struggles and challenges but, for us, trust hasn't been one of them. Rightly or wrongly, I have blind faith in him. Knowing how loyal I am to him, all I can do is assume that he is just as loyal to me. If we didn't have that firm belief in each other as well as in us as a couple, we'd probably both go crazy. Even though having this strong foundation in place helps, it doesn't make it all smooth sailing.

Smooth

Personally, what I find the hardest is not to be able to speak to him whenever I'd like, and not having a shared routine anymore. Routine used to be something I loathed. I saw it as an old couple's problem to be brutally honest. However, now that it's gone, I miss it deeply. Simple things I took for granted like watching a film or cooking a meal together as well as going to sleep and waking up next to him are now what I long for. Luckily, we've been able to see one another every two to three months thus far. I guess it's not too bad considering how far apart we are from. Over the past year and a half, we've diligently planned and booked the next time we'll meet months in advance. We've also set and stuck to the date at which we'll be reunited. I'm convinced these are the two elements that will see us through until we live together again. Our secret recipe for longevity. Impatient though, we've already started counting the months before the distance that now separates us turns into a hazy memory.

Distance

This trip back to Europe is my last before moving to Australia. I will only spend eight days there and will be travelling to four cities across two countries. I'm exhausted just thinking about it, but I know it'll all be worth it. It always is. Back in London, I spend time with handsome guy and catch up with his family as well as a few dear friends of mine. One of them started his own business recently. He helps professional athletes to prepare their life and career after they retire either by choice or by obligation, for example in case of injury. Speaking to him is really inspiring and revives the latent desire I have to start my own venture one day.

Desire

Over the past couple of weeks, handsome guy's two brothers have become dads. Yet another reminder of how quickly time flies and how much you miss out on when you live far away. Meeting one of the new born girls briefly at the hospital is a beautiful and emotional moment, although it doesn't change our minds. Handsome guy and I are ready for an adventure on the other side of the world, not for a family. In Paris, I catch up with my parents and my sister. I'm so grateful to see that no matter how far in the world I plan to move to, they still support me. Unconditional love. Reciprocal love. Simply, love.

Love

Next, handsome guy and I make our way to the South of France for a friend's wedding. There, we first catch up with two of my friends from university: confident girl and sarcastic girl. I haven't seen sarcastic girl since we fell out six years ago. She contacted me a few weeks back and has travelled from Paris to Toulouse just to meet with me. Handsome guy doesn't understand why I've agreed to see her again. Water under the bridge. My anger and sadness have slowly dissipated and my mind has carefully buried her hurtful words. It's hard to explain exactly why, but I feel like I need to hear her out. The first moments of our encounter are awkward to say the least. A short night later, we head out on a walk just the two of us.

Us

After all these years, not only does she explain, she also apologises. It's like an unbelievably heavy weight I had almost managed to forget about, has been lifted off my shoulders. I might not be such an awful friend after all. Her words mean the world to me. They make me more hopeful and a little more confident in my ability to nurture current and future friendships. I might start to let other people in a bit more. I'm not sure whether she grasps the extent of the positive impact our discussion is having on me. I wish I could stay longer and speak to her for days. I have so many questions and I feel like my turn has come to lift her burden. Of course, I forgive her. There isn't an ounce of me that doesn't want to. Plus, I'm convinced there is a reason our paths have crossed again. If only I had time to explore this further with her. Perhaps we could even lay the foundation of a new friendship. Sadly, we've run out of time, handsome guy and I now have a wedding to attend.

Wedding

A couple of French friends we met in London are getting hitched this afternoon. It's with a lighter yet heavy heart that I bid goodbye to confident girl and sarcastic girl. Too many people to see, not enough time... When you move away, you naturally lose touch with countless friends. There are those you contact on and off. There are those you don't but when you see them again, it feels as though you're picking things up where you left off. Finally, there are those you catch up with only to realise that you don't have much left in common. Perhaps a hasty and slightly twisted way to know who your lifelong friends actually are. Upsetting yet realistic perspective.

Perspective

This trip back to Europe had another purpose, resigning from my job. Over the last four years, the company has enabled me to travel all over the place, learn so much and meet exceptional people. Leaving is a nerve-racking perspective to say the least, especially as I have no idea what I'll be doing in Australia. I don't even really know what I'd like to do in the first place. Even if I did, there's no guarantee that option would exist anyway. Despite being overwhelmed by anxiety, there is no way I'm backing out now. I can't wait to be reunited with handsome guy. The prospect of our future life together is what keeps me going. Hopefully I'll figure something out between now and then. If not, it will be a new adventure nonetheless and I love adventures just as much now as I did when I wrote my 'grown-up' list years ago.

Now

Breaking the news one by one to the Human Resources director, to my manager and to my colleagues both in the UK and in

China, I realise that surprise is the most common reaction. It seems as though everyone thought I would stay with the company and simply relocate back to London after my two-year assignment. Their assumption makes me wonder how well these people actually know me or tried to get to know me. Perhaps this explorer side of mine isn't visible to the naked eye. Truth be told, my cheeky alter-ego enjoys keeping everyone on their toes.

Everyone

Everyone but my team. The two girls and I have become even closer with time. I'm dreading telling them. My boss has asked me to keep the news a secret until he comes up with a succession plan. Sure, I thought ironically. I'm certain he'll start spreading the word himself as soon as I turn my back. I even know who will be the first person he tells: his minion. Except this news isn't his to spread. The culture here is turning into something that is so far from my core values. I can't help but look forward to removing myself from this unhealthy environment. The only thing that's holding me back is worrying about what will happen to the girls. I want to make sure their jobs are safe before I go. I break the news to them and to my dearest colleagues separately. Their reactions are so warm and genuine. They fill my heart with pride and gratitude. The one great thing about all this is that we have a few months to make our work relationship evolve into a friendship. Team work makes the dream work. They've unknowingly given meaning to that cheesy saying.

Team

It's that time of year again: major European football teams are on their way to China to play in the International Championship Cup (ICC). I'll be involved in welcoming two of them: Borussia

Dortmund and the French club Olympique Lyonnais. I couldn't have wished for a better final assignment. I know it will involve little to no sleep, but I don't mind. I'm sure that, just like last year, it will be amazing! Having spent a few days in Guangzhou with Borussia Dortmund, I make my way to Nanjing via Hong Kong. There, I meet the travel manager for Olympique Lyonnais and one of his team members. We connect instantly. We share the same objectives, the same outlook on life and the same sense of humour. Quickly, I become involved in far more than I had originally planned. People often ask me why I always try to go above and beyond. I'm not entirely sure. I think it might be the outcome of a combination of my inherent desire to help and please others as well as my perfectionist nature. Regardless, I'm enjoying every moment of every day on the field. Isn't that what life is all about, finding your own version of happiness?

Life
My parents gave me the gift of life. That sentence is wrong. My parents are giving me the gift of life. Their gift is one that keeps on giving. Every moment spent with them breathes life into me again and again. To be honest, I don't think I could have pushed through the tough moments of this experience if it wasn't for them and their numerous visits to the east. This family summer holiday is taking us a bit further. The four of us, Mum, Dad, my sister and I are meeting in Japan for just over a week and will be travelling to Tokyo, Hakone, Kyoto, Nara, and Osaka. Once there, our trip goes so well. Time flies by and before we know it – the day before my birthday – we sadly have to say goodbye again.

Birthday
I came back to Shanghai last night and today is my birthday. A part of me enjoys this day for the love and attention that comes with it. Another part of me hates it for the pressure it puts on those 24 hours. I can remember scuba diving with manta rays and sharks in French Polynesia reaching -14 metres on my 14th birthday. What could ever top that? Probably nothing. My expectations are too high and often can't be met. Especially today, which is a Monday and a work day. However, as often in life, I remind myself that I have two options. I can either have a pity party or, I can make whatever it is I want happen. Believe me, taking things into your own hands is always a viable option and it doesn't get more empowering than that. So this year, that's exactly what I opt for. Determined to both not be alone and do something special, I've organised a food tour with a few close friends.

Food
After work, we meet our guide in one of the streets of Shanghai's Old Town. He's been living here for 18 years and knows so much about both the local food and culture. We taste all sorts of strange dishes. Deep fried snake and turtle jelly are just a couple of examples of what's on tonight's menu. More importantly, we have so much fun! Our last stop is at a Xinjiang restaurant. Located in the north west of China, Xinjiang is the province I'm planning on visiting for my last solo trip before moving to Australia. Once more, I wonder whether finishing our tour here is coincidence or fate. At the restaurant, a group of policemen and other officials are drinking together upstairs. They've had a few too many and invite us to dance with them. It's Monday and we're all pretty sober but who cares, it's my birthday after all! After a second of hesitation, we join them. Could it ever get more random than this?

Random

Tonight, a couple of British girlfriends and I are going to KTV[11]. I'm not sure what the letters stand for exactly but, essentially, it's karaoke. Over here, everyone seems to take it very seriously. Renting a small room with their family and friends, they eat, drink and sing for hours. Singers take the mic one by one and each tries to do better than the last. What to them is a serious competition, to us is the opposite. Once in our little private room, the girls and I sing together wholeheartedly. At one point, I start dancing. Instantly, they burst out laughing. We're letting it all out and it feels so good! I can't believe this life-changing experience is coming to an end soon.

Soon

Handsome guy and I have started counting the days. This is our last trip together. Next time we meet will be in Melbourne and we'll be moving in together again. Almost there… But before that, we're going to see pandas. Yay! Like a kid in a candy store, I hop around the reserve and take hundreds of pictures. They look so fluffy and adorable. I try not to say their name in Mandarin out loud though. Apparently, the way I pronounce it sounds like something totally different: chest hair. It amuses my colleagues but might offend the hordes of domestic tourists that surround us. Despite having to manoeuvre through thousands of other visitors, our trip is wonderful. The following day, we visit the Leshan Giant Buddha and that evening, we attend a Sichuan Opera Show. Determined to make the most of this experience, I agree to dress up as one of the artists – a

---

[11] KTV actually stands for 'Karaoke television' and describes a karaoke entertainment establishment.

once-in-a-lifetime opportunity. I look so different behind all the make-up. I can't even recognise myself in the mirror. A little girl wants to have her picture taken with me. For once, it's not because I look foreign that she asks but because she actually thinks I'm one of the stars of the show. Repeatedly over his week-long stay, handsome guy asks me, "How did you manage to live here for so long?" What feeds his question are mostly things that I've started to be oblivious to: the pushing, the spitting, the roaring crowds and the language barrier. Could I have finally embraced it all?

Finally

To my greatest surprise, as I prepare myself to leave China, an unexpected guest comes to visit: Step-Grandma. I'm looking forward to welcoming her and showing her around the city I've lived in for the past couple of years. Sadly, it doesn't take long for her presence to remind me of what Granddad said all those years ago. Taken back to the past through our conversations, I start to feel like a failure all over again. Her life is impressive and filled with experiences I'll probably never have. Does that make me a disappointment in comparison? Right now, in my eyes, it does. After she leaves, I – once again – have to re-build my bruised ego one step at a time.

Step

I do my best to think of this impromptu visit as a test of life. She is who she is. I am who I am. What is meant to be will be. Perhaps the time has come for me to forgive the words said years before. Perhaps the time has come for me not to think of success as purely relative to that of others and start learning to celebrate my own. Perhaps the time has come for me to quit fearing my future potential failures.

Potential
Packing and panicking, these two seem to go hand in hand. A true match made in hell. I have tried not to accumulate too many belongings over the past two years, but clutter seems to have a life of its own, one that involves perpetual and uncontrollable growth. I've started three piles: one for the bin, one for a local charity and one that will move with me. Boutchou has made it into the latter again. International teddy bear. Perhaps I should interview it for my blog.

Blog
Cool guy has been helping me to create the blog I've been thinking about for a while. He's the one I worked with in Thailand. I told you the world was small, right? The first draft of the website is exactly how I wanted it – clean, simple, and welcoming. Not only is he giving me a hand with the technological side of things, he'll also be my first interviewee. Although he feels a bit camera shy, he has got an amazing story to tell. Born and raised in the UK, he moved to China seven years ago. What was meant to be a six-month internship turned into a job that then led him to eventually co-found a business in VR. Living a life of creativity and passion, I find his nonchalance and cynical sense of humour contagious.

Contagious
Soon, I'll be in Melbourne. Once there, I have absolutely no idea what I'll be doing. That's not like me. I'm the one with a plan and of course a list. That's who I've always been. The closer I get to the date, the more concerned I become. On the one hand, I dream of working in media and finally becoming a TV reporter and broadcaster. On the other hand, I dream of creating my

own business and telling the stories of those who've chosen to live abroad. Anyway, I know how impossible both sound. I'll have to figure this all out later as the time has come for me to relocate.

Relocate
Last night, I handed the keys of my apartment back to the agent. What a strange feeling. I'm moving into a friend's place for a couple of weeks. She lives with her boyfriend in an apartment located in the middle of one of Shanghai's old lanes. Reaching the front door requires walking through the neighbour's kitchen, a truly immersive local experience to conclude these last two years in China. As I lie down in their guest bedroom, it suddenly hits me. Right now, I don't have an address. If someone asked me, I couldn't say that I live in Shanghai any longer but couldn't say that I live in Melbourne yet. It's like I'm lost in an 'in between' time and place, a no man's land that somehow everyone, myself included, is keen on celebrating.

Celebrating
It's with a small group of colleagues that I head to next door's rooftop bar for my farewell party. Offering beautiful views of the river and of the city's landmarks, the place is absolutely gorgeous. As the sun goes down, the buildings light up on both sides of the water. Standing here and staring at the endless urban jungle ahead of me, I can't help but feel immensely lucky and a little emotional. What a privilege it's been to live here for two years! The best part? The truly extraordinary people I've met along the way. Most of them are already here. Aside from them, I'm not expecting a big turn-out. To my surprise, I couldn't have been more wrong. After about half an hour, most of the office is here and our group keeps on expanding. Colleagues mix in with

friends. I'm humbled by all the lovely messages and gifts I receive throughout the night.

Lovely
For the first time, I realise that I'm going to miss being here. Most of all, I'm going to miss them. It's as though I'd finally started to find my feet just before the time had come to leave, unless I'm only feeling this way because I know that this experience is coming to an end. I'll never know. In the meantime, I try to grab hold of these short-lived moments and carefully store them away in my memory. Tomorrow will be my last day at the company after four years. Even that thought is bittersweet. Working there gave me so many amazing opportunities to learn, to travel, and to grow. I might be ready to leave the daily burden of it, but I've become attached to the history and ethos behind the brand and most importantly to a few people I've had the immense privilege of working with. Luckily, the world is only getting smaller. I'm convinced I'll be back. This isn't goodbye but 'until we meet again'.

Goodbye
Before I leave, I've planned one last solo trip. All of my colleagues' parting words have been along the lines of "You *are* insane!" The places I'm heading to are deemed dangerous by many. My expedition along the Silk Road starts today in Kashgar, one of the westernmost cities in China. I will then make my way back towards Shanghai via Urumqi, Turpan and Dunhuang. Determined for this to be an unforgettable adventure, I've booked and planned to do everything on my own. Kashgar, here I come!

Kashgar
Arriving in Kashgar actually feels like stepping into another country. The sky is blue, the heat is dry, and the buildings are low and colourful. Even the people look and sound different. I've heard that one way to make out each of their ethnic backgrounds is by looking at the hats men wear. Food, too, is unlike anything I've had before. The bread, for instance, is absolutely delicious and comes in all shapes and sizes. Thanks to an online travel group, I've been in touch with a couple who I'm due to meet in a small tea shop off the beaten track.

Couple
They are lovely and extremely helpful. They've just completed the trip I'm about to embark on but the other way around: from Dunhuang to Kashgar. They tell me all about it and I write down their tips diligently. Unknowingly, they become the first people I articulate my future plans and hopes to. The concept of being beyond borders strikes their curiosity. As Canadians, they've moved to China to learn Mandarin and say they can totally relate to my thoughts. What if I was onto something? One thing is certain, the more I speak about this topic, the more passionate I become. It has so many dimensions and raises countless questions. I love listening to their story and realise I could easily sit here and talk to them for hours and hours. Having visited Kashgar's famous Sunday market, mosque, and mausoleums, partly with them, partly on my own, it's full of confidence that I reach Urumqi.

Urumqi
To start with, the weather is very different. In the space of an hour-long flight, the temperature has dropped from 30+ to

below 10 degrees Celsius. It's late evening when I finally reach my hotel. There, the service is dreadful, and no one speaks a single word of English. My Mandarin is enough to survive but not quite sufficient to ask about day trips. I've come here hoping to see the breathtaking Heavenly Lake. Sadly, I've been told that I won't be able to reach it on my own. Not many people come here from overseas so moving around hasn't been made easy yet. After hours of struggle, chatting to one of the hotel receptionist's contacts, I finally decide to book myself onto tomorrow's group tour. I was prepared for it to be challenging but didn't quite expect this level of nightmare. Shopping stop after shopping stop, the closer we get to our destination, the further away it feels. When we finally reach the bottom of the lake, the guide keeps trying to upsell all sorts of extra tours. Sometimes, not understanding much actually helps. I pretend not to speak a word of Mandarin, get out of the bus and walk towards the water by myself.

Water

The view lifts all my frustrations instantly. The lake is heavenly indeed! I walk up towards an isolated temple and explore the surrounding nature on my own. It's so cold that there is snow under foot. I don't have a coat, but I don't mind. Nothing can affect my regained positivity. That's what I think until my camera stops working unexpectedly. There are days like this, wherever you are… Days when everything seems to go wrong. Days that probably won't make it into your social media feed. Bad days. The reality of being on the road is that something as simple as taking your camera to a shop so it can be checked and fixed can turn into an overwhelming and nearly insurmountable task. Back in my cold and lonely hotel room that night, a familiar question comes creeping back in: why am I doing this? As the darkness fills the room, I can't help but wonder whether I should continue my trip along the Silk Road or head back to Shanghai instead.

Continue

It only takes an hour and a half by train for me to end up back in the desert. Welcome to Turpan! This place feels like a little forgotten village in the middle of nowhere. Having just arrived at the hotel, the flawless English of the receptionist catches me by surprise. Being able to understand and be understood is so wonderful that I'm tempted to hug her. I'm pretty sure that would be a cultural *faux pas*, so I give her the biggest possible smile instead.

Smile

The magic of solo travel arises again, and I end up finding a few companions with whom I book a tour guide for the following day. He will take us further into the desert. Out of the four of us, one is a German woman who's travelled from Moscow all this way by train. She has been on the road on her own for over three months. Her honesty, courage, and humility blow my mind. The other two are Israeli friends. The man is 71 years old. He started travelling when he was 63 after having five children and working as a farmer all his life.

He tells me not to wait like he did and to go after my dreams without hesitation. "I admire the life you lead," he says with sparkles in his eyes. There is no doubt he's preaching to the converted.

"The great thing about travelling is that there is no expiry date," I state jokingly.

He laughs at my words. All we can hope for is that we both remain healthy enough to maintain this lifestyle for many years to come. Neither of us have chosen to live this way because it's perceived to be 'cool' or 'fashionable'. It's become vital. Not only do we live to travel, we travel to live. Caught up in my daydream, I walk slightly ahead of the group through the alleys of a tiny village.

Village

Turning a corner, I realise that there's a film set in front of me. Taking a parallel lane, I walk to the top of the village and stare at the view for a few minutes. As I make my way back down, I'm stopped by a couple of staff members. They ask me to wait for the end of the scene to be shot. In my broken Mandarin, I accept and enquire whether this will be a Chinese or foreign movie.

"It's a Chinese and French cooperation," one of them says.

"That's funny because I'm French," I reply.

"Oh really?! So maybe you know this guy then," the other continues as he shows me a photo on his phone.

"Of course I do!" Football legend turned actor, this guy is beyond famous. Curious, I look around as I cross the road. I can't see anything. Suddenly, the director announces a lunch break. That's when I spot him. Not thinking twice, I head over and greet him in French. For the first time ever, I'm totally star struck.

Shaking, I stand there and tell Eric Cantona, "I can't believe you're the first French person I've spoken to in days… and you're so famous!" I forget to ask him what he is doing here, what they are filming and when it will be out, but I at least remember to ask for a photo of this unforgettable moment.

Unforgettable

An overnight train journey to Dunhuang is all I have left before reaching my final stop. It was the part of the trip I dreaded the most, wrongly so. Everything goes smoothly, I even sleep pretty well. I'm ready to explore the beautiful sights this last place has to offer, from the mysterious Mogao Grottoes to the enigmatic Crescent Lake and the unbelievable rock formations of the Yadan national park. This journey has most definitely been a crash course in Mandarin. Having spoken to one of the guys I shared my cabin with, I'm now chatting casually to the lady behind the hostel's reception desk. It's not just about the language though. Attitude and confidence have a lot to do with it too, so I've realised.

Realised

As my days of solo travel along this part of the Chinese Silk Road come to an end, I reflect on the fact that this experience has taught me countless lessons. Over the past two years, and even more so over the past 10 days, I've learnt to embrace and cherish being on my own. I've understood both the need to give myself time and space to be upset as well as the way to pick myself up when I'm ready. I've realised that I am enough. To me, being alone no longer means being weak, but being strong. Home may or may not be a place. Home certainly is them – the people I love so dearly. However, when they're not around, wherever I go and whoever I decide to be… Home is also me.

CHAPTER 8

Home is the World

List

Handsome guy and I have made a list of all the places we'd like to see and all the things we'd like to do in Australia. Looking at it reminds me of my 'grown-up' list. Although I stopped keeping track of my progress in the strangely diligent way I had done in the past, I've never forgotten about the list itself. Sadly, there's no denying that I somehow got side-tracked along the way. Perhaps that's what happens when life takes over. Take the past six years for example, I put my career ahead of so much else. Never mind, the time has now come for a change. A new chapter. A new life. A new me?

Me

Everything I own fits into six bags of various shapes and sizes. Staring at it all, I'm not sure how to feel. On the one hand, that's a hell of a lot to carry half way across the world. On the other hand, after just short of 30 years on this planet, I think six bags are next to nothing. By this time, I guess most people own a house, a car and more. Even now, these material possessions don't appeal to me much. Anything that could tie me down to a place for too long makes me want to run away. Perhaps it will change at some point. Sometimes, I wish it had. There are days I hope a simpler life – a nine-to-five job and all that seems to come with it – could fulfil me. However, I know it wouldn't, not for long anyway. Instead, I keep chasing after something though I'm still not sure what. All I can hope for is that I'll know when it comes around. Unless I'm not chasing after but rather escaping from something. I don't think so. I don't feel so. But I don't know. These are the thoughts that are going through my head as the taxi wizzes along Shanghai's streets. My colleague from Malawi, who's become a friend, is sitting next to me.

Next

She's offered to come with me to the airport and I'm so grateful for her help. Her tough love has played a big part in my transformation from master of rapid action to apprentice of slow reflection. Plus, her sense of humour doesn't fail to make me laugh. 'Boss lady', is what she calls me. I can't explain how or why but as we say goodbye, I'm convinced that we'll meet again one day. Hopefully it will be in Malawi. Listening to her story and her passion about a country I had barely heard of before has made me want to visit her there someday. A new destination added to my extensive yet growing list.

Destination

I smile as we take off. I smile when we're up in the air. I smile as we touch down. I can't help it; my happiness and excitement are overwhelming. It's only a matter of hours now before handsome guy and I are reunited. Goodbye long-distance calls at random times, hello cosy routine. Things couldn't be going any better thus far. He's been in Melbourne for about six weeks and has already found a job. The company and role are exactly what he was looking for and the pay is better than what he was earning previously. Not only that; they've already offered to sponsor both of us on a working visa. Goodbye time-bound experience, hello timeless opportunities.

Hello

Thus far, he's been living with the nomadic couple and so will I. It's going to be amazing to see the three of them. Our crew reunited four years later. After all, we pretty much lived together in London before. In six weeks, the nomadic couple will be heading for what I like to call 'the ultimate beyond borders experience'.

Ultimate

To put it simply, they'll be travelling the world for an undefined period of time. Goodbye sedentary life, hello nomadic adventures. I admire both their courage and the hard work they've put in to be in a position to actually go through with it. I, too, wish I could live off my passion. If only I could find a way of supporting myself while I do what I love and help and inspire others to do the same.

Others

Tonight is party time! We're all going out for dinner and drinks. There are about 30 or so of us in the group. Though I've been looking forward to the evening for a while, I'm overwhelmed as soon as we get to the bar. The music is loud, the lights subdued and there are so many people I've never met before. Sitting at the end of the table in silence, I feel like I've just come out of a cave after a long hibernation. The attitude and behaviours others so naturally exude seem familiar yet foreign to me. It's as if they were from a distant past. Back in the starting block. Again. "Where are you from?" someone asks nicely. I can't even begin to explain how much I loathe this question. It's not the worst though. "You're French, aren't you?" is the *crème de la crème*. I never know what to respond. Not that I should be offended, I *am* French, there's no denying that. However, I can't help but wonder why we always need to put people into boxes? I'm guilty of it too but not tonight. Tonight, I'm an alert observer and all I see and hear are stereotypes. Nationality box here. Profession box there. Perhaps the reason I'm so upset is that I don't seem to fit into anyone else's boxes anymore. Multi-cultural and jobless. Out of place. Out of purpose. Out of here.

Here
Adjusting to a new place always takes a bit of time so I decide to cut myself some slack. Instead of focusing on the little challenges and struggles, I make a conscious effort to bring my attention to the positive things around me. What's great is that there are many of them so it's incredibly easy. Take my morning routine for example. Every day, I start with a one to two hour walk to the beach followed by yoga. Both open my mind, enable me to centre myself, and give me space to move, think and relax.

Relax
There is something magical about the sound of the waves, the smell of salt in the air, and the reflection of the sun on the water. The latter isn't a prerequisite though. Rain or shine, I head out and about. Once at the beach, I always take a minute to stare at the immensity of the sea and breathe deeply. Often, inspiration comes and goes along the way. Thousands of steps bring a handful of ideas. Some good, others bad or awful even. I write down the ones I wish to hold onto. The rest, I leave for the wind to blow away.

Blow
What to say? What to do? What to write?
My inner wounds are open.
The pain stings from my blow.
Broken is the tip of my pen.
Feeling lost. Feeling sad. Feeling stuck.
A little. A lot. Too much.

What to do? What to say? What to write?
How to feel complete? How to feel worthy? How to find my way?
What do I miss? What do I need? What can I do?
Who should I be?

Be

'Be the change that you wish to see in the world' are just a handful of Mahatma Gandhi's[1] countless wise words. Together with the profound need to create a place for people like me, these are the reasons behind 'Be Beyond Borders'. A place where people who are leading a slightly unconventional life driven by their love of travel can share their stories and read those of others – a way to inspire people to go out, explore their surroundings and broaden their horizons. But, why? Because made smaller by travel, the world will turn into a place of tolerance, acceptance and ultimately peace. Because the more people live beyond borders, the more borders will become irrelevant. Because we can then focus on both local and global issues rather than all the nonsense in between.

Local

The place we've moved to is called Elsternwick. From there, it only takes 15 minutes to reach the centre of Melbourne by train. Despite this proximity, the neighbourhood feels more like a small community rather than part of a big city. There's a delicious French bakery around the corner, an ice-cream shop that opens till late and a health shop which serves the most

---

[1] Mahatma Gandhi (1869 – 1948) was an Indian activist. He peacefully fought all his life for India's independence from British rule.

delicious soy *matcha* lattes[2] ever, my favourite! I go to these places time and time again. There is something extremely grounding about becoming a 'regular' somewhere. It only takes a few days before the people who work there start recognising me and vice versa. This hasn't happened since I lived in Bordeaux seven years ago. Their simple acknowledgment makes me feel welcomed and appreciated and every single one of their smiles spreads positive energy into me.

Energy
I'm not an unknown, a number or a shadow anymore. I'm a human being, someone they seem keen on getting to know even. Generally, I find people so kind and friendly here. Perhaps it has something to do with the weather. Every time you enter a shop or a restaurant, whether they know you or they don't, they ask you how you are. Surprised at first, it has taken me no time to become used to this warm culture. It's no wonder the nomadic couple stayed here for three years and are struggling to come to terms with the idea of leaving. Life is easy, comfortable and enjoyable 'Down Under'. It's a shame Melbourne is so far away from pretty much everywhere else in the world.

World
Why do people laugh when I tell them I'm from the world? Fact is, we are all from the world. However, every time I say it, I feel the need to justify myself or downplay what I've just stated by adding something along the lines of, "I realise how idealistic I might sound." It seems as though phrases such as 'global citizen'

---

[2] *Matcha* is green tea powder which, after being mixed with hot water, is traditionally drunk at Japanese tea ceremonies. In recent years, using animal or plant milk to make *matcha* lattes has become very popular.

or 'citizen of the world' are perceived as ironic, derogatory or even arrogant. Hopeful nonetheless, I wish to contribute to their resurgence. What if all it needed was a slight change of perspective?

	Before	**After**
World	Knowing	Accepting
Nation	Renouncing	Enhancing
People	Judging	Observing
Self	Better	Different

Being beyond borders doesn't mean that I am no longer French. It means that I am beyond French. It doesn't make me better than anyone else, just different. It defines me as accepting of the world and its people. Other people are the ones I learn from, by observing them rather than judging their every move. One person plus multiple cultures equals one unique culture combination and multiple possible connections.

Connections
Since arriving in Melbourne, I've met so many wonderful people. I love listening to each of their individual stories. It's incredible how everyone has a unique tale to tell. Unique yet linked. Somehow, my belief that all of us are connected and that there is a reason for our paths to cross when they do, has grown stronger. Being new to the city and keen on expanding my circle of acquaintances and friends, I join various groups. One is a brilliant community of girls who live abroad. I first came across it during my solo trip to Seoul when I lived in Shanghai. Another one is made up of walkers. The founder has actually walked several marathons. Hearing about his experience inspires me to sign-up for the upcoming Melbourne half-marathon. My secret

hope is that it will be good practice for a full one later down the line. However, I remember too well what happened last time I started dreaming about marathons, so I'll have to take it slowly this time. Step-by-step.

Step

Slow and steady wins the race. Replace wins by finishes and there you have it, that's all I wish for. Standing in the middle of the crowd waiting for the event to start, handsome guy keeps telling me to stick to the plan. Understandably, he isn't keen on seeing me cross another finish line in an ambulance. It's not a perspective I cherish either. That's why I'm determined to walk the whole distance. No running. Just walking. I don't care how silly I might look. I don't care how long it might take. All I care about is enjoying the moment and eventually crossing the finish line healthy and happy. Adrenaline starts pumping through my veins. Off we go.

Go

There are thousands of us. I hadn't thought about a half marathon as a way to discover a new city though it turns out to be a great one. All the roads of the centre have been closed for us. Walking past, I marvel at the façade of the National Gallery of Victoria and soon after at the clear and quiet waters of Albert Lake. After all the grief my knee has caused me over the years, I'm so grateful to be right here right now. My eyes, my ears and my heart are wide open to each sight, sound, and emotion. Making my way around the lake, a man comes over and speaks to me.

Man
"You're walking really fast, as fast as I run," he says. To each their own race, I think to myself in silence. "If you keep going, you'll complete this race in under three hours," he continues. That's an hour less than the four-hour target I've set for myself. Doing the maths in my head, I realise that he might be right. I'm walking a lot faster than I anticipated! He'd like to carry on talking and I'm more than happy to listen so we keep going, side by side. He tells me that he is from Indonesia and is the proud father of five children including one who is currently studying in Melbourne. After talking briefly about his beautiful country, he explains that he works in the travel industry over there. Our common background is yet another reminder of how small and interconnected the world is. Our paths eventually split but the fire he's lit in me can't stop burning. Crossing the finish line in under three hours is my new target.

Target
With each step, I walk faster and faster and faster. It's as though I had wings growing on my back. I feel ready to take off and fly! After two and a half hours, the end is near. I'm totally exhausted… Every muscle in my body is tense. Finally, I can see the stadium from afar: the iconic Melbourne Cricket Ground also known as MCG. Commonly used for national and international cricket and Australian Football League matches, it is the largest stadium in Australia and can host about 100,000 people. Entering the arena gives me the boost I need to pick up the pace again. I might make it under three hours… Maybe.

Maybe
Regardless, this feeling right there is what I'm doing it for: accomplishment and relief. Crossing the finishing line, I know

that I gave it absolutely everything I had. Never did I give up or in. This isn't just about now, it's about all the years that have led to this moment. I made it! I completed a half marathon in two hours and fifty-seven minutes. No running. Just walking. I'm trying to catch my breath and crying all at the same time as I call handsome guy. He worries instantly but there is no need. These are tears of immense joy.

Tears

There we go. When it rains, it pours… I'm crying again. Same output, totally different trigger. Hiking has become one of my favourite things to do and Australia is the perfect place for it. We're out and about most weekends. Sometimes, I look back and can't believe how different I've become. I'm miles away from my 13-year-old self who hated her parents for taking her on a hike for her birthday. From the way I look to what I like to do, almost everything has changed, everything but my core values of honesty, openness, love, and passion. However, in my mind, even after all these years, a clear difference remains between hiking and climbing. The first one only requires one's feet. The other involves hands too. The nomadic couple hadn't mentioned the extent of climbing this trek up Cathedral Ranges required. I guess it's not something they would think about when they're not terrified of heights themselves.

Terrified

Despite my best efforts, I haven't been able to shake off this irrational and overwhelming fear. Obviously. After a few metres grabbing onto the rocks with my hands and trying to stabilise my unsteady legs, I have to stop. My whole body is shaking. Tears are streaming down my cheeks uncontrollably. It only takes seconds for the panic attack to take over my entire being. My mind is paralysed. I can neither make my way up nor make my way down. I'm stuck. Metaphor of this time of my life perhaps. Trying to steady my breath by distracting my mind, I watch a group of children who are heading down slowly and safely. I wish I could go back in time, although I can't remember ever being that fearless. Eventually and with handsome guy's help, I manage to centre myself and decide to keep going. This mountain now symbolises all of life's setbacks and challenges. I won't let them defeat me. Not this time. Luckily, I've heard there is a longer and easier path. That will definitely be the way I'll walk back to the car. Baby steps.

Baby
Everyone around me seems to be having babies. In the last six months, six friends and three former colleagues have given birth. Handsome guy has become an uncle twice. His younger and his older brother each had a daughter two weeks apart. Right after, my best friend gave birth to a cute little boy in Brisbane. A baby beyond borders, he is the gorgeous outcome of a love story between a French lady and an Australian man who met in the UK. I'm on my way to visit them, feeling thrilled! I'll be spending a week in their new home. Seeing so many families being formed and growing around me is wonderful. Sometimes, I wonder whether it should make me feel broody. I guess this is the natural next step I'm expected to take. Apparently, you know when you're ready. I don't. When I look into the future, I see more travelling and exploring by myself, with handsome guy and with family and friends. Perhaps things will change. Perhaps they won't. Whichever way it goes, I'm finally ready to follow the flow. In the meantime, I'll gladly be

the slightly crazy auntie with her thousands of stories and worldly lifestyle.

Lifestyle
The nomadic couple is leaving Melbourne tonight – sad times. We wave goodbye as the taxi that drives them to the airport disappears in the dark. Handsome guy and I then head back up to the apartment. Without them, it feels empty and strange. Though they're gone, their endearing presence remains. Somehow, it seems like we can still hear their voices. 'You do you girl', is something they used to say quite often. I can't even begin to explain how much these words resonate with me. Living beyond borders is a choice. It's been mine but that's not to say that it would suit everyone. In no way is this a phase or a whim. It won't pass with time. I'm no hero, I'm no villain. My aim isn't to force anybody to do the same. All I hope to achieve is to trigger more understanding and acceptance for those who've chosen to live this way and more support and inspiration for those whose dream it is to do so. Step-by-step, I dream to create a home for their stories and mine.

Home
When I look back, it's undeniable that this life beyond borders has changed me. It's led me to places I'd never heard of. It's broadened my mind in ways I didn't know were possible. It's challenged me on a level I couldn't have imagined. It's introduced me to all the people I love. It's made me want to keep exploring the world indefinitely. And so much more. I might have learnt all these life-changing lessons without moving as much. I guess I'll never be sure, but I doubt it somehow.

Somehow

Handsome guy and I are living together now, just the two of us. It feels so incredible and unreal to see each other every morning and every night. No matter how lost and down I might have felt during the day, I always find myself smiling from ear to ear when I hear his key opening the door of our apartment. We've spent the last couple of weekends coming up with little changes and adjustments to make the place ours. After yet another trip to IKEA© on the other side of the world, it is now. So much so that somehow, it feels like home. What if home was a place after all? Mysterious question.

Question

Looking for home has taken me to so many places over the years and I'm excited to see where it will take me going forward. After almost 30 years of extensive search all over the world, I've realised that...
Looking for answers, I found more questions.
Looking for a home, I found several homes.
Looking for a place, I found a definition.

Definition

Home is a place, people and a person: you. A tripod for life. Although one is sufficient to get by and two would be plenty, it's when all three are fulfilled that we're the happiest. Finding home doesn't have to be an endless worldwide quest – though it can be. In each and every one of us lies the power to define, create, and cherish our own home. So, dear reader, where, what and who is home to you? As I type these words, to me, home is a place – the world. It's people – handsome guy, my family, and my friends. And it's finally beginning to be me.

Beginning
With every goodbye comes a new hello, with every achievement comes a new dream and with every end comes a new beginning. So, as I'm about to bring one more chapter of my story to a close, I can't help but wonder... Where to next?

Acknowledgments

This book is very personal and close to my heart, which is why the first people I would like to thank are my parents, Philippe and Alice Anglaret for their unconditional love and support throughout each and every one of my crazy adventures. The family portrait wouldn't be complete if I didn't mention my dear sister Anaïs Anglaret. Time has brought us closer and it's been amazing to see you grow in the most beautiful way since I left Louviers just over 10 years ago. My infinite gratitude goes to handsome guy Andrew Small. Your love, your optimism and constant encouragements have enabled me to keep going even when I felt useless and hopeless. I'm so glad life brought us together again 'Down Under' and can't wait to see what the future holds. Following in my footsteps, this book too has travelled the world. Thank you to all those across the globe who read my first draft and gave me so much valuable feedback. Alice Miller Dupas, Alison Small, Amélie Pha, Andrea Agrotis, Bonnie Chao, Céline Maimaran, Joanne Profeta, Lindsay Fave, Nina Coutéat, Olivia Ryan, Oriane Freund, Ouissem Belgacem and Simon Taylor, I couldn't have done it without you. To my editor, Amanda Spedding, it's been an absolute pleasure to see my words reach new highs in your capable hands. Now that the *Frenglish* is gone, the sky is the limit! Thank you Nelly Murariu for your precious support. Your magic has turned my manuscript into a beautiful looking book. To Haresh from HRM Graphics, I can't even begin to tell you how much I adore the gorgeous cover you put together. To my mentor, Julie Postance, working with you has been an absolute honour. You've taught me, coached me and most importantly inspired me. Finally, to all of you readers, I am eternally thankful for the precious seconds, minutes, hours you have or will spend reading my humble story. I hope it inspires you to be beyond borders. This was Solène Anglaret, bidding you goodbye and happy travels.

About the Author

Solène Anglaret was a little girl with big dreams. As she got older, they got bigger, and so appeared an odd feeling that she didn't quite belong where she was born. There had to be more to the world than the little town she was growing up in. Determined to find out, she was only 18 years old when she left the place she'd called home thus far. Her first stop was Norway, where she both studied and worked for a year. This extraordinary experience taught her countless life lessons and left her longing for more exploring and discoveries. She fell in love with the place and began to wonder whether it could be the 'home' she was looking for. That quest for where or what home actually is never left her as she then went on to live in the United States, the United Kingdom and China. There, she worked for two large multinational companies and turned out to be a talented, driven and ambitious businesswoman. As time passed, she kept rising up the ranks. Each of her jobs was exciting at first but it took her very little time to figure out what they were about and start dreaming of new horizons instead. Having moved to Australia for love in October 2017, she finally decided to combine her passions of storytelling and living abroad. That is what brought her to launch her unique blog and to write this book, both underpinned by the idea of living beyond borders and everything that comes with it. Doing so, she hopes that her story and those of other world citizens will inspire more people to step out of their comfort zone and help spread a message of tolerance, acceptance and peace.

Interested in having Solène speak at one of your events?
Looking for advice about moving or living abroad?
Keen to keep in touch?

🌐 www.bebeyondborders.com
✉ bebeyondborders@yahoo.com
📷 @bebeyondborders

www.ingramcontent.com/pod-product-compliance
Lightning Source LLC
Chambersburg PA
CBHW032029290426
44110CB00012B/725